Legaginney
Revisited

By
Finbarr M. Corr, Ed. D.

A memoir, written in the present tense,
using the voice of an eight year old.
The voice grows as the author progresses
in years and wisdom to adulthood.

Uncle Jim's Poems

James Brady R.I.P. Lacken

FMC Press Inc

Fort Myers, Florida

Cover Design by Elizabeth Moisan, Harwich, MA.

Dedicated to Mary Woodward, New Hampshire

Printed in the United States of America

FMC Press Inc.

ISBN 978-0-9794324-6-0

Table of Contents

Prologue

What and where is Legaginney? is a question I am frequently asked at book-signings. My answer depends on who asks the question, as the native Irish are wont to answer a question with a question.

Legaginney is a place, not a town, located seventy miles north of Dublin. It is one of five hundred townlands that make up the County of Cavan. Our home is called Legaginney House. The first myth attached to that title is that,"the Corrs are rich." I can testify under oath that this was and is a myth. I was just twelve years old when the majority of Dad's cattle on our second farm died in the blizzard of the century in March of 1947. We ate rice and potatoes for three months until the family economics recovered through the sale of milk from eight cows; fatted pigs ready for slaughter; and a flock of full-grown geese, ready for somebody's Christmas dinner.

Our Legaginney farm, in total approximately one hundred acres, had sixty acres of meadows and arable land suitable to grow potatoes, oats and other vegetables. The rest was rocky ground, suitable for grazing and two acres of bog. The bog provided income, as Dad charged farmers, who came from as far as five miles to cut and save turf to heat their homes during the winter.

What I remember about living in Legaginney, as one of Nell and John Frank's nine children, can be summarized in one word - "Freedom." Neighbors, rich and poor relatives, tinkers - all were free to knock on the kitchen door, walk in and be welcome. We children were free to go out in the fields to play ball; go into the hayshed to play hide-and-seek; and, when we got a little older, go out hunting rabbits and foxes for several miles without adult supervision. When I watch television today or read the newspapers about the lives of children in Syria, Israel, Gaza or Saudi Arabia, I raise my eyes to Heaven and thank God for planting me in Legaginney.

Another phrase that describes life in Legaginney was the "Welcoming Hearth." During the long winter nights, before the advent of radio, television or telephones, people just dropped in and sat for an hour or two for a "Ceilidh" (an Irish folk gathering, sometimes including music and song). The blazing turf fire was a catalyst for the storyteller, the card players, or on weekends the fiddlers and accordion players, who joined our mother Nell in a "session" of gigs, reels and hornpipes.

Prior to 1955, before electricity was installed in all of the homesteads around Legaginney, we children did our homework on the kitchen table, underneath an oil lamp whose lighted wick, assisted by a silver reflector, projected sufficient light for budding mathematicians and future authors. Our mother Nell made sure that we all had our homework done on Friday evenings and the family Rosary said before Miss Berrill arrived to tell us ghost stories before we ascended the dark, rickety stairs to bed. Not all of us went to bed immediately, as we know Miss Berrill would sing a few songs and Jimmy Quinn would arrive to join Mammy as she played her fiddle. No adults looked up to the top of the stairs, where several of us kids cuddled together in the dark and joined the Ceilidh, until sleep overcame us and forced us to sneak into bed.

The parish priest had tremendous influence on my young life. I faithfully served mass and listened to his weekly sermons. We children didn't have to move outside the confines of our farm to meet new people, who came each spring and summer to work in our bog or who joined my dad and our servant Jack Murtagh when we thrashed oats, separating the straw from the grain that would eventually become our porridge.

I hope you enjoy my story, as I progress in years and wisdom to adulthood.

Legaginney House

Chapter I

July 25, 1943

"Hello Dympna, who is this young man with you?" asks Pat Lynch, owner of Lynch's popular country shop at Lacken crossroads. The shop is popular because many people stop there on Sunday mornings after mass for groceries and at other times to hear Pat's latest jokes. "This is my little brother Finbarr, who is eight years old today." Dympna replies. Pat comes around the counter, grabs my shoulders and yells in my ear, "Happy Birthday, Finbarr," and adds, "Didn't I see you serve a funeral mass last week?" Pat is a mortician, along with being a grocer.

I shyly reply, "Yes, I can only serve at masses for the dead because the big red Gospel book used at the other masses is too heavy for me. I am only strong enough to carry the black book."

"I want one pound of butter for Mammy" Dympna announces, "And a pan loaf for our neighbor down the lane, Mrs. McCusker." (*Because Mrs. McCusker and her husband Phil have no children, the Corr children usually stop in to ask Mrs. McCusker if she needs anything from Lynch's shop. We are not being totally virtuous, as Mrs McCusker frequently gives sixpence to the lucky shopper.*)

As we leave the shop, Pat puts a little bag of toffee in with the butter, saying, "This is for the birthday boy." Meanwhile Father McEntee, in his black shiny cassock, is walking past the shop, turning right up the hill to the chapel on the side of Potahee Mountain. He does not stop and speak, as he is reading from a small missal that (I learn later) is called a breviary. Father McEntee's house is just twenty yards away from Lynch's shop.

It is a beautiful sunny day. People frequently stop at the crossroads and chat with each other. Local farmers in carts pulled by donkeys or horses go through the crossroads to shop in the village of Ballinagh two miles away, or to transport their cows' milk to Crossdoney Creamery three miles down the road.

The crossroads is also a hangout for young lads in the neighborhood who gather in the long summer evenings to play skittles or handball at the handball alley, or just to chat about Gaelic Football and the chances of our County Cavan team beating Kerry in the All-Ireland football final. It is very quiet at the crossroads today, as Dympna and I continue walking towards Legaginney Lane. I am carrying Mrs. McCusker's bread, which is about the same weight as the black book I carry on the altar.

"This has to be my godson Finbarr," yells the mustached cousin Frank Corr from his garden of potatoes, cabbage, lettuce and beetroot, as we go past.

"Yes it is" says Dympna "and today's his 8th birthday." "Wait a minute I have to give my godson a birthday present." Dympna gives me a hug and takes the loaf, as I follow Godfather Frank into his house. His wife and daughter Nancy sing "Happy Birthday" to me. Dympna stays outside. She is afraid to come in because she learned from her older sisters Marie and Eilish that Frank likes to embarrass little girls by kissing them with his dirty-looking whiskers. A whole shilling richer, I run down the road to catch up with my sister.

Dympna warns me not to tell Mrs. McCusker that it is my birthday, as it might seem we are asking her for money. We also know that Phil is still upset that last winter our older brother Brendan threw a snowball down the chimney of their thatched house, where it landed in his dinner in the pot hanging on the crook over the fire. Thankfully, Mrs. McCusker thought it was a joke and persuaded Phil not to tell our daddy, as he would have been very angry and would have forced Brendan to apologize and offer to help with some farm project to mend fences with a good neighbor.

A few more yards down the road, in the shadow of St. Michael's Church of Potahee we meet old Jimmy Beatty, who was on his way up the steps past Legaginney National School to ring the Angelus bell at twelve noon. Before Dympna has a chance to stop me, I run over to him and say, "Jimmy, today's my birthday." He is in a bad mood and just sneers at me and says, "You are already too fat, without eating a birthday cake. With that big bum, you are now the fattest kid of all the Corrs."

Realizing that I am about to cry, Dympna puts her arm around my neck and says, "Don't mind Jimmy, he is getting old and cranky, tired of walking up the side of the mountain three times a day to ring the bell at the chapel. I ask Dympna "Why does he ring the bell?" Dympna, not yet wanting to try to explain the story of the Virgin birth to me, says, "When you get a little older I will tell you and then you will understand."

Dympna and I drop off Mrs. McCusker's pan loaf. She gives us each a slice of her currant cake she has baked for Phil's tea, after he comes home from making the hay down the road in the meadow. We don't sit down, as we know our Mammy is waiting to celebrate my birthday. We

3

haven't yet reached the back door of the kitchen when I smell Mammy's favorite currant cake baking in a portable oven on the hob next to the turf fire. I like watching her prepare the dough, using cooking flour, and adding currants, eggs and buttermilk. I know that one day I want to learn how to cook like Mammy.

Brendan, Eilish, Marie, Dympna, Colm and I sit around the kitchen table to have our tea and celebrate my birthday. My older brothers, P. Joe (Peter Joseph) and Jack are home from boarding school but are not here to celebrate. They're out in the fields, cutting the oats with my dad and our workman Jack Murtagh. Mary Farrelly, Mammy's helper is busy feeding the hens, chickens and geese. The latter are been fattened up for our Christmas dinner. Mary hears my siblings sing Happy Birthday from across the yard, where she is preparing the birds' supper. She comes into the kitchen and grabs me with a big hug as she says, "Happy Birthday you wonderful *gosuun* (Gaelic for young lad)." Mammy insists that Mary sit down and have a slice of my birthday cake. She knows that Mary and I are very close, since she had taken care of me and my brother Colm for several months when I was five years old because Mammy was laid up due to the birth of my baby brother Fonsie.

Since my birthday is in July and the summer sun in Ireland stays up in the sky past 10 PM, I am not sent to bed at my usual time of 7 PM. I go outside and play ball with my brother Colm, awaiting my dad and my brothers' return from the cornfields. All of a sudden Colm said, "Look, someone is coming in the lane." It is my Godmother Kitty Osborne, home from England. She is sitting up front on a horse-drawn trap, driven by her brother Joe, all the way from the village of Ballinagh, two miles away. I am very excited, as she always brings nice gifts. Because she has worked in England for many, many years, she talks with a strange voice. My sister Marie calls it a British accent.

Kitty is carrying a large cardboard box and hands it to her brother Joe so that she can have both her hands free to grab me and wish me a happy birthday. I am dying to know what is in the big box. I can tell by my mother's face and her rushing to clear off the kitchen table that she is surprised at Kitty's visit. She is happily surprised that a governess, who spends most of her adult life taking care of rich families' children in England, would come to Ireland just for my birthday??

Kitty hands me the box and added with her distinguished voice, "Here is something that you will enjoy playing with your brothers and friends." I open the box to find a large rubber ball in several colors. I go over and gave her a hug and say, "Thank you, Godmother Kitty, this is the most beautiful ball I have ever seen."

I have a great birthday that ends with Dad, P. Joe and the two Jacks, Corr and Murtagh, eating the rest of my birthday cake. The only sad thing that happens all day is the bell ringer Jimmy's comment about my fat bum. The next morning I wake up early and say my prayers, still thinking about mean Jimmy. I come down the stairs quietly and open the parlor door. This time it doesn't squeak. I run over and stand before the full-size mirror, up against the wall, and turn around to look at my bum.

"Old Jimmy is right", I say to myself, "I am determined to get rid of it."

Chapter II

A Missionary Child

Infant Jesus meek and mild, look on me a little child
Pity mine and pity me and suffer me to come to thee.
Heart of Jesus I adore you, heart of Mary I implore you.
Heart of Joseph pure and just,
in these three hearts I place my trust. [1]

Saying my prayers on my knees, by my bedside, prepares me for the day ahead. My brother Colm is still sleeping; I jump out over him to look for my shirt and pants. I sneak down the creaky stairs past the girls' room, so as not to wake them. I am surprised to find Marie already up and reading her comic book Beano at the kitchen table. Marie always enjoys reading. She giggles and laughs as she explains to me some of the funny things that Beano and his friends are up to in the story. As for me, I prefer to be out in the garden kicking my new football, that I had just received from my Godmother Kitty.

Mammy is busy putting some of the logs Daddy has cut on the fire. She smiles at me saying,

"Did the birthday boy Finbarr say his prayers this morning?" We all know that her first duty is to make sure we all say our morning prayers and then eat a good breakfast of milk and porridge. While all of us kids are sleeping, she cooks a small iron pot of oatmeal, water and a little salt. When the oatmeal is boiled she removes the pot from the crook over the fire and places it on the

---

1   Elsie's corner

hob beside the fire to keep it warm for the whole family to enjoy the next morning. Whether we are on our way to school or just going out to play, as we do during the summer months, she reminds us that a good breakfast of porridge keeps us from being hungry all day.

"You had a great birthday, Finbarr," she says. "I am surprised that you are up so early this morning. Aren't you tired?"

I want to tell her, it was a fun day, except for old Jimmy calling me "a fat ass", but I can't use the word 'ass' talking to my mother. That is a bad word I learned from Brendan.

Mammy goes over and puts a few pennies in the Mite-box at the corner of the kitchen dresser.

"This is for you Finbarr, to thank Jesus for you having a great birthday and you being a good boy." As the little black statue on the Mite-box bobs his head I give her a big hug and ask her, "Now that I am eight years old can I go out today and sell some raffle tickets for Noogey?"

(The Mite-box is a gift sent to Mammy from St Patrick's Missionary Society, because she sends money each year from the raffle tickets she sells and from deposits in the Mite-box to support the Irish missionaries { priests, brothers and nuns} in Africa. The bobbing black statue tells the donor who drops in the change "Thank you for giving money to support the priests and nuns who come to my country Africa, bringing the good news of Jesus." 'Noogey' is the fictitious name of the missionary who edits their monthly magazine called "Africa")

Mammy replies, after a slight hesitation,

"Both daddy and I feel you have the gift of gab and will be a good salesman one day. But I don't want you going to any families who don't know you. Why don't you go first to Miss Berrill? If she buys some tickets and I expect she will, as she always puts some change in the Mite-box when she visits us, you can go down the road to Michael Cox, the McCall's, Lizzie Corr and McFaul's."

I get excited as Mammy sits me down and teaches me what to say.

"Think about the little black baby on top of the Mite-box, who would never learn his prayers or know about Jesus if we don't send missionaries to his country of Africa. Ask Miss Berrill if she would like to help Noogey, who sends priests and nuns to Africa, to baptize people and teach them how to pray to Jesus. She will say, "Yes". Then open your little bag and take out the tickets explaining that the tickets cost three pence each. Ask her to print her name and address on the stub of the tickets she buys. Be sure to thank her and tell her how what a nice house she has and how friendly her cats are."

(Miss Berrill {which is what everybody calls her} is a short, charming, fat lady who works for the Irish Railroad as a gatekeeper. Her neat bungalow, which serves as her residence, compliments of the railroad company, is situated about thirty feet away from the railroad tracks. As the train comes north from Crossdoney on its way to Dublin the train conductor blows his shrieking whistle and Miss Berrill waddles out and opens both gates, blocking traffic going to and from the village of Ballinagh. As children, we imagine the steam driven train is saying "Push me up Legaginney, Push me up Legaginney" as it travels through our farm.)

There is neither a sight nor sound of trains, as I take the short cut from our yard across Scott's field to the railroad tracks. *(The Scott family owned this field, before*

Phil McCusker bought it.) I am barefoot; carrying a small purse Mammy gave me to hold the tickets and the money from the tickets I hope to sell. It is a sunny day. I have been walking barefoot to school since the beginning of summer. The grass in Scott's field, soft and mossy, feels good under my bare feet. I am already worried about walking along the railroad tracks about 300 yards to Miss Berrill's house. The path along the tracks is covered with rough sand and little stones. My legs are still too short to walk on the tracks, as the railroad ties are too far apart.

When I arrive, Miss Berrill is working in her flower garden. Her flowers are lovely. Her favorite flowers are dahlias and rambling roses. To enter her home you go underneath an arch of wire netting covered with rambling roses.

"Who do we have here? You are one of the Corrs, right?" she asks.

"I am Finbarr, Miss Berrill" I reply.

"For a minute I thought you were Brendan. You are getting so tall. Come on in and tell me what you have in that nice purse."

Remembering what Mammy told me to think about and say while selling the tickets, I say to her. "You remember the statue of the little black boy on the dresser in our kitchen?"

"Yes, indeed I do Finbarr."

I move on and tell her, "You know that a priest named Noogey sent that Mite-box to Mammy, because she sends him money every year to make sure that little boys and girls in Africa learn about Jesus and how to say their prayers, just I like I do each morning. Now that I am eight years old I want to help Mammy by selling these tickets at three pence each and make sure missionaries go to Africa to teach all the children about Jesus."

"Finbarr you are only eight years old and you are already a missionary. I will, of course, buy two tickets." I am sitting there looking at all the decorations in her kitchen, dolls she made herself and colored vases full of flowers from her garden, while she goes to her bedroom to find the sixpence to pay for her purchase. Her three cats look friendly, purring at me from under the kitchen table. I ask her to fill in the ticket stubs, as I am not sure how to spell Berrill and don't know what her first name is. She fills in the stubs with Bridget Berrill and hands me the sixpenny piece, which I put in my purse.

"Before you leave my house Finbarr" she says, "you have to eat one of my freshly made buns and drink a glass of milk". Remembering Mammy's words to be nice and thankful to Miss Berrill, I eat the bun and drink the milk and walk down the hill to the bog road where Michael Cox is also lives alone.

Michael is a bachelor, living in a thatched house, very close to Legaginney bog, which my daddy owns. Michael supports himself by working on other peoples' farms and in the bog in summertime. He loves children, even though he has none of his own. His only known weakness is that he loves to gamble on horseracing. He likes teasing children and asking them silly questions. When I walk down the Arva road I turn right at Legaginney Crossroads and take the same path that all of the local farmers take to go to the bog to cut and save the turf, they will use to cook and keep their families warm the following winter. Michael is in his garden milking his goat, when I arrive. I wait for him to finish milking, as I don't want to frighten the goat. I expect to be teased.

"This has to be Finbarr that Pat Lynch has been raving about," says Michael. "He told me about your birthday." With a grin he says,

"How old were you last year?" I reply, "Michael, I was seven years old."

"How old will you be next year?" I reply, "Nine"

"What happened to your eight?"

"I celebrated that yesterday" I said with a smile. Michael gave a big laugh and said "I can see why Pat Lynch thinks you are the smartest kid in Legaginney. What is in the little purse you are carrying?" I repeat my story and ask him to support Noogey. He gives me three pence, fills out the ticket stub and I continue down the bog road to see if Mrs McCaul is home. She also has a goat in her yard. She looks at me as if to say hello and goes back to gobbling the leaves of cabbage left over from Mrs. McCaul's kitchen.

I don't know Mrs McCaul, only my Mammy and Daddy know her. They have a half door and a full door at the entrance to their kitchen. The full door is always open, except at night. The half door is closed to prevent chickens, the goat and any other birds or animals going into the kitchen. *(This is similar to Dutch doors, except with the Dutch door there is only one door, divided horizontally in the middle.)* I have to stand on my tippy toes to be able to speak over the top of the half door. I call out in a loud voice, as I cannot see anybody inside. "I want to speak to Mrs McCaul please". A girl, as tall as my sister Marie, comes to the door and smiles down on me on the other side. She has long white hair hanging over her shoulders.

"My mammy is not home. She is at work. Can I take a message for her?"

"I want her to buy a three pence raffle ticket for Noogey."

She laughs at me and says "Who is Noogey?"

I wish my mammy was here, as she didn't teach me how to explain Noogey to someone just a few years older than me. I try to answer the right way saying,

"He is a priest, who sends other priests and brothers to Africa to teach people like you and me about Jesus and how to pray to him each morning."

"Miss Gaffney, who teaches at our school up the road in Legaginney, told our class about priests, brothers and nuns going to Africa to baptize black babies. If you tell me who you are I will tell Mammy and she will help you and give three pence to Noogey."

"My name is Finbarr Corr. Maybe my sister Marie or Eilish is in your class"

She gives me a big smile and says, "I know Eilish, she has hair just like mine. If you come back on Saturday or Sunday my Mammy and Daddy will be home."

Disappointed but hopeful, I walk back toward the crossroads, past Michael Cox's home and turn right on the way to Arva. I am now walking on a road that has some of my Daddy's meadows on both sides. The meadows have cocks of hay, that my dad, Jack Murtagh, P Joe and my brother Jack have built, now ready to be taken home by shifter to feed the cows and horses during the winter.

My next stop is going to be fun. Lizzie Corr, Daddy's cousin, lives with her husband Eddie and her bachelor brother James Peter Corr in a thatched house, just ten yards off the road. My Daddy loves Lizzie and smiles every time someone mentions her name. Mammy is not too happy to have her children visit Lizzie. She says Lizzie curses and uses bad words, that should not be said in front of any child. Lizzie and Eddie have one son named Aidan and a daughter named Ettie. Aidan is younger than I am and is quiet like his father.

Lizzie sees me coming into their front yard, which is full of flowers just like Ms Berrill's, and runs to meet me.

"O my God! she screams, "I cannot believe that your mother Nell let you, Finbarr, come alone all this way from Legaginney." They live in Lacken, which is another townland, much bigger than Legaginney.

"My Mammy says I am a big boy now, since I am eight years old and she told me yesterday it will be safe for me to go out selling tickets for Noogey and his missionaries in Africa, as long as I go to houses where people know me."

I don't have to give a long explanation to Lizzie, as she comes to visit us often and always puts a penny or two in Noogey's Mite-Box. Today I see that Lizzie has a big belly. She notices that I am staring at it and she tells me that she is making another baby, so that Aidan has his own brother or sister. That is the first time I hear that babies are made in their mothers bellies. I still believe what Mary Farrelly told me that Mammy's nurse Mrs Day brings babies in her bag attached to the back of her bicycle. I still remember playing with Dympna in Scott's Field and seeing Mrs Day coming in our lane, getting off her bicycle and taking the bag with baby Colm in it upstairs to Mammy's room.

Eddie and James Peter come from the fields, where they are cutting and putting the oats in stacks before bringing them home for thrashing. They don't need watches to tell them it is dinner time (1.00 PM). The

Angelus bell, being rung on Potahee Mountain, can be easily heard at noon in the town-land of Lacken. As my Mammy would say,

"Your stomach will tell you it is time to eat. It is already four hours since breakfast."

Eddie takes my hand and gives me a handshake and says,

"I see we have one of John Frank's (my father) sons visiting us today. You are welcome lad."

Lizzie insists that I sit down with the two men at the dinner table as she prepares Aidan's meal, while he is sitting in his crib beside his dad. I feel like a big man sitting with Eddie and James Peter. At home, I am treated as a little child, while sitting at the little children's table on a three legged stool. Lizzie puts bacon, cabbage and a small boiled potato on each of our plates. I am not hungry enough to eat all she gives me because I had eaten Miss Berrill's bun just an hour ago.

Lizzie does not sit down with us; she takes Aidan on her lap and gives him his dinner. Aidan gurgles as he drinks his bottle of heated cow's milk. Lizzie announces with a giggle,

"I have a new name for Finbarr. I am going to christen him the 'Little Noogey,' as he is out today selling tickets at three pence each for the missions in Africa." (*She changes the name later to 'The Three Penny Beggar Man'.*)

Eddie and James Peter have a good laugh.

Eddie says, "Oh Lizzie, stop picking on the lad. Give him a shilling from the egg money, you received this morning from Pat Lynch." *Pat comes around each week and buys eggs from the farmers wives and if they need groceries like tea leaves or pan loaves of bread, he*

14

exchanges the groceries for the fresh eggs. I get excited as Lizzie goes to her bedroom and returns with a shiny silver shilling (twelve pence) enough to buy four tickets. She fills out the stubs, putting Aidan's name on them, she said "for luck".

I ask Lizzie, "Do you know if Mrs McFaul is home?"

"She is of course," she replies. "She is almost blind and cannot go anywhere unless her son Jack takes her. She is a prisoner in that house, since her husband Jim died last year." I thank Eddie and Lizzie for their kindness to me and for supporting Noogey and go back on the same road, turning right at the first lane, up to meet Mrs McFaul.

I knock on her door and get no answer; I begin to ask myself,

"Did Lizzie say she was hard of hearing, as well as being partly blind?" After what seemed like a half hour but probably only five minutes I hear a shuffling noise coming toward the half door.

"Who do we have here?" says the grey haired, stooped woman.

"I am Finbarr Corr, Mrs McFaul, how are you today?"

"Are you one of the Corrs from Legaginney?" This was the name given to us to distinguish us from the Corrs of Lacken or Drumbrade.

"Yes I am, Mrs McFaul. My Mammy let me out today to sell tickets for Noogey, a priest who sends other priests to 'Africa' to tell little boys like me and girls like my sisters Eilish, Marie and Dympna all about baby Jesus."

"I know about Noogey. We get his magazine 'Africa' every month. I can only see the pictures Finbarr, my son Jack reads the stories to me. My eyesight is getting worse every day."

"I am sorry to hear that Mrs. McFaul, I wish I could help you."

Then she surprises me replying,

"Yes, you can help me. Do you know how to put thread in a needle?" I think I surprise her too, when I say,

"I have watched my Mammy several times. Let me try, I think I can"

"That's great", she says and then goes to her kitchen closet and takes out a large black spool of black thread. She then reaches over the fire place, careful not to disturb the big sheep dog stretched out before the turf fire and pulls down a small cushion full of short and long needles. I begin to think to myself, I came into her kitchen to help Noogey now I am about to help Mrs. McFaul. I remember how my mammy takes the end of thread across her mouth, causing the thread to become straighter and smaller, making it easier to put it through the tiny hole in the needle. On my first try the thread splits open and gets stuck in the hole. I wish my Mammy was here now to help me. I do what I think my mammy would want to do, I don't complain, as I know it could be worse.

Mrs McFaul could have said, "Finbarr, even with my bad eyesight I see you have a big backside"

Chapter III

Anybody to play Skittles?

I thread ten needles for Mrs McFaul. She thanks me, gives me a hug, and buys two of Noogey's tickets. Having sold ten tickets, I am proud as a peacock (as Mammy would say) as I walk up Legaginney Road. I choose to walk the road rather than go by Miss Berrill's and risk hurting my feet on the stony path along the railroad tracks. As I go under the railroad tracks, I turn left up Legaginney Lane. As I walk past McCusker's, I meet Phil, as he is bringing his three cows home for milking.

"What are you up to, young man?" asks Phil.

"I have been out all day selling raffle tickets for Noogey, the missionary priest."

"Come on inside Finbarr, I am sure my wife will buy a few." This time I am embarrassed, as we Corr kids are always taking money from Mrs. McCusker.

When she hears about my day, she asks, "Aren't you quite the young missionary Finbarr? How many tickets did you sell?"

I reply, "Ten, Mrs McCusker. You don't have to buy any, as you are always giving us money. I wasn't going to come at all today, until your husband told me to come in."

"We won't go bankrupt if we buy two tickets. You will make your Mammy very happy, and your brothers and sisters will be jealous to see that you are such a good salesman. Since you started serving mass, Phil and I enjoy seeing you up there on the altar every Sunday. If you don't

17

get attracted to girls in the neighborhood, maybe you will be a missionary priest yourself some day."

While she goes up to her parlor to find sixpence, I sit by the fire thinking of my brother Brendan throwing the snowball down the chimney into Phil's dinner. I don't tell her what I am thinking, and I decide not to tell her that I like girls. She fills out the ticket stubs, putting Phil's name on one and her own Bridget McCusker on the other. I shake her hand and say, "Thank you Mrs McCusker. Noogey is going to be very pleased that you and Phil are helping him teach all the young boys and girls in Africa about Jesus."

I cannot wait to tell Mammy how well I did selling Noogey's tickets. She laughs and says, "Your daddy knows you better than all of us when he says, 'Finbarr has the gift of gab.'"

"What does that mean, Mammy?" I ask.

She smiles again, saying, "Daddy feels you can talk people into buying things that they don't even need. You must have told them a good story about Noogey and the missionary priests and how he will use the money you collected to send missionaries to Africa to teach both the little children and their parents about Jesus."

Marie looks up from reading her comic book and says, "Well done Finbarr, you little salesman."

Feeling very good about my success and not really tired, I go out into the garden in front of our hall door. I grab my grandmother Kitty's colored ball. I am excited about beginning to do another good thing today - getting rid of my fat bum. I kick the ball in the air. It goes up a mile, carried by a slight breeze towards Potahee Mountain. Trying to catch the ball before it lands, I run as fast as I can in my bare feet towards the end of the garden. Like most things I try to do, except selling Noogey's tickets, I fail the first time, the second time and the third. Looking back at the large kitchen window, I wonder if Brendan, a very fast runner, is looking out and laughing at his little brother doing something as silly as running after a ball in the garden that he kicked towards nobody. What will I say if he asks me why I am playing football alone? I cannot say, "I am doing it to get rid of this fat bum."

When I kick the ball a fifth time, I take off like a rocket. I run so fast that I am actually waiting for the ball to drop into my arms. I keep kicking, running and catching until Marie comes out to tell me that Mammy wants me to come in for the family Rosary and bed.

Daddy, P. Joe and Mary Farrelly are busy milking the cows. When Daddy comes into the kitchen for his tea, the first thing he asks me is, "Finbarr, are you enjoying Kitty's big ball? I saw you running after it like crazy when I was taking in the cows for milking."

"I like it a lot Daddy" I say. "I am trying to run faster and win races at school, just like Brendan does. Did you win races, Daddy, when you were the same age as Brendan?"

He ignores my question. Years later I learn why he didn't want to reply. He was already, at Brendan's age, a member of the IRA [*The Irish Republican Army*], a volunteer army whose goal was to drive the British Government out of Ireland by whatever means, legal or illegal.

I keep playing football by myself several times a week. Sometimes Brendan plays with me, other times he invites me to go up to Lacken Crossroads as he joins older boys who are playing Skittles. Skittles is usually played by having teams of two players compete against several other teams to see which team reaches the score of 41 first.

Brendan teaches me all about the game. He shows me how the five wooden pins (standers) are placed in the form of a square with four pins on the corners and a fifth pin in the center. Each pin, made of circular wood, is six inches tall and about twelve inches in circumference. The players stand behind a white chalked line twenty feet away from the square target. The purpose (or goal) of the game is to for each player, on their turn, to try to knock over as many pins as possible by throwing a three-foot-long skittle towards the square target. Each player throws four skittles underhand to the primary target, the pin in the center of the square. This earns the highest number of points for the lucky striker.

On weekends there are usually twenty or thirty adults sitting on the ditch with their backs against the fence and cheering the different teams. The male customers who buy their groceries at Lynch's shop frequently stop and cheer their local hero, who may be in the process of knocking all five pins, using all four skittles. Brendan tells me that on certain evenings Johnnie Moore, an older player, serves as referee and sees to it that the winners receives a modest financial reward. Johnnie collects three pennies from each player. Another adult, Toddy Maguire keeps the score.

Brendan, knowing that I just don't like to sit and watch others play, asks Johnnie if it is okay if Mel Lynch, Pat's son, and I replace the pins after each player has thrown their four skittles. "No problem," says Johnnie, "but make sure that they are not hit by one of these skittles."

Brendan joins Mike-Joe Mulligan and they form a team. Brendan starts off with a flourish. Using an underhand swing, with his first throw he knocks the center pin down the road. Toddy marks down a five on his score chart. Mike Joe is not as lucky. He knocks down two of the side pins, but referee Johnnie rings his bell, saying, "Points disallowed; the player had both feet inside the foul line."

As the evening darkens, I say to Brendan, "We'd better go home or we will get in trouble with Mammy, if we miss the Rosary."

My eighth year is going by very quickly with playing football, helping with the game of Skittles at Lacken Crossroads, serving mass on Sundays and, on week days, with an older boy strong enough to move the red mass book to the Gospel side.

I love going to school, as it means learning to read, write and add up numbers. My brothers and sisters and I are lucky that we don't have to walk far to school. Mammy says it is less than half a mile. You simply walk out Legaginney Lane and when you reach Legaginney Road you turn left and walk up the hill in the direction of Potahee Mountain.

The parish hall is on your left, while Beatty's house is to the right. The school is on the left side of the road, sitting beneath Potahee Mountain, where the parish Church of St. Michael's is situated.

Legaginney School is old. It is large enough to hold seventy students in its two classrooms. Miss Gaffney teaches grades one through four, while Master McCarthy teaches fifth through eighth. Father McEntee is the manager, and Master McCarthy is the principal.

I love Miss Gaffney. She is like Mammy, who tells me I am a special child and supports me when I am struggling with some addition or subtraction in my homework. As we begin the day before we start our lessons, Master McCarthy comes into our room or sends an older student from the eighth grade to take roll call. Miss Gaffney then starts the day by leading us in our Morning Prayers. She then checks the homework of the third and fourth grade sand gives them an assignment that they are expected to complete while she teaches my second grade how to read sentences and write sentences.

Because the boys and girls in first grade have just started school Miss Gaffney asks one of the smarter girls in fourth grade to keep them quiet using crayons in a coloring book until she is free to start teaching them the alphabet. We sometimes hear Master McCarthy get mad and scream at one of his students. Miss Gaffney listens for a moment and then shakes her head. She never loses her temper. On Friday, September 30th, she announces, "I want you all here on Monday. You will see why."

Chapter IV

Father McEntee versus Miss Gaffney

All of us students come to school early on Monday morning, as we all love Miss Gaffney and don't want her to be upset with us. Dympna and I come in together. She is in Third Class and sits in a row behind our class. For some reason Master McCarthy is in our classroom rather than his own. He starts a big discussion with Miss Gaffney. We cannot hear what he is saying, as both of them are facing the blackboard, with their backs towards the students. Miss Gaffney does not like whatever she is hearing, as she keeps shaking her head and saying "No, No!" He finally marches out of our room and says to her as he opens his own door,

"Alright, have it your way."

Miss Gaffney is shaking, she is obviously upset. Without telling us why, she starts Morning Prayers. We were almost finished when Father McEntee, the school manager, enters our room, using the door that faces Legaginney Road. There is a strange woman walking behind him. She is years younger than our Miss Gaffney. Fr. McEntee does not say hello to our teacher or to all of us her students. Miss Gaffney is ignoring him, until he begins to talk to us.

"Good morning children. I am here this morning to introduce your new teacher Miss Kelly." At first there is complete silence. None of us know what is happening. Fr. McEntee continues, "You will love her as much as you love Miss Gaffney." That does it. The Fourth Class students shout immediately, "We want Miss Gaffney. We want Miss Gaffney."

Fr. McEntee tries to get the screaming students to stop, waving his hand and putting his finger to his lips, signaling to be quiet. It doesn't work, as the rest of the students in the room, including me, join the fourth graders yelling, "We want Miss Gaffney, we don't want Miss Kelly," repeating it several times.

Hearing the noise, Master McCarthy enters in the room, all flustered and not knowing it was Fr McEntee who caused the uproar. Miss Gaffney is sniffling.

"Good morning Fr. McEntee." Says the Master. Fr. McEntee ignores his hello. He is upset that the children of his school, Legaginney National School, not only didn't accept his decision to replace the aging Miss Gaffney, with an attractive young teacher from County Galway, but are bold enough to express their anger by yelling at him "We want Miss Gaffney." I am upset that the priest whose masses I serve several times a month on Sundays and week days is so cruel to our favorite teacher.

After several minutes of silence, except for Miss Gaffney sobbing and several girls in each class crying, Master McCarthy asks Fr. McEntee to step outside the classroom into the cloakroom, where our coats hang and the turf for winter are stored. Miss Kelly starts speaking softly to children in the First Class. Miss Gaffney sits behind her desk and puts her face her in hands. After several minutes the master returns to the head of the class and says something quietly, first to Miss Gaffney and then Miss Kelly. They each nod their heads and he announces to the class,

"Until further notice, there will be two teachers in this

room, Miss Gaffney will teach First and Second Class, while Miss Joyce will teach Third and Fourth. I want the boys in Third and Fourth to move their desks back to make room for Miss Kelly to teach you." Hugh Finnegan, in Third Class starts to clap his hand and we all join in. Miss Gaffney, realizing that it wasn't Miss Kelly that caused the confusion, walks over and gives her a friendly shake-hand. Fr. McEntee doesn't return to our classroom on this day.

Miss Kelly spoke to her new students in a low voice, so as not to disturb Miss Gaffney. Miss Gaffney tries being relaxed, as she corrects each of my class-mates homework. I am happy, as I got all my additions correct. We all love Miss Gaffney and don't want Fr McEntee or anybody upsetting her. As Dympna and I walk down Legaginney road after school she explains to me what she thinks is happening in school today.

"Miss Gaffney is getting old and Fr. McEntee, the manager of both schools in our parish, hired Miss Kelly to take Miss Gaffney's place. Our old teacher feels that she is well able to teach all of us, as she has done for forty years, since she succeeded her aunt in this job. Fr. McEntee feels differently. He is following the custom in this Diocese of Kilmore, where each teacher usually retires on reaching the age of seventy. The master knew that Fr. McEntee was bringing a new teacher in to take Miss Gaffney's place. He was trying to get her to accept the manager's decision to retire and accept her pension. That is when she kept saying No, No, No, before Fr. McEntee came into the school with Miss Kelly."

Then Dympna says something that makes me very sad. "I am afraid that Miss Gaffney is going to lose this battle." I am really angry but say nothing.

Mammy can tell by looking at my face that I didn't have a good day in school.

"Where is your usual smile Finbarr and all your funny stories from school?" She asks. I bang the kitchen table with my fist. She knows I am mad about something.

"I am very angry at Fr. McEntee. He was nasty to Miss Gaffney today. He tried to throw her out of the school and replace her with some teacher from Galway; we don't know or want in our school. We kids stood up to him and all yelled together, "We want Miss Gaffney, we don't want Miss Kelly."

Dympna goes upstairs to talk to Marie who is changing from her school clothes. Marie is in Fifth Class and didn't take part in our fight with Fr. McEntee. Dympna knows that I have a quick temper, just like our daddy. She does not want to get in the middle of the confrontation that is going to take place between Mammy and me. Mammy comes over and puts her hand on my head saying, "I know you love Miss Gaffney, we all do; but I don't want you joining other boys and girls in school yelling at Fr. Gaffney. You have three uncles priests, who like Fr. McEntee are God's anointed messengers. As a Corr from Legaginney people are going to expect you to show more respect for priests. I am sure that we will find out very soon that Fr. McEntee is doing the right thing."

I couldn't hold back any longer. "I am sorry, Mammy you tell us all the time that God, who created us, wants us always to treat other people with the respect. Fr. McEntee didn't treat Miss Gaffney with respect today."

"I cannot argue with you Finbarr, I wasn't in school today to see what happened."

I wasn't going to win, no more than Miss Gaffney is

going to win in her battle with her manager, as Dympna said. So I finished my discussion with mammy by asking, "Mammy is it all right if I change my clothes go out in the garden and kick the ball around, before I do my homework for Miss Gaffney?"

"Go ahead son, maybe you will feel better about Fr. McEntee when you are finished."

How is that Mammy knows more about my feelings than I do myself?

She does not bring up the issue about Fr. McEntee and Miss Gaffney to Daddy at tea time. She is afraid that Daddy would be very angry at me disrespecting Fr. McEntee. She may talk about it with Daddy after the family Rosary this evening, when we have gone upstairs to bed.

For the next two weeks school goes on as usual, with one exception there are three teachers instead of two and Fr. McEntee is no where to be seen. We kids notice that the school master spends more time in our room to make sure there is no conflict between Miss Kelly and Miss Gaffney. He doesn't have to worry, as Miss Gaffney reaches out and makes Miss Kelly feel comfortable. On one occasion, when I had to back into our classroom to find something I needed during recess, I discover both teachers having lunch and chatting at the front of the room.

My life continues as usual serving mass, going to school and playing football by myself in the garden after my homework is done. When I serve mass with Fr. McEntee he does not say anything to me regarding Miss Gaffney or that he is upset with me, taking the side of the rebellious students, who want her to stay on teaching, while he wants her to retire. Fr. McEntee continues to meet beggars and poor people from the area after mass in the sacristy. He is so kind and generous, living up to the message of Jesus, to give to the poor, while ignoring his own needs. Sean Mulligan and Hugh Finnegan, who serve mass with me and are in my class at school, are both very upset at all the beggars who take advantage of our priest. Hugh says, "Everybody knows Fr. McEntee is a saint. Some of us think he gives away too much. Rather than ordering a new cassock from tailor Phil Miney in Lacken to replace his old greasy one, he chooses to give all of his money to poor people and doesn't care how he looks."

Sean agrees with Hugh's comments and adds more information that he learns from his family, "My Daddy says that some of these beggars are thieves and not really poor. They read the papers daily and if some very well off parishioner dies they know that the offerings taken up at the funeral will be big and they cue up outside the sacristy after the burial, to get their "share" of the spoils."

In the Diocese of Kilmore, the practice of taking up financial offerings, in memory of the deceased at funerals, is a definite benefit to the priests in the parish. The offerings are divided between the top priest, called the Parish Priest and his assistant called the Curate. In our parish of Ballintemple we have three churches, St Michael's, Potahee, St Mary's, Bruskey and Ahaloora with two priests serving the three churches.

The same year that Fr. McEntee is having a conflict with Miss Gaffney, one of the most distinguished and oldest parishioners Mr. McKiernan dies. He owns one of the most popular grocery and hardware shops in our County of Cavan. The funeral is announced in the national papers, The Irish Press and the Independent, along with our local county paper The Anglo Celt. Fr.

McEntee announces the death from the altar on Sunday morning and invites parishioners to attend the funeral, as the deceased has being a big supporter of the parish. The celebration of the deceased's life includes a concelebrated mass on Tuesday morning at 10:00 AM. Master McCarthy sends four of us altar boys up the hill to serve the mass at Potahee. He chooses my brother Brendan and Brian Mulligan, two senior servers, along with Sean Mulligan and me, two juniors. The church was packed. For the first time I saw standing room only at St. Michael's Church. At least thirty guys were standing near the vestibule where old Jimmy Beatty rings the Angelus Bell. When it comes time to pay their offerings, they march up behind the others and drop paper money on the table, just inside the altar rail. Sean Mulligan guesses the total offerings comes up to 500 pounds (sterling).

Besides Fr. McEntee and our curate Fr. Smith two other priests concelebrate the funeral mass. Fr. McEntee gives a beautiful eulogy, listing all of the deceased's charities, his devotion to attendance at mass and other liturgical functions. At that moment I have mixed feelings about Fr. McEntee. He can be so complimentary speaking of a rich dead parishioner, who is less than a half hour away from being buried in the cemetery, that surrounds the church and yet shows so little feeling towards a poor teacher Miss Gaffney, who has given her life to educate hundreds of us children for over 40 years.

As the funeral mass is completed, Fr. McEntee leads the concelebrants through the main door of the church. We all process with the coffin, the deceased man's family first after the coffin, followed by close friends. Brian Mulligan and Brendan lead the procession to the cemetery, one of them carrying the censer, the other the incense. Brian and

I walk behind them carrying the holy water, so that Fr. McEntee may bless the grave as the coffin is lowered into it. Back in the sacristy, Jimmy Beatty, our long time sacristan and bell ringer is sitting guarding the funeral offerings in a leather bag. Fr. McEntee invites his fellow concelebrants to go down the hill to what we call the Priest's House, for a cup of tea.

As we four altar boys are removing our soutanes and surplices, Fr. McEntee comes over and gives each of us a whole shilling. Meanwhile over twenty "beggars" are lined up outside the sacristy door. Brian Mulligan surprises all of us by going over to them and says, "Please come back tomorrow. Fr. McEntee has invited his priest friends to go down to the Priests House for tea" They grumble a little and leave. As I am saying my night prayers, I am thinking a lot about our still favorite priest Fr. McEntee. I say to God "Lord, if I grow up to be a writer I want to write about our saintly and generous parish priest Fr. McEntee."

Chapter V

Christmas in Legaginney

Hail and blessed be the hour and moment
In which the Son of God was born
of the most pure Virgin Mary
At midnight in Bethlehem in piercing cold,
At that hour, vouchsafe Oh My God to hear my prayer
And grant me my petition. Amen.

The popular Irish author Alice Taylor describes the uniqueness of celebrating Christmas in Ireland in her 1995 book "An Irish Country Christmas" She writes,

"The magic of Christmas was out in the haggard with the cattle and down the fields with sheep, but most of all it was here in the holly-filled kitchen with the little battered crib under the tree and the tall candle lighting in the window. The candle was the light of Christmas and the key that opened the door into the holy night."

Christmas season begins each year in Legaginney with our mother Nell inviting all of us children, who are willing, to join her in reciting the *Hail and blessed* prayer four thousand times prior to Christmas Day. When asked to explain to us why so many times she replies,

"I believe that people of the world, who loved God, waited 4,000 years for God's Son to take on human flesh in the womb of his virgin mother Mary." To make sure that I keep my commitment to Mammy and more importantly baby Jesus, I kneel by my bedside each day, starting November 1st, the Feast of All Saints, and keep a record of the number of times I say the prayer. I tell Miss Gaffney and the kids in my class about this prayer. Miss Gaffney surprises me by saying with a big smile,

"Finbarr, I have been saying that prayer four thousand times each year, since I was in second grade, just like you are now."

Besides helping her children prepare for Christmas spiritually Mammy makes sure to get Legaginney House, both physically and spiritually, ready to celebrate the birth of the Christ child. As early as December 1st she orders ten white candles, about one foot in height, at Pat Lynch's shop that she will place on Christmas Eve in the ten windows of our home called Legaginney House. She is not surprised when I ask the question,

"Mammy, why do we put these candles in the windows on Christmas Eve? Why do we not do the same at Easter or for St Patrick's Day?" She smiles at me and replies.

"Leave it to you Finbarr to ask the right question. We light these candles on Christmas Eve to give light to the Blessed Virgin and St Joseph as they are on their way to Bethlehem. I will ask your brother Brendan to take you out on that evening to go up on the side of Potahee Mountain so that you can see the lights in all the houses in Legaginney and Lacken. You cannot stay out too late as you must be in bed by 8 o'clock, before Santa comes over the mountain with his reindeers bringing toys for all you little children."

Long before this takes place, I join Mary Farrelly in feeding the geese, which have to be fattened up to be sold at the market or to be cooked for one of the three special dinners during this holy season. The first of these special dinners is Christmas Day, followed by New Years Day and then January 6, the feast of the Epiphany, which we in Ireland call "little Christmas." This year two mother geese and a proud nasty gander produce eleven goslings. Starting in mid-November the fourteen geese are put in a cubicle in the pigsty and fed cooked potatoes and oats. During the first week in December Daddy takes eight of the newly fattened geese in the horse and cart to the market in Ballinagh. The lucky gander and the two mother geese are released to feed in the local fields, while their now three fattened offspring have their necks broken, as a first step towards them being cooked for Christmas dinner.

I am a little sad at first seeing the three geese lying dead in the haggard. Mary Farrelly notices my mood and reassures me that the way daddy killed them is painless. She takes the dead geese in one by one to the dairy, about twenty yards away from the kitchen door. She spreads a cover on the floor and starts the laborious task of plucking their feathers. I try to help her, but I don't have the strength in my fingers to do so. Brendan comes home from school and after changing from his school clothes, he sits on the dairy floor and helps Mary finish the job. Mammy comes over to supervise our work and asks me to help her gather the feathers and put them into white flour bags.

"What are you going to do with the feathers Mammy?" I ask.

"You should know Finbarr, as you sleep on a pillow each night, filled with feathers from last year's geese." She replies. "I make my own bed pillows and whatever is left over I use to make couch pillows that we use in the parlor."

As Mary and Brendan finish removing all the feathers, I notice that there is a whole covering of furry hair left on each goose, that must be removed before the job is finished. Brendan remembers how to do it. He goes out into the vegetable garden, where Daddy grows his cabbage, onions, lettuce, beats and brussel sprouts. He gathers a small bundle of dead branches and lights them with a match, creating a small flame that Mary uses to singe the fur of the three geese. Mary then takes the geese back into the dairy, slits their throats and rear ends, removing their hearts, livers and gizzards. Brendan and Mary take the chickens into the kitchen and with some twine tie the geese to hooks over the fire place to be smoked for the two weeks leading up to Christmas.

Now that the principal ingredient for the Christmas dinner is hanging in the chimney, P. Joe goes down the railroad tracks past Miss Berrill's to Reverend Battersby's farm to get some red- berried holly to decorate our kitchen and parlor for Christmas. Eilish and Marie take over cutting up the holly branches, careful not to knock off any of the berries. Standing up on kitchen chairs they hang the berried branches behind the picture of the Sacred Heart of Jesus, that takes up almost a quarter of the wall along the kerosene lamp, which lights up the whole kitchen. They place some holly on nails over the geese, hanging in front of the chimney. The picture of grandma and granddad Corr gets decorated along with a long stream of holly sitting on top of the kitchen dresser that holds all of the plates, cups and mugs used at meals. With some direction from Mammy, my two older sisters take four rolls of colorful paper, attaching the ends to the four corners of the kitchen ceiling and stretch them towards the centre and attach them with a large bow to the center of the ceiling, like a mistletoe.

The next room for decoration is the parlor, where the Corr family spends most of Christmas Day. The mirror over the fireplace and the very large mirror on the back wall get their share of red-berried holly. My favorite picture in the parlor is Father Michael Corr, pictured in his US army chaplain's uniform. He is my idol; both as a priest and for the way he combs his hair in the picture. The split in his on the left hand side is just perfectly straight. I have not met him, but hope to some day, as you will read in a future chapter. Today Marie decorates his picture with red-berried holy. I check my reflection in the large mirror and I ask Marie, "Does the split in my hair look like Father Michael's hair?" "It does of course." She says. The final decoration in the parlor happens when Mammy takes down the old crib that she hides from year to year over the clothes' closet in her bedroom. She warns Eilish and Marie not to break any of the delft statues of the Virgin Mary, St Joseph, the Child Jesus in the crib or the two animals that make up the holy crib. She tells us all,

"This was a gift my mother in Longford gave me, when I came to Legaginney to marry your daddy." To make the scene look natural, Eilish goes down the lane to Scott's field and gets some dry moss and spreads it over the big sideboard in the parlor. They remove all of the little statues from their covering of white tissue paper and place them on the moss, first the crib and baby Jesus in the center and then his Blessed Mother, Saint Joseph and the animals, all looking towards the crib. Mammy then places a small stumpy candle, she calls a votive light in front of it. It is not lit until all of the family is ready to sit down in the parlor for Christmas dinner.

One of the last things Mammy does in preparation for Christ's birthday celebration is prepare her Christmas pudding. She gathers all of the ingredients on her cooking table in the kitchen, having shopped in Murray's grocery shop and Connolly's Market in Ballinagh. She does not want to be distracted by all of us children, especially me asking her, "Mammy what is that black stuff you are adding to the fruit and flour?" She sends everybody, except Eilish and Marie, out to the haggard to play hide and seek in the hayshed. We have fun playing hide and seek with Dympna and baby Colm. When we return to the kitchen, we discover all of the ingredients that were spread all over the cooking table are gone and Mammy just points to the Christmas pudding sitting in a white bag being cooked in a big pot of boiling water over the fire.

Christmas Eve is spectacular. There is not a cloud in the sky, which is very unusual for our beloved homeland. Brendan and I walk up the steps towards Potahee chapel and turn around every few steps to look at the lights in Beatty's home, then my godfather Frank Corr's, followed by Maguire's and Pat Lynch's in Lacken. As we go higher we can see all the way down to Legaginney bog, with just a single light in Michael Cox's thatched cottage and several flickering lights in McCaul's and cousin Lizzie's. I cannot help thinking that God, who directs us and everything from heaven, gives the holy family this spectacular night to make the journey to Bethlehem more pleasant and we do our share by lighting the road for them.

Brendan reminds me that Santa is on his way and we better get home and be in bed before he comes down our chimney.

Chapter VI

Christmas 1943

It is pitch dark when I wake up in the boys' room in Legaginney. My sleeping partner P. Joe, home from St. Patrick's College, is still snoring. In the other bed Brendan and Colm are unconscious. I reach up to touch the brass railing to see if Santa had come and filled my Christmas stocking. "Why wouldn't he?" I say to myself. "I am a good boy". Unable to reach the brass railing, I stand up and in doing so I step on P. Joe's arm and wake him up. "I'm sorry." I say. He whispers back to me,

"Don't wake your brothers. Santa came. I saw him. Wait until you see the beautiful colored sweater, and you're stocking filled with a big orange, a banana and two bars of chocolate."

I am so excited, I can't go back to sleep. I know P. Joe likes to tease me, his little brother, but I also know he is not going to be mean and lie to me on Christmas morning. I lie quiet in bed, looking at the dark ceiling for almost an hour. I hear Colm waking up, moving around and check his Christmas stocking hanging over his head. He lets out a squeal. He apparently pulls down his stocking and discovers a toy train and his stocking filled with sweets and fruit, which he had told Santa he wanted for Christmas.

P. Joe, realizing that it is a waste of time trying to go back to sleep, gets up, finds a box of matches in his pants pocket and lights the candle Mammy has placed in the window to light the road for Blessed Mary and Saint Joseph on their way to Bethlehem.

The sweater Santa brought is gorgeous.

"Put it on," says P. Joe. Leaving my night shirt on, I pull the sweater over my head. I discover to my delight it is a perfect fit. The sleeves reach down to my wrists, while the back reaches down to my fat butt. Colm starts playing with his train on the wooden floor by his bed. I run across the corridor to Mammy and Daddy's room. Daddy is already up and has the candle in the window lit. He is sitting on the bed having his morning cigarette.

Mammy says, "Finbarr you look great in Santa's fair isle sweater."

"Thank you Santa", I respond. Daddy dresses and goes to check on the cows before he leaves for mass.

I keep my sweater on and hop into bed to cuddle with Mammy. Baby brother Fonsie, too young to know anything about Santa, is sleeping in his crib. It is still dark outside when Brendan gets up and helps Colm get dressed. He tells me to get ready. He is taking Colm and me to the early mass. I am wearing my Santa sweater, as we walk out the lane and up Legaginney Road towards Potahee. The stars seem to be even brighter than they were last night. Brendan takes Colm's hand and we walk up the steps from the road to St. Michael's on the side of the mountain. Half way up, Brendan stops, turns around and says,

"Look at the beautiful new moon that wasn't there last night, when you and I came out to see the stars," I say,

"Oh yeh, it is only part of the moon. It looks like half an orange."

"That's right," says Brendan. "In less than two weeks it will look like a full orange."

Jimmy Beatty rings the church bells as we reach the

entrance. The choir up in the church loft is singing "Silent Night". Brendan and Colm climb up the stairs to take their seats on the choir loft. I go around to the front of the church to the sacristy and put on my cassock and laced surplice over my new sweater. Sean Mulligan is waiting to serve with me.

He says, as he laughs, "You must have been a good boy for Santa to give you such a beautiful 'ganzee." (*That is what we call crocheted pullovers in our part of Ireland.*) We have the candles lit on the altar and the cruets with altar wine and water all set up when Fr. McEntee arrives to vest in white vestments for the joy-filled Christmas mass. The choir is singing "O Little town of Bethlehem," when Sean and I process out of the sacristy in front of Fr. McEntee. We three genuflect as Father begins the prayers "Introibo Ad Altare Dei" (*I go unto the altar of God*) on the ground level.

He preaches a short sermon, all the time smiling, as he looks up toward the choir and ends up saying, "I feel like I am celebrating the birth of the Christ child with the angels in heaven, because of the beautiful music we have had this morning from our choir upstairs."

Sean and I get the altar ready for 10 AM mass. Fr. McEntee shakes our hands, gives us each a six penny piece,

"Happy Christmas," he says. "I am sure that Santa Claus was generous to both of you, as you are both good boys and faithful altar servers."

Brendan and I babysit Fonsie while Mammy, Daddy, and my three sisters get ready and go to 10 AM mass. While we are at mass, I know Daddy takes one of the smoked geese from the chimney. He chops off the wings, which Mammy and my sisters will use to dust the parlor and kitchen after all of the Christmas celebrations. Meanwhile, Mammy is busy preparing the stuffing for the goose, our annual ritual. She has already cooked the giblets, *(the neck, lizard and gizzard.)* She saves the stock to moisten a loaf of bread cut into three-quarter inch cubes. She adds one chopped onion, four spoons of her home made butter, one chopped apple, some sprinkling of sage, salt and pepper to the stuffing.

She places the stuffed goose and the extra stuffing that she couldn't fit inside the goose, in a large flat bottom pot placed on top of a three pronged stand, with hot coals below and an equal number of coals on the lid. Before she leaves for mass, she warns Brendan to make sure that there are sufficient hot coals, underneath the pot and on top, because she wants to be ready to serve the traditional Christmas dinner in the parlor when Uncle Father Lawrence arrives at 1:00 PM.

I love the feeling of anticipation of this day. When Mammy returns from mass, she puts on a colored apron and supervises Eilish and Marie as they take the good delft from the parlor sideboard and set the table for our most elegant dinner of the year. Mary Farrelly peels the potatoes and puts them in a pot over a blazing fire. Brendan gets coal that Daddy has bought for the tiny fire place in the parlor. He lights the fire, gathers Colm, baby Fonsie and I to sit in front of it, probably to have us out of Mammy and my sisters' way, as they continue preparing the dinner.

Meanwhile, Daddy sits in the kitchen to the side of the hob looking at the blazing fire. I guess he is thinking of Christmases past in Legaginney and his brothers, Father Michael and Joe, both in America. He is waiting for his younger brother Father Lawrence to arrive after having said two masses in his Church in Stradone, almost twenty miles away. I'm cuddled up with my baby brother Fonsie, wearing my beautiful sweater on the couch, looking at the tiny flames coming up from the coal fire. Brendan has the gramophone going, playing Christmas carols sung by Irish tenor John McCormack. The smell of the goose cooking in the kitchen reaches the parlor, making me feel like I am starving, as I haven't eaten anything since I had my porridge after 7:00 AM mass.

At exactly 1:00 PM Dympna runs up to the parlor and announces Father Lawrence is here. Brendan stops us from running down to the kitchen saying, "Wait here until he comes up. If we go down we will interrupt Mammy, who is trying to get the dinner ready now that Uncle Father Larry has arrived" We respect Brendan's wishes.

For reasons I don't understand, Mammy is always nervous when her brother in-law, our Uncle Father Lawrence visits us. Before he arrives she tells us how to behave, what to do and what not to do. On some Sundays she will even try to stop Brendan and me from going fishing or hunting because she says, "Father Larry may stop in to see you all today."

One day when I wasn't supposed to be listening I hear Marie ask Mammy,

"Why are you afraid of Father Lawrence? Dympna and I think he is a lot of fun. We look forward to playing games with him when he comes at Christmas."

Mammy hesitates for a minute or two and says, "I want you two to enjoy playing with him. Because he is a priest he will never have children, maybe he thinks of all of you as his children and wants you to grow up to be responsible. When you are all gone to bed and Daddy is outside some place he lectures me saying, "Since all of your children are part of the "Corrs of Legaginney", much more is expected of them than all the other children from families who go to Potahee Church." I don't know what that means. Maybe I will ask Mammy when I get older.

Mammy comes into the parlor and asks all of us to be seated with Father Lawrence around the big table in the parlor. That is everybody, except herself, because she is going to serve the dinner. P. Joe decides to stay in the kitchen and eat with Mammy and Mary Farrelly. The table looks gorgeous. The white table cloth, with the lace border, is decorated with a lighted stumpy candle, set in a crystal holder in the center. There are eight silver knives and forks with cloth napkins in front of each person's seat. These knives and forks have been shined with brasso by Eilish and Dympna during the annual house cleaning 'campaign' in preparation for Christmas. Mammy and Eilish serve the food, carrying the goose that Daddy carved, on a silver-plated platter. Father Lawrence says the prayer, blessing the food before we all eat. Fonsie is unaware of all that is happening. He is just lying happy in his crib, drinking warm milk.

I love Mammy's mashed potatoes, covered with her homemade gravy. The stuffing is very popular, and several people ask for seconds. Eilish goes to the kitchen a couple of times to refill the container. Because Father Lawrence has been fasting since midnight and offered two masses he takes a second helping of goose and stuffing. I eat too much of the mashed potatoes and don't leave enough room for Mammy's delicious Christmas trifle. Daddy excuses himself and joins Mary Farrelly and P. Joe milking the cows in the byre.

It is dark by 5:00 PM when Father Lawrence announces that he is not staying late this evening. He says he is afraid of having to drive home to Stradone in a fog. Mammy persuades him to wait until Daddy returns from milking the cows, so that he can serve him a Christmas cocktail before he leaves. Marie giggles. She knows Daddy does not drink alcohol and Mammy will have a half a glass of Port Wine, so that Father Lawrence will not be drinking alone. Daddy returns and pours his brother a glass of Paddy's Irish whiskey. Mammy puts on a guilty face, drinking her annual half glass of Port Wine.

I ask her later, "Mammy, why do you put on that face? Don't you like the taste of wine?"

"It is not the taste of the wine. I have a brother in-law, that you have not met yet and when he drinks alcohol he gets nasty with my sister Julia. I don't want any of you to ever start drinking alcohol."

Marie is the first to notice that Father Lawrence is beginning to tease her and Dympna. Marie jumps on his knee and starts to take off his Roman collar. Everybody is laughing except Mammy. She calls Colm and me outside the parlor and quietly ushers us with a lighted candle upstairs to bed. I am tired, being awake since five or six o'clock. I don't know what time my uncle left and if he had to drive through the fog to get home to Stradone.

Chapter VII

Saint Stephen's Day

I get up early, as I am expecting another busy day with a lot of fun. Mammy explains to me, as I am eating my porridge, that here in Ireland we celebrate the feast of Saint Stephen by remembering how this holy man was betrayed and later martyred when a little bird, called a wren, revealed where Stephen was hiding in a thorny bush. She says,

"People, called Wren Boys come to our home wearing silly costumes, face masks, sing and dance as they collect money to supposedly bury the 'mean' wren."

I hadn't finished eating my porridge when a car drove past our kitchen window and stops at our hall door. A tall man, with a big red face, gets out with a wrapped package in his hand. I ask Mammy,

"Is this man a wren boy?"

"Oh no" she replies "that is Mr. Morton, a Protestant friend of Daddy's. He comes each Christmas season and brings Daddy a gift. Mammy invites him in for a cup of tea. He asks Mammy all kinds of questions about us children, while he waits to speak to Daddy. I keep quiet, as this is the first Protestant I ever met. I wonder if all Protestants have red faces, like Mr Morton. The gift of chocolates may have been for Daddy, but he shared them with all of us.

As Mr. Morton drives out our lane he is met by our first set of laughing, singing Wren-Boys. Brendan runs outside, anxious to know if he can recognize any of them.

Mammy puts on a big smile and says to Brendan,

"Let them come in and sing or play their instruments. They should earn their money, we are going to give them."

There are six in the group; their leader is very tall dressed in pajamas, a mask and wig. Brendan says in a whisper,

"I bet he is Vincent, Father McEntee's workman and I am sure he is wearing an old pair of Father McEntee's pajamas."

Mammy speaks to the smaller fellow carrying the melodeon,

"I would like you to play a gig and have a couple of your friends dance."

"No problem Mrs. Corr" he replies in a muffled voice, trying to hide his identity. While he plays the jig the others dance around our concrete kitchen floor. I wouldn't say it is great dancing. My sisters Marie and Dympna, who take dancing lessons, do a lot better. When the Wren-Boys finish they bow towards Mammy, while the rest of my siblings and I give them a big round of applause. Then big Vincent leads them all singing the Wren-Boys theme song,

"The wren the wren the king of all birds, Saint Stephen's day was caught in the fir.

Now up with the kettle and down with the pan, a penny or two to bury the wren."

Mammy gives them a shilling and they all thank her. Brendan thinks he knows all of them saying,

"They are part of the gang that plays skittles and hang out at Lacken Crossroads.The little guy is Mike-Joe Mulligan. The fellow with the woman's dress and cap turned backwards is Michael King, who lives up the hill from Mulligan's. I am guessing that the other two are Toddy Maguire and Joe McCusker."

I say to Brendan, "Why don't we all get dressed up and go up the lane to McCusker's. Marie and Dympna will dance the jig and Mammy can play the fiddle."I thought Brendan was going to choke laughing at my suggestion. He then says,

"When Mammy comes back from feeding the hens, and let's see what she says." I can tell by the smirk on his face that he is teasing me. Colm is too busy playing with his toy train that he got from Santa. Eilish, Marie and Dympna are occupied washing the 'good dishes,' which Mammy just uses for special occasions. They put them and the silver plated knives and forks back in the drawer of the sideboard of the parlor, ready to be used at Easter, or if some of our "Yankee" relatives come home to Ireland during the summer.

Mammy returns from feeding the hens, carrying four fresh brown eggs. She is very happy, as the hens don't usually lay many eggs during winter. Brendan asks her with a straight face,

"Mammy, Finbarr wants to know if you will join Marie, Dympna, him and me and go up to McCusker's as Wren-Boys. He wants you to play the fiddle, while Marie and Dympna dance the jig."

Mammy puts on a big smile saying,

"I cannot leave Colm alone with Fonsie and I am expecting more Wren-Boys. If you like I will take down the fiddle after we have our tea. Marie and Dympna can teach you and Finbarr how to dance the "Stack of Barley" and the "Siege of Ennis", which they have learned last month at their dancing classes."I am delighted, as I always want to learn how to dance. I asked Daddy last year, on my seventh birthday, if I could take dancing lessons. He replied,

"Dancing lessons are for girls and 'sissy' boys. I don't want any of my boys to grow up sissies." I shot back,

"Daddy, I saw you dance once. How did you learn?"

He replied angrily,

"I learned by watching other boys and girls dance at country dances."

While Mammy and Mary Farrelly are preparing our evening tea, there is a loud knock on the kitchen door. Four adults and two young Wren-Boys come in. One adult starts blowing on his mouth organ, while the second adult joins him playing a on his tin whistle. The two younger ones, who turned out to be girls, dressed as boys with their long hair tucked under their caps, dance a beautiful two hand reel. Brendan doesn't have a clue where they had come from; he asks one of the adults, "Where are you from." The gentleman replies, "We are from Ballinagh. We have been on the road since 9:00 this morning. This is our last stop, as we are starving."

That last statement was too much for Mammy. She cannot stand any children being hungry, starting with us her children. Speaking directly to the two adults,

"Please all of you sit down. We have plenty of Christmas trifle left over since yesterday. This will carry you over until you get home to Ballinagh. I cannot stand seeing two young people being so hungry."

After our evening tea, which includes all of us sharing Mammy's left over Christmas pudding, Daddy and Brendan move the dining table back towards the big dresser, which is attached to the back wall. Mammy takes down her fiddle, she has carefully hidden away from all of us over the wardrobe in her bedroom. While she tunes it and adjusts the strings, Marie and Dympna put on their special dancing shoes. Mammy announces, "Ok girls; take your places for the Reel. Keep your arms by your sides, just as if you were dancing in competition at the Cavan Feis."

Marie stands up straight and looks as if she is in a trance; beginning her steps with a nod from Mammy. Dympna is not as serious. She smiles at all of us, sitting or standing around the kitchen, all the time keeping in perfect rhythm with her older sister. Daddy is sitting on the hob near the fire. Before he sits he grabs me, knowing that I will be tempted to join Marie and Dympna on the dance floor. He whispers in my ear, "Finbarr when Mammy calls for all of us to get on the floor for the "Stack of Barley" you can be my partner." This is the first time ever that my daddy makes me feel special.

Rt. Rev. Msgr. Michael J. Corr
R.I.P. 1966

Chapter VIII

Father McEntee wins;
Miss Gaffney loses

The Christmas season in Ireland begins on Christmas Eve December 24th and ends on January 6th, the feast of the Epiphany, or as we call it "Little Christmas." Although we eat goose on Little Christmas, the holiday is not as special as Christmas Day. Our uncle Father Lawrence doesn't come; instead we frequently get a surprise visit from his older sister, our Aunt Nora Brady. Both she and her husband Jim Brady, who live over two miles away in Lacken, are a lot of fun. We just love it when they visit! Uncle Jim owns a big mill, which converts the oats grown by Daddy and other farmers, into oatmeal, which Mammy then uses to make our porridge. You will be reading several of Uncle Jim's humorous poems at the end of this book. Just like Father Lawrence, Nora and Jim have no children and, as Mammy says, "They spoil the Corr kids of Legaginney, as if they were their own."

I serve mass on the feast of the Epiphany with a new altar boy named Brian Smith from Legaweel. Father McEntee is not in his usual jovial mood. He doesn't even welcome Brian. I should have guessed that his mood is related to Miss Gaffney. As soon as he finishes reading the gospel, Father McEntee addresses the congregation, saying, "I hope you all had a happy Christmas, visiting your family, receiving guests and most of all spending time praying to the infant Jesus in the crib."

He hesitates for a moment and then in a firm voice says, "I had no choice but to ask Miss Gaffney to retire on reaching the age of seventy. It is the rule of the Diocese of Kilmore and the National Education Office in Dublin. She refused to retire, leaving me with no choice but to transfer her to teach the lower grades at St. Mary's School in Bruskey, the second school in our parish. I know the boys and girls at Legaginney School won't be happy with this news. They love Miss Gaffney and told me so back in November when I introduced the new teacher Miss Kelly from Galway. I am announcing it today from the altar, particularly to you the parents, and I ask for your support."

I don't hear or want to listen to his sermon on the readings of the feast of the Epiphany! I am mad and feel like yelling out in church, "Father McEntee, Miss Gaffney does not ride a bicycle. How do you expect her, a seventy-year-old woman, to travel four or five miles to and from Bruskey five days a week?"

I continue to serve mass like a robot, an angry robot at that. Father McEntee does not speak to us after mass. When we leave after extinguishing the candles and hanging up our soutanes and surplices, we are greeted by ten or twelve angry parishioners, waiting to attack Father McEntee, before he walks down the hill to have his breakfast.

I am not looking forward to going back to school on January 7th. I have no choice but to accept Father McEntee's victory over our beloved Miss Gaffney. The only good news we hear after the horrific announcement from the altar is that Johnny Cullen, a graduate of Legaginney National School and a former student of Miss Gaffney's, has volunteered to drive her in his taxi to and from Bruskey at a much reduced fare.

There is another surprise announcement at the Corr

dinner table. P. Joe announces that Miss Kelly is taking up residence in our Aunt Nora and Uncle Jim's home in Lacken. This is a lot more convenient than Miss Gaffney's new assignment, as Miss Kelly will only have to walk less than a mile to her teaching job in our school.

Brendan gets suspicious that something else is going on and asks P. Joe, "How do you know about Miss Kelly's new residence?"

P. Joe gets all flustered and his face turns red. Brendan, knowing that P. Joe is attracted to beautiful women who move into our neighborhood, starts teasing him. "P. Joe, you have a crush on Miss Kelly."

P. Joe says, "Stop bothering me, I have to leave now to bring in the cows for milking." I don't know what a "crush" means; I am guessing that P. Joe wants to kiss Miss Kelly. You will learn later that both Brendan and I are right.

Our school gets off to a surprisingly good start in 1944. Master McCarthy comes in to check on our classroom, now totally under the guidance and teaching of Miss Kelly. Father McEntee does not come to visit us that day, as he usually does. We do not actually see him in our classroom until three months later when he comes on March 16th to wish us a Happy Saint Patrick's Day (March 17th.) He reminds us all to wear real shamrocks to mass.

I have a hard time keeping my mind on my arithmetic, writing and catechism. I keep thinking of P. Joe wanting to kiss Miss Kelly. For the first time in my life I feel an attraction to a woman, and this woman happens to be Miss Kelly. I want to do something to her or for her to make her happy. I don't know what that something is. I never had feelings like this for Miss Gaffney, although I loved her like a mother. Fortunately, those warm fuzzy feelings towards Miss Kelly subside after a few days and I get busy learning how to create sentences and write a story.

Within two weeks Miss Kelly knows all of our names. When I tell her, "My name is Finbarr Corr," she smiles and says, "You are the first Finbarr I've ever met."

I don't know what to say. I just laugh. She then says, "Finbarr! That is a name I will never forget."

Flustered, I say, "Thank you Miss Kelly."

It is now the middle of January, and the weather is getting colder. There is white frost on the bushes on each side of our lane, as we walk to school with our books and a sandwich for lunch in our school bags. To keep the classrooms warm Master McCarthy and Miss Kelly light fires in the fireplaces in the front of their classrooms. Some children have to carry a piece of turf to school to be burned in the fires each day during the winter. Other families, like ours, bring a pony-cart full of turf just once each winter. Since my daddy owns Legaginney Bog, he is happy to do more than his share to keep the school warm for the forty-six children who attend Legaginney School.

Two months later we have a big surprise. It starts snowing on Sunday evening and doesn't stop for three days. When we get up on Monday morning to go to school, our Daddy says there won't be any school that day. My sister Marie, who loves school, does not believe him and says, "Master McCarthy always tells us 'rain or shine Legaginney School will be open.'"

"Okay, Marie, if that is what you think, I will walk with you to the school, as soon as I have finished milking the cows. The rest of you can spend the day playing hide-and- seek in the hay shed." Brendan is already finished with his education and leaves for work wearing his long wellingtons. Eilish, Dympna and I, cuddled up near the fire; sit on the hob eating our warm porridge. I wish Brendan would stay home because he could help us build a big snowman.

Daddy and Marie are back home about a half hour after they walked down the snow-white lane. He is not angry at Marie. He knows she likes to study and that one day she will be a teacher like Miss Gaffney or Miss Kelly. He tells Mammy and all of us, "The master was there in the school, but he didn't light a fire. He said Miss Kelly came to the school but he sent her home because one of his neighbors, who is good at forecasting the weather, told him this is going to be the worst storm in forty years. P. Joe and I are going to take the cows down to the stream for a drink and then bring them back to the byre. We are not going to take them out to graze until the storm is over. We will feed them plenty of hay and give them buckets of water to drink. According to the master, the school may be closed for a whole week." Marie does not say a word; she goes up the stairs to the girls' room to read a big book that was a birthday present from her godmother, Maisie Phillips.

It is still dark in the boys' room when I wake up on Tuesday morning to the sound of hail and wind crashing on our bedroom window. I let P. Joe sleep. I know he will have a busy day taking care of the cows. Mary Farrelly tells me that the cows give just as much milk during a snowstorm as during a sunny day. I try to go back to sleep, but I am too curious to know why the usually soft snow changes to ice as it bangs on the window.

About an hour later I get out of bed quietly and go over to Mammy and Daddy's room. Daddy has a candle lit and is sitting on the edge of the bed, smoking a cigarette, while Mammy is feeding my baby brother Fonsie at her breast. Fonsie stops sucking and falls asleep. Mammy hands him to Daddy, who puts him back in his cradle and tucks him in.

Daddy does not seem surprised when I ask, "Why does the snow make such a loud noise on the window this morning, which it didn't do yesterday?"

Daddy smiles over at Mammy before he replies. Mammy interrupts, saying, "That is your curious son Finbarr; he notices everything."

Daddy then slowly answers my question. "This snowstorm is very different than anything I have ever seen before. My guess is that the temperature dropped way below freezing last night and turned the soft, wet snow into ice, and that is what is hitting the windows this morning. This storm is now called a blizzard. With all of the snowdrifts outside, I have my doubts that you, Finbarr, will be able to reach the hayshed to play hide-and-seek today."

The wind and icicles are still bouncing off the kitchen window as we eat our porridge at the kitchen table. Mary Farrelly, her furry hat all covered with snow, comes in from milking the cows. She walks up behind me and puts her cold wet hands on my face. She addresses all of us. "You kids won't have school for several days. There now are banks of snow three feet high outside the byre and four- or five-foot drifts up the lane."

Marie goes back upstairs to read her book, while Dympna takes out the box of playing cards and teaches Colm and me some new games. Eilish joins us after she finishes making the beds upstairs. I like the game called "The Old Maid going to the Bone-yard" where the leader divides all the cards among the three players. The winner is whoever first gets matches for all of their cards.

Dympna's favorite game is "Tommy Come Tickle Me." With one quarter of the stack of cards in your hand, your goal is to get rid of all your cards by matching the card numbers in Hearts, Spades, Diamonds and Clubs and then throwing them one by one onto the center of the table, saying, "This is a very good Ace for me," then the second one "As good as thee", followed by the third, "The best of the Three," the fourth "Tah me." (*Gaelic for 'that's me'*) The game ends when the loser, the last person with a card in hand, says "Tah me." The other players jump all over the loser and tickle him or her as they say "Tommy come tickle me."

By Thursday morning the snow has stopped falling. Marie, Dympna, Colm and I put on the warmest clothes we have and head off for Legaginney School. When we go past McCusker's house, we have to walk single file down the lane as there is still a four-foot snowdrift against the hedge on the left. When we reach the school, we are surprised to find only the Mulligan and Lynch children. The rest of the families presume there is no school today. Master McCarthy has swept the snow of the steps going into both classrooms. He and Miss Kelly, dressed in woolen scarves, gloves and rubber boots, are waiting outside the school. The master announces, "Unless we get twenty more students during the next hour school will have to be postponed until tomorrow. We have not lit any fires yet. In the meantime Miss Kelly and I will help you build a snowman as a surprise to any students who may turn up." I can tell by Miss Kelly's face that she is the most surprised by the master's proposal.

Mike Joe Mulligan gets the snowball rolling down the little hill between the school and Legaginney Road. We help him turn it on its side and everybody, including the master and Miss Kelley, picks up armfuls of snow and put it on top of Mike Joe's round snowball. The master makes a round ball of snow and places it on the top, as the head of the snowman. Dympna finds two small stones on the side of the hill, which is now partly bare and places them in the snowman's head as eyes. Mel Lynch gets a piece of stick out of the hedge and places it in the snowman's mouth, to look like a pipe.

We are all laughing and admiring our creation when Miss Kelly attempts to climb back up the hill but slips and falls on her backside down the hill. Master McCarthy laughs and attempts to lift her up. He also falls, loses his hat and exposes his bald head. Mel Lynch, thinking it is part of the fun begun by the master, picks up some snow and throws snowballs at both the master and Miss Kelly. We all – that is, everybody except Marie - join in pelting them both with snowballs. Marie, disgusted with our childish behavior, chooses instead to find her school bag and walks home. Dympna and I walk down Legaginney Road past Miss Gaffney's cottage. We notice her doorstep is swept clean of snow. I am feeling guilty, as I am beginning to really like Miss Kelly. When we get home I decide I am going to ask Mammy if I am being disloyal to Miss Gaffney.

Chapter IX

I receive the Holy Ghost,
March 7th, 1947

I continue to enjoy school and sports. My ambition is to grow up to be good enough to play Gaelic football for my own county of Cavan. My brother Jack, who played with the local Cornafean team, was almost good enough to play for the county team. I no longer play alone, as I did for two or three years. Playing alone and running up and down our garden causes my big butt to disappear. I cannot show the good results to old Jimmy Beatty who, you will remember, brought my big butt to my attention. After ringing the church bell for the last time on Christmas Eve he died on his kitchen floor. Sean Mulligan and I served his funeral mass, celebrated by Father McEntee.

I now have plenty of friends at school, who are just as ambitious about sports as I am. My good friend Brian Smith, a year younger than I am, has similar dreams and is always available after school to kick and catch the big rubber ball that I got from my godmother Kitty.

Mel Lynch, who helps his dad and mom serve customers at his father's shop, prefers to play handball at the ball alley down Lacken Road near the railroad. Toddy Maguire, who lives beside the crossroads, is more than ten years older than Mel or me. He plays handball and prefers it to risking getting hurt playing football. Toddy stops me one day and says,

"Finbarr, I hear that you and Mel want to learn how to play handball. I am available to teach you if you come get me at my home anytime after 5 o'clock." Toddy works with his dad on their little farm.

Two days later Mel and I go to Toddy's home and the three of us walk down the road to the ball alley. Toddy is a good teacher and says,

"You two are going to be great handballers, if you keep practicing like you did today." Toddy throws the small hard ball against the wall and shows us how to hit it back against the wall with the palm of our hand, using an underarm swing.

He explains,

"Fellows, to win the point you have to return your competitor's shot, as it returns from the wall and makes one hop, before you hit it back towards the back wall. To make it harder for your competitor to return your shot you will learn how to aim your return shot to the bottom of the back wall, making it impossible for him to return the shot. Mel laughs and interrupts Toddy,

"It is easy for you Toddy, you have been playing handball for over ten years and we are only eleven years old."

"I should be better. Wait until you see Johnny Moore and some of the good handballers play on Sunday after mass."

People are still talking about the snow blizzard of 1947, reported in Chapter VIII, and which lasted for several weeks. While we, who attend Legaginney School, enjoy building snow men and having extra days off from school, the people from our local village of Ballinagh do not have such happy times. On the second Monday of February, hundreds attend the screening of "The Bells of St Mary" at the local dance hall on the Crossdoney

Road. As the patrons are leaving the cinema, walking up the road towards the village crossroads, there is a light sprinkling of snow falling. A big truck driven by a driver, not familiar with the zigzag crossroads, mistakes the light snow on top of McDermott's pub for the Main Street, he thinks is leading him to Granard. Meanwhile, several of the happy movie goers are walking on the sidewalk in front of McDermott's Pub, not yet visible to the truck-driver. The unfortunate driver applies the brakes and turns abruptly right onto the sidewalk to avoid landing inside the pub. Only a miracle could save the up-until-then-happy moviegoers.

Fortunately, none of my older brothers or sisters attends the movie this evening. We do have a cousin among the casualties. Tom Fitzpatrick, age 21, whose family nickname is the "Whits", is a native of Ballinagh and Kevin O'Reilly from Bruskey. The local Gardai (police) asks the driver to back up the truck a few feet, as the one of the wheels is sitting on top of Tom' chest. The same officer sends Owen O'Reilly from Drumbrade over to Father Dan Reilly's rectory, requesting that he come over, and anoints our cousin Tom and Kevin. They are obviously dying.

Somebody must be praying for the moviegoers this evening, as cousin Tom and Kevin are the only fatalities. R.I.P. Tom Smith whose nickname is "Tom the Bun," has a broken arm and a bruised leg. While P J Duffy from Garrymore has injuries to his face and arms.

.........Back at Legaginney School Miss Kelly is busy preparing all of us, age 12 and above, to receive Confirmation. She explains that when Bishop Lyons anoints us all with the chrism, the third person of the Blessed Trinity, the Holy Ghost, descends from heaven on each of us, giving us the spiritual strength to be soldiers of Christ.

I ask Mammy, "What does it mean to be a soldier for Christ?"

"That's easy, Finbarr," she says, "We have a picture in the parlor of your uncle Father Michael, who was a chaplain in the US Army. He is a soldier, who is prepared to fight to defend his country. When you and all your class are confirmed by Bishop Lyons on March 7, you are expected to imitate Jesus in loving your neighbor and forgiving those who hurt you, while continuing to serve your church, like you do when selling raffle tickets for the missions." I ask Mammy a question that I think may be too difficult for her to answer,

"Will the Holy Ghost inspire me like he does my uncle Father Michael?"

"He will of course Finbarr," she replies. "He is already inspiring you to be a little missionary when you help the Kiltegan priests send missionaries to Africa." I now feel more confident, as I say my daily prayers, knowing that the Holy Ghost is guiding me daily.

Besides studying the catechism and preparing ourselves for the oral exam given by a diocesan priest, Brian Smith, Sean Mulligan and me, are recruited by Master McCarthy to serve the mass on March 7. I know my catechism and am not anxious about the oral examination.

Sean is a little anxious about serving the Bishop.

He asks, "What will happen to me if I drop the Bishop's crosier?" (*A crosier is a staff, traditionally used by shepherds and now by Bishops on occasions of ceremonies to symbolize their role as shepherds of their flock in their diocese.*) All Brian is concerned about is passing the oral test so that he can be confirmed.

As Brian and I walk home down the railroad tracks, he lets out a yell "Whoopee! We passed. I don't care if this is the only exam I ever pass in my life."

I feel honored as March 7, 1947 approaches. Mammy and Daddy buy me a new grey suit and black shoes. This is probably the first time I don't have to wear hand-me-downs from my older brothers. I should have worn my new shoes a few times before March 7, since walking in new shoes with stiff leather causes me to have blisters on both heels on Confirmation day.

The second honor is given to me by Master McCarthy when he asks me to carry the sacred chrism. I walk one step behind the Bishop, as he dips his thumb in the heavy oil and anoints each of my classmates. Unfortunately, my godmother Kitty Osborne is unable to attend, because she is busy in England being a governess for a rich family's children. My godfather, Frank Corr, honors me with his presence; he shakes my hand and says "Finbarr, I am proud of you. Maybe you will end up being a Bishop one day if you don't fall in love with one of those nice girls in your confirmation class."

Chapter X

I dream of going over the Hill

Life in Legaginney is never stagnant; it is always changing. Miss Gaffney dies about two years after losing her battle with Father McEntee. I'm relieved to learn that Father McEntee asks his curate Father Smith to celebrate her funeral mass. Sean Mulligan and I both cry on the altar, as Father Smith eulogizes our favorite teacher. My Mammy tells me that,

"Of all the teachers I ever met, Miss Gaffney is the best at teaching children the art of good handwriting."

"I agree Mammy", I say. "I will always try to make Miss Gaffney proud of me."

My brother Jack, eight years older than me, is also a graduate of Legaginney National School. Unlike some of his siblings, he makes Miss Gaffney proud by the artful way he writes his letters. He accompanies our older brother P. Joe to St. Patrick's College, Cavan in September 1940 and five years later goes on to Saint Patrick's College Carlow (a seminary to train priests for English speaking foreign countries). Like me, he is influenced by the life and ministry of our uncle Father Michael J. Corr in New Jersey. If he was a better student in Gaelic (*Irish*) he might decide to sign up for our home Diocese of Kilmore and follow in the footsteps of our uncle Father Lawrence. Having failed the subject of Gaelic in his Leaving Certificate Examination, he is no longer eligible to go to St. Patrick's College Maynooth, the seminary for priests destined for dioceses in Ireland. He chooses instead to sign up for the Diocese of Paterson, New Jersey, which is next door to the Archdiocese of Newark, where Father Michael is stationed.

After two years studying Philosophy and other subjects, preparing him for the priesthood, he comes home in June, 1947 and surprises both my parents and his siblings sitting around the kitchen table having evening tea.

"Bishop McNulty of the Paterson Diocese wants me go over to America this summer and finish my four-year seminary training, before ordination." My parents are in shock. They don't understand the bishop's request. In retrospect Jack could explain the bishop's rationale better by saying,

"While I am studying theology I can learn more about life in the United States." But he does not say it. Daddy is not too upset, as he has known for two years, or more, that Jack has no intention of becoming a farmer. Mammy starts crying and says,

"Does that mean, Jack you are going over the hill to America and we will never see you again?" Jack does not know what to say and blurts out,

"Don't you want me to become a priest like Father Michael?"

There is a cloud of sadness over Legaginney. Father Lawrence comes over on Sunday afternoon and tries to explain to Mammy why Bishop McNulty is making this request. Mammy cries again, making me cry, even though I don't feel as close to Jack as I do to my two older brothers, P. Joe and Brendan. Since we are on holidays from school I decide to go down to our bog with P. Joe, as a distraction from thinking about Jack going to

America. Jack Murtagh, our workman, is already down there preparing to cut the wet turf from the bank, where he left off last year.

P. Joe takes a short cut through Phil McCusker's bog to the bog road past Michael Cox's home. Michael comes out to chat with P. Joe saying,

"P. Joe, I see you are bringing your "Noogey" brother with you to teach him how to catch turf." P. Joe just smiles. Michael adds,

"I hear that we may be losing Jack. Is it true that he may be going to America next month?"

P. Joe says "I don't want to talk about it". I think to myself that sad news travels quickly in Legaginney. Then Michael adds, "Mickey Rourke, the postman tells me that your mammy is very upset about it."

We walk down the road to where Jack Murtagh is waiting for P. Joe to catch the wet turf. Even though Daddy owns the whole bog, there are more than ten farmers who pay him rent, cut their turf here and take it home when dry to burn in their homes the following winter. The Fays from Denbawn arrive an hour after P. Joe and me. They come several miles in a pony and cart. Their son Kevin is a year older than I am and a nice guy. I know immediately that we will be good friends. I watch him catch the wet sods of turf as his dad pitches them to him. He places about ten of them on the wheel barrow; yells to his dad, "Enough" He then wheels the barrow about ten yards to an area covered with heather, lifts the right handle and dumps the wet sods in the row where he left off yesterday.

"I can do that." I tell P. Joe. Jack Murtagh does not believe that I, now almost thirteen, am prepared to do an adult job of catching turf and wheeling them out to a higher bank to dry. Kevin Fay stops pushing his wheel barrow when he sees me take over catching from P. Joe and yells,

"Well done Finbarr"; he puts his index fingers in his mouth and gives a loud whistle for everybody in Legaginney Bog to hear. P. Joe and Jack Murtagh just laugh. P. Joe then takes out a magazine out of his jacket, sits down and reads, until Daddy arrives later with our dinner.

The Fays have to cook for themselves. They light a fire with sticks and withered heather. They hang a kettle of water over the fire to boil for tea and later to cook their eggs. Daddy comes down the bog road on his bicycle to drop off the dinner that Mammy has prepared for P. Joe, Jack Murtagh and me. For the next hour Legaginney Bog is just one giant picnic, with small fires burning, men and boys eating and drinking. Before work resumes, we younger folks walk along the bank visiting and chatting with our neighbors.

I enjoy my summer, working in the bog and later watching Daddy cut the hay with Maggie, my favorite horse, and her son Silver pulling the mower. There is a holiday atmosphere in the meadow, as Mary Farrelly brings our tea out about 4:00 PM. I just love it when Mammy comes out with the tea; she always brings something special, like tasty raisin bread or toast with raspberry jam. As time goes by, she gets more relaxed about Jack going to the US. She organizes a going-away party the night before he is due to travel. Several of the neighbors come along with some of Jack's friends from Ballinagh, who attended Saint Patrick's College with him. Miss Berrill, of course, attends and without too much encouragement sings a very sad Irish lullaby.

Jack starts to cry, gets up from sitting near the fire, walks over and gives Mammy a big hug. Several of his buddies from the Lacken Crossroads are there. They talk football and how well Jack played for Cornafean against Mullahoran at the beginning of July. The phrase "Good Bye" never comes out of their lips, even as they shake hands with Jack as they leave the party. Daddy sits close by the fire and chats with his political colleague Stephen Shanaghy, who is drinking his second bottle of Guinness. While Daddy never drinks alcohol, he doesn't mind his friends having a drink or two. While the party is still going on, I sneak upstairs at 10:00 PM and go to bed.

Jack is lucky not to have to travel alone to the US for his first trip. Jim and Alice Finain, friends of my Daddy's, who emigrated to Massachusetts several years earlier, are returning after a two week holiday with Alice's family in Corduff, two miles up the road from Legaginney. They offer to take Jack with them in their hired limo the following morning, on the drive south, over one hundred miles to Shannon International Airport. The next day our whole family has the sad experience, common to many Irish families, of saying good bye to emigrating children and siblings, not knowing whether they will ever see that family member ever again. Jack is overcome with grief as he hugs Mammy and Daddy. He kisses Eilish, Marie, Dympna and Mary Farrelly on the lips and then surprised Colm and me by kissing us on the cheek before he takes his seat in the big limo. Jack is usually not that affectionate.

Summer is over, Jack Murtagh and P. Joe bring home the turf and stack it in the turf shed about ten yards away from the kitchen door. Daddy pulls the cocks of hay in the meadows onto the shifter and Maggie pulls the lot to the haggard to be stored for winter food for our eight cows and two horses. After the oats are harvested and allowed to dry in the field, they too are taken home and stacked in big reeks.

The last event that marks the end of the harvest is when the Halton Brothers arrive on schedule with their threshing machine and spend the whole day separating the oats from the straw. This event is like the picnic in the bog, as several of the local farmers come in to help my dad, P. Joe and Jack Murtagh execute the job. Two of the younger farmers get up on the stack of oats and heave the sheaves of oats toward Tommy Halton on top of the thresher, who feeds the sheaves of oats into the thresher. The middle-age farmers, like my dad, make sure that the oats run into the heavy bags, attached on the side of the thresher, while two more take the straw that is ejected from the rear of the machine. The oats are then transported by horse and cart to my Uncle Jim's mill in Lacken. The Haltons move on to their next customers, when the project is finished. The local farmers are invited for high tea into our home, served by my Mammy and Mary Farrelly. This is always a fun evening, the one time during the whole year when the local farmers work together, eat and spend a few hours exchanging stories and teasing each other.

As summer ends we start another school year. I move from Miss Kelly's room to Master McCarthy's, since I am now in fifth grade. The master lets our class know immediately what is expected of us, saying, "You have less than two years to prepare to take the most important test in this grammar school. The Primary Certificate Examination is the only public exam sponsored by the Education Department in Dublin, that certifies that you are qualified to continue your studies at a secondary school." The master says,

"Finbarr I expect that you will continue your education at St. Patrick's College in Cavan, following in your brother Jack's footsteps. You will not be accepted as a student unless you pass your Primary Certificate Examination."

He didn't scare me at all; as I know I will study hard and pass the exam. Master McCarthy does not know yet how much I like going to school and learning.

The weather is getting colder. We have rain several days each week. Daddy asks Dympna and me to help pick the potatoes. Dympna does not like it. She says, "Daddy, I would prefer to stay home, help Mammy cook, take care of the hens and chickens." Being a boy, I keep quiet and join P. Joe and Jack Murtagh in the White Field picking the potatoes and piling them in a pit. If I had repeated what Dympna said he would have called me a sissy.

What I really wanted to say was, "Daddy I don't want to spend my life picking potatoes in wet soggy fields, cleaning cow shit out of smelly byres. I want to get away from it all. I dream of one day crossing that hill (*pointing toward Potahee Mountain*) and never coming back.

Chapter XI

One Step away from College

It is no coincidence that I develop a devotion to our Blessed Mother in my early teens. The recitation of the Family Rosary in our home is as much a part of every day as eating warm porridge before we go to school. Mammy gives us a two-minute warning to get our Rosary beads so that we can begin this special family prayer before we younger children need to go to bed. If Daddy is absent because of a political meeting or other reason, he will fetch his Rosary beads when he arrives home, get on his knees at the dining room table and say his own Rosary.

Mammy also offers a thirty-day Rosary novena for some special intention. Because of Mammy's example, and possibly because I am moved by the Holy Ghost I received in Confirmation, I ask Mammy to buy me a Rosary Novena booklet. I begin praying the Rosary Novena on my thirteenth birthday.

I am happy with my life. Now in the sixth class at school, I am working hard and preparing for my Primary Certificate examination. My sister Marie, who is now in the eight class and passed this exam two years earlier, helps me with my homework. The intention of my first thirty-day Rosary novena is that I will pass this exam.

I don't see Miss Joyce every day and am surprised to learn that Brendan's prediction of P. Joe having a crush on her becomes a reality. I no longer feel an attraction toward her. P. Joe has become her boyfriend. I am attracted instead to a tall, buxom girl in the sixth class. I am too scared to tell her to her face that I like her. When Master McCarthy is not looking, I leave notes on her desk that say "Patty, I like you" signed "Finbarr." When she receives them she looks back to my seat and smiles.

The days, weeks and months at Legaginney School go by very quickly. All of a sudden it seems Master McCarthy receives a big brown envelope in the mail in mid-June from the Department of Education in Dublin. It contains four copies of the test to be presented the following morning to my cousin Nuala Phillips, Sean Mulligan, Hugh Finnegan and me. My good friend Brian Smith has to wait until next year. He is still in fifth class. I finish the test during the allotted time of two hours. I feel confident that I did okay in the exam. The four of us watch Master McCarthy seal our responses in an official envelope to be mailed back to the Board of Education.

We don't have to do any homework during the last two weeks of the school year. We just sit in the last row with the eighth class and work on arithmetic problems given to us by the master as the school day begins. The master does not stop teaching, but now focuses on the students in the fifth class, reminding them they have just one year to prepare to take the Primary Certificate Exam.

At home, family life is not running so smoothly. The winter blizzard of 1978 causes the deaths of twenty of Daddy's two-year-old cattle. When the calves at Legaginney farm reach one year old, they are driven five miles down the road to our second farm in Kilmore, where they graze on good pasture in the summer and have plenty of good hay in the winter. The sale of these cattle as three-year-olds provides a substantial part of the income my parents use to feed our family and pay tuition for two of my older siblings in boarding schools.

It needs to be said here that the winter weather in Ireland is usually moderate, with a light frost, a little snow and plenty of rain. Ordinarily, two-year-old cattle don't need to be housed during the Irish winters. But the winter of 1978 is very different. The snow drifts are three feet high. With no housing, the cattle are forced to walk and lay in the snow. Even with plenty of good fodder and water recovered from the frozen Kilmore Lake, half the cattle get sick and die.

At first Daddy does not tell Mammy or any of the younger children about this financial loss that will affect all of us. He tells me later, "You didn't need to know about it, Finbarr; you were busy the whole year preparing for your big exam."

He does not want to tell Mammy. He knows she will be traumatized, worrying about having no money to buy groceries for all of us. Each day he goes down to Kilmore by horseback and with the help of the herdsman Jim McCaul, buries the cattle who died during the previous twenty-four hours.

My daddy is too proud to borrow money from his brother Father Lawrence or his brother Barney the dentist in Cavan town seven miles away. Instead, he does not rehire Jack Murtagh to work on the farm; and he tells all of us that we will have to survive eating oatmeal, potatoes and other vegetables for a couple of months until he gets the monthly checks for the milk we take each day to the Crossdoney creamery.

When I learn the truth in May, I feel bad for Daddy. I know he is a hard worker and a proud father. He takes me aside and says, "Finbarr I don't want you telling any of this to your friends the Smiths or Mulligans. If Pat Lynch hears about it, you might as well have the priest announce it from the altar on Sunday morning."

"Daddy, you don't have to worry, I will keep it a secret. I can help you Daddy," I add. "Since I have taken my exam and expect to pass, I can take the last two weeks of school off and catch the turf from P. Joe in the bog."

"Okay. Finbarr, he will be starting next Monday." What Daddy does not tell me is that we will be cutting the turf in a different bog, much closer to our home than Legaginney Bog." I want to tell him I would prefer our regular bog, as I will miss seeing and playing with Kevin Fay, but I decide that he will not be receptive to that request after the terrible winter he endured.

Our faith community of Saint Michael's, Potahee, also has a sad loss. Father McEntee, our beloved P.P. (Parish Priest) – forgiven by now for his treatment of Miss Gaffney - is found dead in bed by his housekeeper. I will miss him. I learned a lot from him during the times I was an altar boy at his masses. His example of serving the poor and sharing part of his funeral income with beggars will inspire me for the rest of my life.

Our diocesan bishop from Kilmore, Bishop Lyons, comes to lead the thirty or forty priests in celebrating the mass of Resurrection on the day of Father McEntee's funeral. Since I am busy out catching turf with Pl Joe, Master McCarthy does not ask me to serve the mass, but I do attend the funeral with Mammy and Daddy. There are no funeral offerings taken up at priests' funerals, so the usual beggars won't be waiting at the sacristy door to ask the bishop for handouts.

Bishop Lyons gives a brief eulogy. He lists Father McEntee's virtues - his humility, devotion to the Blessed Mother Mary, caring for the sick and poor. The only good news I receive this year is a letter from the Board of Education in Dublin containing the Primary Certificate and congratulating me for passing the exam. While rejoicing over my academic success, I (at the tender age of thirteen) immediately feel pressure to focus on choosing a career.

Should I become a priest like my hero Father Michael in New Jersey, or should I get married and have a big family like Mammy and Daddy? Becoming a priest obviously means that I can never have a girlfriend. If I am honest with myself, which I must be for such an important decision, I have to admit that I like girls and I do get excited just thinking about buxom Patty in sixth class. But I am only thirteen. so I conclude that I don't have to decide yet.

On a Sunday afternoon that summer, Brian Smith and I are returning home along the railroad tracks. Kicking the football in Scott's Field for a couple of hours has left us both exhausted. Brian suddenly snaps to attention when he notices fresh footprints that lead from the railroad track down to the stone ditch between the railroad property and Scott's Field. Shushing me not to make any noise, Brian beckons me to follow him. To our surprise, P. Joe is lying in the ferns with his arms around Miss Joyce and is busy kissing her. I motion to Brian to be quiet and to follow me back to the railroad tracks. The "guilty couple" don't notice us. We laugh hysterically and admit to each other that this is the first time either of us saw a couple "make love."

I return to school in September only to discover I am totally bored and learning nothing. The master is not focused on teaching me or any of the students in the last seat of his classroom. Cousin Nuala, Sean Mulligan and

I spend our time playing a stupid game of Xs and Os. I once read that "an idle mind is the devil's workshop." I discover this statement is true because of trouble I get into early in October.

There are too many children in the master's classroom. Half of one class has to stand up along the wall on their turn and read their lessons, just like those sitting down. On this particular morning about seven girls from the fifth class stand reading their English book. I suggest to Sean Mulligan that we tie a string from the metal base of our seat, pull the string across the aisle, and tie its other end to the metal foot of the seat up against the wall. Our plan is to have the seven girls trip over it when the master announces, "Off you go for recess."

The prank works exactly as we intend. The girls don't see us setting up the trap. The first to fall is my cousin Eithne Phillips, followed by Margaret Mulligan and Rose Sorahan, who falls on top of Eithne. Unfortunately, the master catches Sean and me laughing. He makes me the culprit and yells, "Finbarr Corr, you may think of yourself a big shot, being a Corr from Legaginney, but one more act like that and you are going to be expelled from this school." Mammy doesn't think our little prank is funny either.

Our new parish priest, Father John McGauran, arrives in Potahee just a few days after we celebrate the customary Month's Memory mass in honor of Father McEntee. My first impression is that he is not like Father McEntee. Father McGauran does not seem interested in getting to know us altar boys. His first words to us are, "Boys, I want you all to wear appropriate footwear on the altar when you serve my mass. Wellingtons, big winter boots or bare feet are not suitable for the altar. I want you all to wear black rubber-soled canvas shoes."

I feel like telling him "My parents cannot afford to buy me new shoes. My Daddy lost twenty cattle in last winter's blizzard." To our surprise, Father McGauran is very friendly with all the children, during his first visit as manager of our school.

Over my childhood years, I always enjoy the summer whatever the activity, whether making the hay, harvesting the oats, or playing football or swimming in the river Eireann during the long summer evenings after a hard day's work.

I am not so happy when fall and then winter arrive. Picking potatoes out in the cold October evenings after school is not much fun. I still dream of getting away from all these dark days and long winter nights. Praying the daily Rosary novena is helping me clarify what I want to do with my life. I feel drawn toward following the footsteps of my hero uncle Father Michael in the U.S. and my recently deceased parish priest Father McEntee.

My hope is that if I am ordained a priest, the grace of the sacrament of ordination will be curb my attraction to women. In the meantime if anybody asks me what I am going to be when I grow up, I tell them I am going to join the Palestine Police, a British colonial police service who served in Palestine from July 1st 1920 to May 15th 1948 My little lie works for the first six months, until one smart aleck tells me that the Palestine Police no longer exist.

My first step toward the priesthood is to become a student at our local Saint Patrick's College in Cavan. When Daddy asks me why I want to go to college, I reply, "I want to become a priest like Father Michael." He looks disappointed. My guess is that he thinks I would make a good farmer. He doesn't realize that one of the reasons I work hard in the hayfields is to get the job done by 5 or 6 so that I can play football in the evening.

"I am sorry to disappoint you, Finbarr. Your Mammy and I don't have the money to pay your fees at the college."

What he doesn't know is that Mammy has a possible resolution. "Finbarr, I know you have a vocation for the priesthood," says Mammy. "Why don't you ask your uncle Father Lawrence? I am sure that he and his brother Father Michael won't let you down."

I reply, "All he can say, Mammy, is Yes or No."

Two days later I borrow my Uncle Jim Brady's bicycle and begin the seventeen- mile trip through the town of Cavan and on to the Cootehill Road to Tullyvin. Because of all the months of praying, I feel pretty confident. The weather is perfect, and the only place I run into heavy traffic is driving through the town of Cavan, past the new cathedral, turning right on to the Cootehill Road. Even though I started my trip early (8:30 AM) I am surprised how quickly I reached the sign TULLYVIN on the Cootehill Road. Father Lawrence's rectory is on the main road. I have no fear of missing it.

His housekeeper Katie is surprised and gives me a warm welcome. "Your uncle will be very happy to see you. He will be available in a few minutes. He opens his sitting room door as soon as he is finishes reading his morning prayers. I expect that you are staying for dinner at 1 PM. I am cooking a leg of lamb."

I am very relieved to find that he is home and not away at a funeral in some other parish. His door opens in less than five minutes. He seems to know that someone is waiting to see him, probably because he heard the doorbell ring.

He greets me with a big smile and handshake. "Hello Finbarr, to what do we owe this surprise visit? I can see you rode a bicycle. You must be in good shape, being here all the way from Legaginney before 11 o'clock."

I decide not to reveal the real reason for my visit up front. I want to get a feeling first of what kind a mood he is in, before I pop the question. I respond, "I borrowed Uncle Jim's bicycle. Daddy needed his today to go down to Kilmore. The only traffic I ran into was going past the Cathedral."

I take off my sweater and sit on his big couch while we chat for over an hour about all the recent events in Legaginney and Potahee. I keep my promise to Daddy not to share the news about the death of the twenty cattle, not even with his brother.

Chapter XII

Getting ready for a new journey

At exactly 1:00 PM, Katie puts her head into the living room and announces,

"Father, dinner is ready!" I feel like adding "So am I, Katie!"

I'm starving, having eaten nothing since having my porridge five hours earlier and sixteen miles away in Legaginney. The lamb is delicious. This is only my second time eating lamb. Father Lawrence says *Grace before Meals* and I dig in. I am careful to follow what Mammy taught us, especially when we have guests in the parlor at home. Katie's home made apple cake adds a special finishing touch to a tasty dinner. Father Lawrence invites me to go for a walk, taking his multicolored hunting dog along. Meanwhile, I am planning how and when to pop the question. I don't want to ask him while we are walking, as I want to see his face when I make my request.

Even though the summer evenings are long in Ireland, I don't want to ride my uncle's bicycle in the middle of the night. Uncle Jim is expecting me to drop it off at his home this evening or early tomorrow morning. I say a little prayer to myself as we return to the rectory to sit in the living room. Father Lawrence sits on his big reclining chair and I sit five or six feet away on the couch.

"Father Lawrence," I begin, "I have a big favor to ask of you. I have been praying to our Blessed Mother to guide me, saying Novena Rosaries, to decide what I am to do with my life. Daddy wants me to be a farmer, because he thinks I am a good worker. I feel God is calling me to do something very different; to be a priest like you and Father Michael. Daddy told me last week he and Mammy don't have enough money to pay my tuition at Saint Patrick's College in Cavan. I rode over here this morning to ask if you could help me out."

I keep looking at him, hoping for a "Yes." Instead I get response that shocks me. "Finbarr I am not surprised. Your parents have never been good at managing their money." I feel angry and want to yell,

"Daddy didn't cause the blizzard that killed twenty of his cattle in Kilmore last winter."

I hang my head instead and wait. After what seemed like a ten minute pause, which was probably really no more than a minute or two, he changes his tone and says affirmingly,

"OK, I will call the college and tell them that I will pay your tuition to be a boarder. It is too far for you cycle to and from the college each day and do your homework. I believe my nephew Brian, my brother Barney's son, is also going to be a boarder in September."

I stand and grab his hand and say, "Thank you Father Larry, I will do my best to make you proud of me."

I can't wait to get on my bicycle and get home to tell Mammy the good news. Before I leave, I go to the kitchen and thank Katie for the beautiful meal. As I ride through Cavan town I make the decision not to ever tell my Daddy and Mammy that his brother Lawrence said, "They were always poor managers of money." I also recite one decade of the Rosary, one Our Father, ten Hail Mary's and one Glory be to the Father, Son and Holy Ghost, as thanks for the help.

Going through Ballinagh, I go full speed down Main Street, then cycle as fast as I can up the hill to Legaweel and down the hill past Miss Berrill's railroad crossing to Legaginney Road. The 6:00 PM Angelus Bell is ringing as I cycle into Legaginney Lane. I can see Daddy working with P. Joe in the haggard. I ignore them and go straight into the kitchen; feeling exhausted, and give Mammy a big hug saying, "Father Lawrence is going to pay my tuition."

"Finbarr, my prayers and yours are answered. Now we must get busy organizing your clothes, so that you will be ready to be dropped off at the college the first week in September."

"I am looking forward to it Mammy." I reply.

When I tell P. Joe about my good luck he laughs at first, saying, "I wonder what nickname the second year students at the college will give you. Mine was not very complimentary, i.e., "Dead Cow." When Jack came in the following September they nicknamed him "Suckey Calf."

Daddy shows no reaction when Mammy tells him the good news. For a change, I keep my mouth shut, guessing that Daddy is disappointed with my decision.

I get up at the usual time the next morning and continue helping P. Joe build up the hay in the hayshed to be used for feeding both the cows and horses in winter.

On Sunday, Uncle Barney, the dentist, and Aunt Maura, drive out from Cavan with their sons Brian and Felim to visit us. I warn Mammy not to tell them why I am going to join Brian in Saint Patrick's College or who is paying my tuition. I feel good about having my cousin Brian with me at the college. He is a year younger than I, but probably a lot more advanced educationally than I am. The Christian Brothers' School he attends in Cavan has a reputation of being very demanding in comparison to the public schools out in the country. We "bog men" (what the "townie" students call us) have not even heard of the subjects of Algebra or Geometry, which we will have to start studying during the first week in September.

Uncle Barney takes his two sons with Colm and me in his car over to Scarvey on the river Eireann for a swim. The economic difference in the two families is obvious. Brian and Felim put on swimming trunks, while Colm and I jump in nude. Uncle Barney does not comment. When he was a young lad forty years ago growing up in Legaginney with my daddy, Father Michael, Father Lawrence and others, his parents couldn't afford fancy bathing suits either.

The news that I am going to Saint Patrick's College spreads throughout Legaginney and the neighboring town lands. Pat Lynch is very complimentary and gives me a half crown (30 pennies) to be put in my savings to take to college. Old Mrs Beatty, Jimmy's widow, adds two half crowns, as does our generous neighbor in our lane, Mrs Bridget McCusker. Four days before my new journey begins on September 4, 1949, I have 30 shillings in savings. Daddy hears about my good luck and asks, "Finbarr, are you going to take all of that with you to college on Tuesday?"

As he is asking that question, I remember where he inherited his penny-pinching attitude. He told us a story a few months ago about how as a twelve year old he was been escorted by good neighbors to the Cavan Horse-Jumping Show, his mother gave him a mere six penny piece and told him, "Have fun at the show."

81

Uncle Jim Brady, our local poet, is happy to hear that I am continuing my education at Saint Patrick's. He still regrets after all these years working the Lacken Mill that he didn't accept his parents offer to send him to college.

He asks me,

"Finbarr, are you sure you have enough pocket money? When I ride my bicycle around Cavan town I frequently see Saint Pat's students walking up town to football games at Breifne Park."

I reply,

"Thank you, Uncle Jim. I have thirty shillings. In fact, Daddy says it is too much to take with me next Tuesday." He just laughs in response and adds, "I have something you can use. My sailor uncle Pat brought back a beautiful trunk from the island of Saint Croix. I will have your cousin, Thomas Francis Corr, who works here at the mill, drop it off at your home tomorrow."

"Thank you Uncle Jim, I can certainly use it."

I feel bad for Mammy, because not only am I leaving her for a few months, but also because Mary Farrelly announces she has to go home to Clones in County Monaghan to take care of her aging mother.

As Mary leaves to catch the bus at Miss Berrill's crossing, Mammy says,

"Don't any of you cry about Mary leaving, she is will be returning shortly to marry Josie Beatty (old Jimmy's son) who she has been meeting with regularly in our lane for several years."

One of Mammy's habits is taking the local bus into Cavan town about once a month to do some family shopping. She usually asks Daddy for some extra shopping money. This time she doesn't approach him, as she knows that the cash box he keeps in the drawer below his clothes closet is practically empty. She is very fortunate to have developed a trusting friendship with Mrs. McDonald; whose husband Philip owns a clothing shop on Main Street in Cavan.

Mammy takes me along for her mid-August trip. She shares my secret with her friend, that Father Lawrence is paying my tuition. She does not have enough money to pay for the navy blue college jacket required, the grey dress pants to go with the jacket and brown corduroys I will wear daily to classes. Mrs McDonald is very gracious. She tells Mammy, "Just give me one pound today and when you sell the geese at Christmas time you can pay me the balance of four pounds."

Even I know that the actual cost of these items is twice that amount.

Mammy packs my Saint Croix trunk on Monday with bed sheets, pillow covers, towels, three shirts, socks and corduroy pants. While my cousin Brian will be transported by car from his home in Cavan two miles down the road to the college, my transportation is going to be my favorite horse Maggie, pulling the four-wheel trap the eight miles to the College. Since the Saint Croix trunk will take up the total floor space, Daddy has to tell Mammy,

"Sorry we don't have place for you to join us in the trap, as Finbarr's trunk is leaving no space for anybody except the two of us."

I am naturally sad as Maggie struts out Legaginney Lane. I am thinking to myself, is this just the beginning of me crossing that hill, to get away from the negative side of farming in Legaginney?

As is usual for my daddy, John Frank, we arrive at the college one hour before the suggested time of 4:00 PM. A middle aged priest, named Father Gargan greets us.

"This must be Father Larry Corr's nephew Finbarr," he says. "He called me over a month ago telling me to look out for an attractive horse and carriage that would be delivering you to the college." Speaking to Daddy, he said "Mr. Corr, you don't have to wait; Larry, one of our janitors, will take your son's luggage up to room 35 on the second floor. He will be sharing the room with his cousin Brian, who has yet to arrive."

John Francis Corr and Fonsie Corr, the author's
younger brother, host a US visitor, Louise Roth,
at the fireside in Legaginney (1954)

Chapter XIII

My first Year at Saint Patrick's

I feel melancholy as I watch Maggie trot out the college driveway, carrying Daddy home to Legaginney. Janitor Larry takes my heavy trunk on a two-wheeled gurney up the elevator to room 35. He says to me, "Mr. Corr, this is the only time you will be on this elevator. Students are not allowed to use them."

"I am not surprised Larry," I reply. He laughs. I offer him a sixpenny piece as a tip, but he refuses to accept it.

Since there are two beds in the room and Brian has not arrived yet, I choose the bed that is away from the window, as I prefer sunlight before shadows. I start to unpack, hanging my shirts in the closet and begin to make my bed.

This is my first time making a bed, as Mary Farrelly or my sisters always make the beds at home. I think I am doing a good job until Aunt Maura, Uncle Barney and Brian arrive a half hour later. While Uncle Barney and Brian are cordial Aunt Maura looks at my bed in disgust and says, "The pigs' bed in Legaginney looks better than that."

She strips the sheets and blankets off the mattress and shows me how to make it from scratch. To my surprise, Brian makes his bed perfectly.

I jokingly say to him. "It is obvious, Brian, that you don't have sisters." Uncle Barney and Brian laugh, while Aunt Maura says nothing, just scowls.

Two brothers, Pat and Kieran Scott, move into room 36 across the corridor. Their home is in Cootehill, which is three miles away from Tullyvin, where my uncle Father Lawrence is a parish priest. Like Brian and me, they are both first-year students.

They will probably be classified half Townies and half Bog-Men, as they are from the town of Cootehill. Since they grew up and went to a school in their town, but didn't attend a school taught by the Christian Brothers, they don't qualify as one hundred percent Townies.

We're summoned to the dining room about 7 PM by the tolling of a big bell on the outside wall. Father Gargan greets us all and directs us first-year students to sit at the tables close to the kitchen. Brian introduces me to John Joe Reilly and Hubert Maultsby, two of his classmates from the Christian Brothers School in town. Brian whispers to me that while Hubert is from a ghetto area of Cavan called the "Half Acre," he is here on a full scholarship and will probably be the smartest student in our class. I immediately make a resolution to be friends with him and use him as a model on how to study and get ahead.

While waiting for my meal, I remember P. Joe telling me before I left home that the food we receive at the college will not be as good as what Mammy serves us at home. I learn this evening that P. Joe's judgment is accurate. Our first supper at Saint Patrick's consists of two slices of a white loaf pressed together with jam in the middle. Mammy would never have served such a trifling supper to us, even during the time our food was rationed at home, after Daddy's cattle died during the blizzard in Kilmore. We had no choice but to eat it and hope for a better meal in the morning.

After Father Gargan gives a blessing over the meatless sandwiches, he welcomes all of us, with a special welcome to those of us who are first-year students. He asks the second-year students to treat the new students with respect. He instructs them to stay in their dormitories and avoid going into the first-year student dormitories. When he finishes his little sermon to the second-year students, the older students sitting at the other end of the dining room start to speak up and yell things like, "Not fair, Father, we must baptize the first-year students."

Father Gargan first smiles and then in a strong voice warns them, "If any student is caught or reported to me as physically abusing any of the first-year students, he will get the usual punishment of six strokes of my cane on each hand and his action will be reported to the president of the college and to his parents at home.

Brian explains to me how, over the summer, he heard that the second-year students frequently grab a first-year student, bring him into the toilet area, hold his head under a running water faucet and give him a nickname.

Both Brian and I go to sleep early. We agree that whoever gets out of bed first in the morning uses the wash basin first. Having inherited my Daddy's genes, I have no trouble jumping out of bed, when the senior prefect goes down our corridor ringing a large hand bell at 6:30 AM. The lights come on automatically in our bedroom. It is still dark outside. I wash my face and hands in the basin, get dressed in my new corduroys and make my bed before Brian gets up. In fifteen minutes the bell ringer comes around again to ring his bell, which Brian says is a last warning to go to the chapel for Morning Prayer and Mass.

We go directly from the College Chapel to the dining room. To my surprise, a full pot of porridge is placed in the center of each table. P. Joe could not share that good news with me, as he never received porridge during his three years at Saint Pat's.

Father Gargan, who offers the blessing before meals, announces, "Gentlemen, all of you who have been here for three of four years will notice that we are experimenting with a new menu for breakfast. After consultation with a local dietitian, we are switching from tea and toast to cooked oatmeal, commonly called porridge in many of your homes. We realize that some of you won't be happy with the change. The good news for those students is that it is just an experiment for one month. Then all of you can decide if you want to follow the dietitian's idea, that porridge is better for young people. It has more nutrition than tea and toast. If you don't agree, you can vote against it in October." Needless to say, I enjoy my porridge, even if it isn't as tasty as Mammy's.

Knowing that I will no longer be wasting my time sitting in the last desk in Legaginney National School, I am excited about going to my first class, I make sure I sit in the first row to keep focused as Father Bob McCabe outlines how he plans to teach us English literature and Poetry. I like him from the very beginning. At the end of each paragraph, he engagingly asks, "Is that clear gentlemen?"

The next teacher we meet is a younger priest with black curly hair. Father Carroll is dressed in a spotless black cassock and Roman collar. His responsibility is to teach all students in his class how to read and write classical Greek. The "Townies" don't have any advantage over us "Bog Men" because this lecture is the first time any student in the class has participated in studying Greek. To introduce the subject, he talks to us first about Greece, its capital Athens, its culture, and its drama and poetry.

The next class is a total surprise, or should I say the teacher is. Mr Breen is an older gentleman whose job is to introduce us to Physics and Chemistry. His teaching approach differs totally from the approach of Fathers McCabe and Carroll. Instead of speaking to us about the subjects to be studied he interviews the twenty-five of us about what grammar schools we attended, whether we were the first of our family to attend Saint Patrick's, and why our parents decided to send us here?

The first student to introduce himself is Francis McBrien, who explains, "Mr. Breen, I am Francis McBrien from Knockbride, County Cavan. I attended the local public school in our parish. I am the first in our family to go to college. Father Brady, our parish priest, whose masses I served, told my parents to send me here. I don't know why. Our school master thinks I am smart."

Mr. Breen replies with a smile, "We will know very soon if you are as intelligent as your master thinks you are."

John Joe Reilly is next. "My name is John Joseph Reilly. I am from the town of Cavan and attended the Christian Brothers School."

Mr. Breen does not wait for John Joe to finish his introduction. "Oh we have one of the Brothers boys here. They think they are the smartest kids in the school. Some of us call them "Townies," they call the rest of you from the countryside "Bog-men."

Cousin Brian looks over at me and nods his head as if to say, "Now you know who created the nicknames Townies and Bog-men."

When Mr. Breen comes to me, I say, "My name is Finbarr Corr. I am the third from my family to come to

Saint Patrick's. My brother Jack left here in 1945 and is now in America studying to be a priest. My older brother Peter Joseph works on our farm in Legaginney, helping my Daddy." Mr. Breen interrupts me, so, fortunately, I don't have to announce to the whole class that I am here because I want to be a priest like Father Michael in New Jersey.

Mr. Breen says, "I remember Jack Corr; he was quite a character and a good footballer. Welcome Finbarr. Are you related to Dentist Corr in town?"

I reply, "Yes Mr. Breen, that is his son Brian sitting over there."

With a sarcastic tone Mr. Breen adds, "This is an historical moment in the school to have two Corrs, one a Bog-man and the other a Townie, in the same class." There is no applause.

When he finishes all the introductions, he takes us downstairs and shows us the large Science Laboratory. Adopting a serious attitude he says, "Boys, here is where your knowledge of Physics and Chemistry begins. The test tubes and electric wiring over there is where I will be teaching the third-year students this afternoon how to divide water into its two components, hydrogen and oxygen. Before we break for the Christmas holiday they will be learning how to create water by passing dry hydrogen over heated copper oxide, which is the reverse of what they will be doing this afternoon." He gives us copies of our text book and says, "See you all next week."

I like Mr. Breen, even if he can be rude at times. I know I am going to love Science and learn a lot from him. I won't share my feelings of liking Mr. Breen with cousin Brian, as I am sure he won't like that he has a set on the Townies.

Off we go to lunch and, to nobody's surprise, we are treated to the same jam sandwich as we had last evening. I feel lucky that I like porridge and am not that really hungry after having a generous portion of it for breakfast at 7:30 AM. We have a one-hour recreation period before we return to the classroom for two more classes. I go up to the ball alley, which is next door to the college farmyard. I watch some of the second year and older students play handball.

One of the players recognizes me and comes over to ask, "Aren't you one of the Corrs of Legaginney?"

I say, "Yes, I am Finbarr."

"I am Hugh Finnegan from Garrymore," he replies. "You must play handball. I know you have a fine ball alley in Lacken, down by the railroad."

"I do play, but having seen how well you play, Hugh, I know I wouldn't give you any competition."

The big outdoor bell rings, calling us all in for afternoon classes. Our next teacher is a tall, grey-haired priest named Father Gaffney. His subject is Irish, or as we traditionally call it, Gaelic. This is a subject I am very familiar with, as my sisters Marie and Dympna are fluent in speaking Gaelic. Dympna spent a month last summer in part of County Donegal called the Gaeltaght, where all of the residents speak their native language.

Father Gaffney is the most direct of all the teachers we meet today. He begins, "As long as you are a citizen in Ireland, you don't have a choice. The study of the Gaelic language is mandatory. You must pass this subject of Irish to obtain your Intermediate Certificate less than three years from now. The same rule applies to you receiving your Leaving Certificate five years hence. If you want to go to the National University in Dublin you must pass Irish to be admitted." I am familiar with this rule because my brother Jack failed Irish in his Leaving Certificate examination, which I believe caused him to sign up for the priesthood in a United States diocese rather than our home Diocese of Kilmore, headquartered in Cavan.

Father Gaffney outlines his goals for the semester. He wants to make all of us more comfortable in speaking Gaelic, writing compositions in Gaelic, and learning Gaelic poems and reciting them from memory. He explains to us that several of the poems about our homeland Ireland don't mention Ireland or *Eire*, the Gaelic word for Ireland. While our country was under the control of the British Empire, the British government forbade it. To get around this repressive rule, the poets wrote poetry about a fair maiden that people of Ireland knew to be their native country. As the class ended Father Gaffney spoke his final words in Gaelic, "*Sla~n lat, Agus beannact Jay Lat,*" literally translated, Good Bye and God bless you.

Brian and I are joking about the nice surprise I received for breakfast. Since he spends part of his summers with us on the farm in Legaginney, he is familiar with Mammy's porridge. He knows I enjoy my porridge. He says, "Finbarr, you are having all the luck! First you get your favorite breakfast of porridge, and then, when we go to the study hall, you are assigned a seat diagonally across from Hubert Maultsby, the student you want to imitate. What do you hope we will have for dinner this evening?"

I respond with "Anything but jam sandwiches."

Our first surprise is that a fifth-year student, a prefect, is assigned to our table. He introduces himself and adds, "Gentlemen, I would like you to keep the same seats you have this evening. I am here for a few weeks to help you get accustomed to life in a boarding school. As you can see, we are having potatoes for dinner along with the meat and cabbage to be served in a few minutes. To make sure everybody gets their fair share, we pick our potatoes in turn each evening. This evening we start with Dan Gallogly on my left and tomorrow evening Pat Scott, sitting beside him, will have first pick. I know some of you are disappointed already with the food you received at lunch today and supper last evening. Many of you will have family and friends visiting us, bringing cakes, sweets, apples and other fruit. I would like to inform you there is a very nice custom at this college of inviting classmates to come to your room for what we call a 'Feed'. I encourage you not to be selfish. So let's go, Dan, pick your spud."

Chapter XIV

Getting Acclimated to College

Two months go by. The food still stinks. Fortunately, the Scott brothers invite us over to their room for a "feed" on their mother's delicious apple and rhubarb pies. Cousin Brian returns the Scott's hospitality a week later by inviting them to our room for another tasty feed. Uncle Barney comes loaded with biscuits, cakes and bananas from a big grocery store on Bridge Street, Cavan.

He whispers to me, "Do not to tell your parents about all this. I don't want them thanking your Aunt Maura, since she already thinks I am spoiling both of you."

I am enjoying all my classes even though I know I have to work hard in geometry and algebra to catch up with the Townies. I become good friends with Pat and Des Scott, and I also spend valuable time communicating with Hubert Maultsby, our star student. I watch him each evening in the study hall, where he sits diagonally from me across the aisle. I take note that he spends the first thirty minutes learning his English and Irish poetry. He tells me it is easier to learn poetry while your brain is fresh.

He adds, "Finbarr, my brain gets tired studying math and science for two hours. I am incapable of learning anything difficult after all that. For your information, Finbarr, I purposely leave geography and history until the end of the study period. It is easy for me, as I have learned most of it already with the Brothers."

Meanwhile, the college senior team is running, practicing free kicking and developing their game plan to meet Saint Patrick's College Armagh on Saturday. Cousin Brian has been with his daddy at several of our college's home games at Breifne Park in town. He tells me that there is a long history of rivalry between Armagh and us.

I am looking forward to going to the park to watch my first college football game. How lucky I am to have all the money our neighbors gave me before I left Legaginney! It is a long time until we go home for Christmas; I decide to take just one shilling with me to the game.

Two days later, Father Gargan, the dean of the college, calls a meeting of all of us first year students to say, "Fellows, there is a long tradition here at the College of having the first year students take on the second year students in Football. I have heard that you have some good football players, who are day students. They are, of course, eligible to play with your team."

James Brady, a day-boy from Cormore, about ten miles away from the college, asks, "Father Gargan, can we play on a Wednesday, when we have a half day? I would get home too late on full days, and I don't think my parents would be happy to see me cycle ten miles to and from the college to play football on a day we don't have classes?"

Father Gargan smiles at James and replies, "Of course you can, and we expect you to be a good footballer like your brother Phil, who played last week in the Senior County Championship in Breifne Park."

James smiles. "I hope to, Father."

Father Fay comes over to me as I am watching our senior team practice on Wednesday. He says, "Finbarr, I see you enjoy watching our team practice. I remember your brother Jack was a good footballer. I am looking forward to see you play next Wednesday with the freshmen against the second year lads. "I explain, "First of all, Father, Seamus Keogan, our chosen captain, has not picked his team yet. I am not expecting to make the team. I play too many sports to be good at football. I play handball and run track, which does not involve getting beaten up each day at practice. But if I am ever chosen to play on the college team while I am at Saint Patrick's, I will give it my all, even if that means getting my shins kicked and my knees bashed." Father Fay does not seem happy with my reasoning.

That same week I'm walking around the football field with a classmate from Dublin named Michael Smyth. A second year student, a very jolly fellow named Alphie Gallogly, a cousin of one of our classmates, comes up to us accompanied by a student I don't know. Speaking to Michael and me, he says, "Welcome to Saint Pat's. I don't know if you know about a meeting we are having at 1:30 PM, a few minutes from now, with some of your classmates, to see how you are enjoying being at the college. We are meeting on the second floor in room 201, near the end of the corridor. Come on over now."

I am slightly suspicious, as I know that classroom is close to the toilets at the end of the corridor, but I don't share my suspicions with Michael. Michael and I agree to follow them. When we arrive at room 201, my suspicions turn out to be valid. The classroom is empty, except for Alphie and his friend. Alphie grabs me, while his buddy grabs Michael.

Alphie announces, "We are not planning to hurt you or embarrass you. We are just going to do to you what happened to us last year. We are going to baptize and christen you. Who wants to go first?"

I look over at Michael. He looks scared, so I volunteer to go first by raising my right hand. They march both of us from the classroom to the washbasins in the room outside the toilets. Alphie pushes my head under the tap and turns the water on as he proclaims, "Shazam, I baptize you in the name of the Father, the Son and the Holy Ghost." Laughing, he looks at me to ask, "How do you like that nickname?" "Sorry, Alphie, I don't know him," I reply.

Alphie says, "If you look in the dictionary, you will find out Shazam is a character in a comic book created by Bill Parker for Fawcett comic books. He is an ancient wizard whose given age is 3,000. Both my friend Pat Carey and I feel that you, Finbarr, are going to be a very wise student and will have a great career like Shazam, no matter what you decide to do after college."

Pat "baptizes" my Dublin colleague Michael and christens him "Slasher" after Myles "The Slasher" O'Reilly, the High Sheriff of County Cavan who became commander of the ill-fated Irish rebellion against the English to regain lost territory in 1641. My friend Michael is thrilled with this new nickname. Even though Michael's family lives in Dublin, his family roots are in Cavan, where his uncle Tom Smyth still owns a hotel. Michael's interest in local history makes him well aware that the nickname is a real honor.

We are both happy and relieved that we didn't get something negative like Our classmate Francis McBrien, now stuck with "Bull-ram Drawers" as a nickname. Michael and I finish our walk around the college grounds and agree that our "christening" is not something that we should report to Father Gargan as abuse.

I discover the following weekend that college can be full of surprises. When we arrive in the chapel on Sunday at 7 AM, a priest completely new to us walks to the altar to celebrate our mass. He begins the introductory prayers on the ground floor, where he faces the tabernacle on the altar. In a deep resonating voice, he intones "*Introibo ad Altare Dei (I will go unto the Altar of God)*."

After reading the Sunday Gospel, he introduces himself. "My name is Father Duggan, a member of the Redemptorist Order. I was invited by your president Father McNiff to give your annual retreat. I welcome you all, especially the first year boys, who are about to participate in their first college retreat."

I am familiar with parish missions, as we had several at St. Michael's Potahee during my time serving masses for McEntee and Father McGauran. We had mostly Franciscan priests, who spoke very softly and encouraged all of us listeners to support their missions in Africa and the third world. I am getting the feeling from this retreat master's loud voice that we are going to get more of a good scolding than the loving forgiving voice of Jesus.

I get another surprise on Friday afternoon. A young female member of the college staff comes to the study hall and tells the prefect sitting in front of the study-hall that "Finbarr Corr has a guest waiting for him in the visitor's room, situated next to the main door of the college."

I am very excited as I run up the corridor towards the main door. I know it cannot be my parents because Daddy wouldn't take several hours off from farming during the working week. The surprise guest is my oldest sister Eilish, who is home from her job in Dublin. She took the bus to Cavan from Miss Berrill's in Legaginney and walked the two plus miles from midtown to the college.

She has a large shopping bag filled with Mammy's currant cake, biscuits from Pat Lynch's shop and apples from our orchard in Kilmore.

I tell Eilish how much I love her and appreciate the sacrifice she made coming all the way into the college to feed her younger brother. Having spent three years in an all-girls school in Monaghan, she knows all the questions to ask me, her hungry little brother.

There is another surprise. Eilish tells me that she has another reason to come to the college. "Last time I was home in Legaginney I met this very good looking guy from Bruskey. His name is Edward Anthony Smith, and he plays on the college football team."

"You are right, Eilish. He is a very good footballer, and I am going to see him play tomorrow against Saint Patrick's Armagh in Breifne Park."

Finbarr on O'Connell Street, Dublin,
on the way to the Seminary

99

Chapter XV

Catching up with the 'Townies'

I answer all of Eilish's questions about my first few weeks at Saint Pat's. She laughs hysterically at my knickname "Shazam". Then she adds,

"I think you did better than your brothers P. Joe and Jack, who were knick-named "Dead Cow" and "Calf" respectfully." She starts picking up her shopping bag in which she brought in all the food for the "feed" I will be organizing for the Brian and the Scotts.

I say,

"I wish that I knew one of the priests at the college better, so that I could ask them to drive you Eilish back into town. To make up for it, I promise to have Edward Anthony Smith come in to meet you the next time you come visit." Eilish smiles, knowing I am only just dreaming about having such a relationship with any of the priests. After we share a big hug, she saunters down the avenue towards the college gates, knowing that this Friday visit to the college is very affirming for her younger brother launching, for him, a major educational journey.

At 11:00 AM the following day the whole student body, except the football team, line up, dressed in our college blue jackets and caps, walk two-by-two to Breifne Park. My new friend Michael Smyth asks Father Gargan for permission for him and me to break ranks and visit his Uncle Tom Smyth and his aunt at the Railway Hotel. To my surprise he says Yes, with the stipulation that we get to the park before I: 00 PM when our team is scheduled to

100

play Saint Patrick's, Armagh.

Tom Smyth gives us a warm welcome, first to his nephew Michael and then to me. Walking from behind the bar he says,

"I am guessing you are Dentist Barney Corr's relative."

"Yes Mr. Smyth, he is my uncle. I am one of the Corrs of Legaginney."

"I know you, I actually know your daddy; he comes in here sometimes for a meal when he is in town selling his cattle. His name is John Frank right? And by the way you don't have to call me Mr. Smyth; everybody calls me Tom or Tommy. whichever you prefer."

The Smyths have two children, Pat who goes to a boarding school in Dublin and Mary who goes to a local girl's school called the Loretto. My friend Michael embarrasses his cousin Mary by saying to me in her presence,

"Finbarr you cannot have Mary, because she has a crush on your cousin Brian."

Mrs. Smyth, a friendly woman, just like my Mammy, serves us a cup of hot tea and a slice of currant cake and we leave for the football game.

When we arrive at Breifne Park which is just beyond the "Half Acre", our blue college jackets are enough to gain us admission. Personally, I don't want to spend the shilling I have with me for admission, I want to buy sweets for Michael and myself. The game is just starting, as we wind our way around the field to seats with the rest of our blue jacketed colleagues.

Just as we sit in the bleachers our fullback Mike Sullivan makes a tremendous leap, catching the ball on the square, preventing a shot on goal from a mere five yards away. He kicks the ball out to Eilish's beau Edward Anthony Smith, who is playing center field. Looking up at the scoreboard, making sure we didn't miss anything coming late to the game, I am relieved to see the score is zero-zero. I don't know all of our players' names. Fortunately, Alphie Gallogly, who christened me Shazam, is sitting behind Michael and me, informs us, calling each of us Shazam or Slasher.

At half time we are leading Armagh 1 goal and 5 points to 3 points. Our side is going crazy, waving our blue college caps and yelling our team on. Alphie yells,

"If we keep up the same defense in the second half we will beat Armagh."

During the break I go over to the food and candy stand and buy six pence worth of toffee sweets. I share them with Michael and Alphie. Alphie, of course, jokes saying,

"Shazam, you didn't have to pay me for christening you."

He is also correct in his forecast, that if our team keeps up the same defense we would win the game. While the two Armagh midfield players are upstaging our two midfield players, the six Armagh forwards are no match for our defense. James McCabe, knick-named the Curry McCabe from Bruskey, my home parish, is declared the man of the match for the outstanding job he does as the center half back. The final score is Saint Patrick's, Cavan 2 goals and 8 points, Saint Patrick's Armagh 1 goal and 9 points. We were a very happy bunch of fellows, walking back out the Clones Road to the College.

Having missed most of my study time on Friday, because of Eilish's visit and Saturday's, because of our time spent in Breifne Park, I decide to do my Geometry homework after the lights go out, by sitting on the steps under the corridor light outside our bedroom,. As I am working on the Geometry I am thinking to myself, if I am going to catch up and pass some of the Townies in the Christmas exams, due in a few weeks, I will have to put in extra time on Geometry and Algebra. With no distractions, I finish my homework in less than one hour and get into bed by 11:00 PM. I am not worrying about sleeping in, as the bell ringing outside my door tomorrow morning is loud enough to waken the dead.

Father Duggan is the celebrant of the Sunday mass, which is happens to be the day he finishes the retreat. He first summarizes all of the homilies and instructions he has given during the week and then announces in his deep booming voice,

"I have something very important to share with you this morning. I would not be doing my duty as a priest if I didn't warn you that there is a very sinful behavior prevalent in this college and other boarding schools I visit throughout Ireland. Senior boys are taking advantage of junior boys and abusing them. I believe you call it "Mugging" here at Saint Pat's. No matter what you call this behavior it is a grave mortal sin, punishable in Hell for all eternity. Am I making myself clear?" There was no response from the pews.

I don't have a clue what he is talking about. I ask my cousin Brian if he knows what it is all about. He replies,

"He cannot be talking about sex, because sex happens only between boys and girls and there are no women or girls in the school, except the maids, who work in the kitchen and clean the toilets. I don't think they would attract any of the senior boys."

103

I was tempted to ask Alphie Gallogly what it meant but when I approached him on the corridor he was already laughing and imitating Father Duggan's deep voice and yelling to his friends,

"Remember Duggan and stop the mugging."

Brian and I decide instead to go the library after breakfast and look up the word 'mugging' in the dictionary. According to Webster's New World Dictionary mugging means "Assaulting a person with the intent to rob." A second definition is that mugging is a slang word used in Britain meaning "to study hard and hurriedly as in preparation for an exam." Another definition in the dictionary is also a reference to exams, i.e. to 'cram' for an exam. Brian and I decide to let it go, since we didn't see any connection between what Father Duggan preached about and the possible meanings of Mugging in the dictionary.

I get back to working hard, doing my homework, studying my Latin and Greek. I am a little scared of my Latin teacher, who will remain nameless. Each Monday morning he comes to class with a long cane hidden inside his black cassock. God help any student who is not able to recite the assigned homework. e.g. *Menso, Mensas, Mensat, mensamus, mensatis, mensant or the verb Amo, Amas, Amat, Amamus, Ammatis Amant.* The student who is unable to recite the assigned homework will receive three strikes of the Father's cane on each hand. The second year students tell us the priest-teacher is crueler in his punishment on the days after his favorite team i.e. the Cavan County team is beaten. This usually means most Monday mornings, after they lose the game on Sunday.

Seamus Keogan invites all of us first year students to meet him after our last class on Monday. We all know he wants to talk about the 'big' football game on Wednesday against the second year students. I don't envy his job of picking the best fifteen footballers from a population of twenty players. He begins with,

"Fellows, I appreciate the confidence you have in me, choosing me as your captain. I have seen most of you during practice over the past few weeks. Several of you are much better players than me your captain. I have drawn up a proposed team of fifteen players, and two substitutes. If any of you feel that you would do better in a different position, like playing as a back versus a forward, please speak up today. He begins by listing Phil Lawlor as goalie. Phil is a "Townie". His dad is the golf professional at the Cavan Golf Course. Phil just smiles and says,

"I will be happy to give it a shot as goalie. I just hope you have a good full back in front of me."

Seamus replies,

"My guess is that our full back, Paddy Sullivan from Denbawn is better than the full back for the second year team. You will all remember how well his brother Mike played as full back on Saturday against Saint Patrick's Armagh. I do expect his baby brother Paddy to do just as a good a job for us on Wednesday." Paddy replies,

"Seamus, I have played full back for our local school in Denbawn. I hope I can handle any of the second year's forwards. They are welcome to shoot points from twenty or thirty yards out but between Phil our goalie and my fellow backs and myself we plan on zero goals against us."

Seamus goes on to list Paddy Delaney and James 'Sticky' Brady to play center field, while Francis 'Bull-ram Drawers' McBrien will play center half-back. As he kept the list going, I was honestly hoping that I would be a substitute. If the contest is to run a mile, I believe I could beat all of the players in both teams in that competition. My hopes are realized as Seamus announced we have two good substitutes, if any of you get in trouble, i.e. Des Scott and Finbarr Corr.

I have no reason now to be distracted from studies. After the lights go off in our room I go out again to the steps outside our room and study Geometry, one more hour under the light until 10:00 PM. The next day I get compliments from my math teacher, which helps build up my confidence. While some of my classmates were surprised that I was not disappointed that I was passed over and didn't make the roster of fifteen for Wednesday football game, I thought to myself that I came here to Saint Patrick's not to become a great footballer but to pass my exams and be ready to go to a seminary in five years, to be ordained a Catholic priest.

Chapter XVI

November 1949

November begins with a surprise. Our president, Father McNiff, is transferred from the college to head a big parish in Manorhamilton, County Leitrim. Father Patrick Gaffney, our class's Irish teacher and the next priest in seniority, takes Father McNiff's place. Although Father Gaffney's smile and jovial personality make him seem easygoing as a teacher, he has the reputation of being a demanding administrator.

In my few months at the college I've become friendly with the farm supervisor John Brady. He tells me, "You all better watch out! Father Gaffney is going to shake up the college. Last week he asked me if the sow gave birth to her pigs yet. I said she did. Then he asks, 'How many pigs did she have?' I say three. He says, "That sow is like everybody else around the college, they get away with doing the minimum." I know what Father Gaffney means, as Dad's sows in Legaginney have at least eight pigs each year.

Today I regret to report that the second-year football team whipped our butts. While our centerfield player James "Sticky" Brady was clearly the man of the match, their center-half forward, Jim McDonnell, was far superior to our center halfback Francis "Bull-ram Drawers" McBrien. Jim would jump one foot higher than McBrien, and tip the ball over to Bernie Doyle. Between them, they score one goal and eight points in the first half. Our team, unfortunately, score only three points. Des Scott was called in as a substitute for the second half, as our captain

Seamus Keogan had to leave because of a knee injury. I feel relieved not to be called in to play.

Even with some of Mrs. Scott's good cooking frequently and "feeds" every week, compliments of Uncle Barney, we are all still hungry. Once again Alphie Gallogly comes to the rescue. He tells us that last November three of his colleagues and he went out to the bishop's orchard and filled up their laundry bags with beautiful yellow and red apples from the trees.

I speak up, "Alphie, I am ready, count me in."

Des Scott chimes in "Me too."

Alphie says, "Next week we will have a full moon. We can steal out at midnight with our laundry bags. It is safer to have the raid on a week night, as some of the priests could be out on Friday or Sunday evenings and catch us sneaking back into the college in the moonlight."

I tell Alphie about my big wooden trunk. "I got it as a gift from our Uncle Jim. It is now empty and hidden under my bed. Whoever wants to use it to hide their apples should feel free to do so."

Alphie warns us not tell any of our friends about the planned raid, because if any of the prefects find out about it they will have to report it to Father Gargan, and we might possibly be expelled from the college for our behavior.

I am careful not to let the planned raid distract me from my studies and my goal of catching up with the Townies. I continue my plan of sitting under the lights on the corridor two nights each week.

One night I get stuck on an algebra problem. The next morning I ask help from our model student, Hubert Maultsby, and within five minutes he has me back on track. Learning algebra and geometry is much easier than I envisioned, while studying physics and chemistry under the tutelage of Mr. Breen turns out to be the joy I expected.

Mr. Breen continues to pick on the Townies, while he seems to favor us Bog-men (although he never calls us that). If one of the Townies misses a question on a quiz, he sarcastically says something like, "What would Brother Patrick think of your response? Would he be proud of you? … I don't think so."

For some reason I compare Mr. Breen with Master McCarthy at Legaginney National School. I realize that Master McCarthy has an almost impossible job. He has to focus on preparing the 6th grade students for their Primary Certificate Exam at the beginning of June, while keeping the 5th, 7th and 8th graders progressing in all subjects except algebra and geometry. I conclude that Mr. Breen's job is much the easier one, but I doubt the Educational Department in Dublin compensates Master McCarthy as well as the college compensates Mr. Breen, for only teaching the one subject of science.

On Sunday morning after mass, Alphie tells us that the orchard raid is scheduled for Wednesday night. "We'll meet at midnight in the basement locker room. Remember to bring your laundry bags and I will have a flashlight in case a cloud blocks the moon and leaves the orchard in almost total darkness." I'm excited at the thought of having my big trunk full of rosy apples from the bishop's orchard.

Meanwhile, Father Kennedy, who teaches music to all classes at the college and directs the college choir, comes to the dining room on Monday evening at dinnertime.

"Gentlemen, all of you, except the first-year students, are aware that we sponsor a student opera each year here at the college. This year we will invite your parents for a special celebration of Gilbert and Sullivan's *Mikado* on December 18th in this dining room. This will be two days before you go home for the Christmas holiday. I need the ten best singers in the college to volunteer for lead roles in the opera, and twenty to twenty-five other singers who we will train to sing in the chorus. This year we are fortunate to have two fine tenors in the first-year class, who I will be grooming to take lead roles in *Mikado.* For the rest of you, who wish to sing in the chorus or try out for a leading role, I will meet you on Monday evening after dinner in room 201 for an audition."

I already know one of the two tenors. His name is John Joe Reilly, one of the Townies. Cousin Brian told me about John's beautiful singing voice and sang in several concerts at the Christian Brother school in Cavan. I am not planning to have an audition, as singing is not one of the gifts my creator gave me. I do look forward to attending the opera. I have, of course, heard of Gilbert and Sullivan's operas, but we didn't have operas in Legaginney School.

I tell my roommate, cousin Brian, about the planned orchard raid on Wednesday at midnight and that it has to be kept confidential. He cautions me, "I have been told that some students go out to town, food shopping through the woods, but this is the first time I heard of a group going out at night and raiding the bishop's orchard. I hope you fellows are aware that the bishop has a big sheep dog, that wanders around outside his residence protecting his property."

"I am sure that Alphie is aware and has a plan to handle it," I say.

Fortunately, I have a spare pair of older pants that I can wear. I don't want to risk wearing my almost new corduroys and tear them while climbing the apple trees. I borrow Brian's alarm clock and set it for 11:30 PM. I need to get a couple of hours sleep before our adventure and a few hours afterwards; otherwise, I will be falling asleep during Thursday's classes.

Des Scott and I leave our rooms simultaneously and sneak down the back stairs to the basement. Alphie and his classmate Jim are already there waiting for us, with their laundry bags and Alphie carrying a flash-lamp. Alphie leads us up the hill past the football field and ball alley. The bishop's residence is to our right. When we reach the upper right hand corner of the walk-around, which all of us use daily, he takes a sharp right turn into the woods. He uses his lamp to guide us under tree branches and towards the fence that surrounds the orchard.

The night is quiet. There is not a cloud visible in the sky. Much of the ground underneath the apple trees is covered with apples. Alphie whispers to us not to pick them, as they are probably infected by bugs and worms. I start picking apples of the tree and filling up my laundry bag. In the moonlight I can see trees with red apples and others with large yellow apples.

All of a sudden I see the bishop's big shepherd dog enter the orchard by squeezing his hairy body under the iron gate. He jogs over towards us and barks in a very low whining tone. I take no chances and begin climbing the nearest apple tree. Alphie takes on a completely opposite approach. He walks towards the dog, whistling in a very low tone.

The big collie falls for Alphie's seductive whistling and continues to walk towards Alphie, wagging his gold colored tail. Alphie keeps his cool and talks to the dog, patting his head and rubbing the rich mop of hair on his

111

back. Alphie calls out to Des Scott and me, "Come down you cowards, the bishop's puppy wants to meet you."

I pick a couple of apples off the branch I am sitting on, jump down the couple of feet to the ground and put the apples in my laundry bag. The bag is already over half full and almost as much as I can carry back to college and upstairs to my bedroom. I pat the dog's head and wish I knew his name.

I finish filling my laundry bag with apples I can reach from the ground. Alphie and his colleague Jim have collect their load and come over to help Des fill his bag. Alphie does not want to risk his good luck any further. The bishop's dog goes back to his kennel outside the orchard. Alphie whispers, "Let's get out of here with our booty and get back to the college before anybody catches us."

I sling my bag of apples over my shoulder and walk with Des, who is following Alphie and Jim to the corner of the orchard.

The moon is still lighting our way as we walk down the hill toward the door, leading into the college basement. We walk single file close to the hedge to avoid any priest or prefect noticing us.

Suddenly we hear a loud scary scream from a bush close by. A big owl flies over our heads, scaring the know-what out of us.

Chapter XVII

Christmas in Legaginney

Thanks to Alphie Gallogly and my colleague Des Scott, from Cootehill, my trunk is full of delicious apples from his Excellency Bishop Lyon's orchard. My cousin and roommate Brian Corr is enjoying his share of our spoils. He says, "If you guys are going again, I will be happy to join you."

Alphie is all smiles when I run into him at breakfast the next morning. I say, "Thank you for last night."

He puts on this silly grin and says, "Excuse me, who are you? I don't remember ever meeting you." Alphie is not only being humorous, he is following his own instructions, "Don't tell any of your students about the raid."

It is only two weeks until we take our Christmas exams. This will be my first time taking exams with six subjects, i.e. Irish, English, Geometry/Algebra, Science, History and Theology. I am not worried about Irish, English, Science or Theology tests. I believe I can pass them with flying colors. I imagine the questions or essays on the History or Geography tests will on broad subjects and involve topics like the Easter Rising of 1916, also known as the Easter Rebellion, which was an armed insurrection lead by Irish patriot Patrick Pearse. I am more familiar with this topic than many of my classmates, since my Daddy and Uncle Barney served as volunteers in the Irish Republican Army (IRA) during this period of Irish history.

The Algebra and Geometry tests will be a challenge, especially for us Bogmen, who only started studying these subjects a few months earlier. I try to convince myself that I have done my best to focus on these subjects in class and to follow up studying them, even staying up past my bedtime to keep up.

On Wednesday afternoon we students get a big surprise. Instead of our weekly walk, going two by two down the Belturbet Road, Father Kennedy invites those students who are not in the opera to attend its first dress rehearsal in the college cafeteria. What a nice treat for us Bogmen, who have never seen an opera on film or even heard one on radio. I am sitting excitedly, in the second row and facing center stage, when the curtain goes up. The full chorus of sopranos, baritones and basses sings the opening theme to Gilbert and Sullivan's *Mikado*. Wow, it is fantastic! The diminutive Father Kennedy, playing on the grand piano, is the lead musician. He is accompanied by two students, one playing a trumpet and the other a saxophone.

Our next surprise is when one of our classmates John Joe Reilly enters the stage all decked out in a beautiful girl's dress and fully made up with powder and lipstick. While he is singing in a beautiful boy's soprano's voice, I poke my buddy Michael Smyth, who is sitting beside me, and ask, "Do you think she goes out at night?"

Michael shakes with laughter and says, "Finbarr, you are nuts - remember Duggan and stop the mugging!"

The opera lasts over two hours, including a short bathroom break. Father Kennedy addresses all of us as the opera ends saying. Thank you all for the loud applause. I am sure your classmates in the opera appreciated it. I know I did. There were a couple of errors this afternoon, which

114

I don't expect you noticed. They will be corrected before the shows on Friday evening and Saturday afternoon, when your parents, brothers and sisters or whoever comes to experience our best opera ever at Saint Patrick's." We applaud again.

The following morning I congratulate John Joe Reilly, which he appreciates. I don't make any reference regarding his beautiful girls dress and his makeup or about the comments I made to Michael Smyth during the opera. I am sure he wouldn't appreciate me hinting that he was sexually attractive to us his male classmates.

Because of the distance between Legaginney and the college and the risk of driving a horse and trap twenty miles round trip, some of it in the dark, my parents decline Father Kennedy's gracious invitation to attend the opera. I am disappointed, especially because I know my mother loves music, but to be honest, I am relieved not to have any distractions over the weekend, as I have only two days left to prepare for my first set of exams at the college.

Our first test on Monday morning is relatively easy. Our outgoing president who is also our teacher, Father Gaffney, invites us to write a one-page essay, in Irish, on our first semester's experience in a boarding school. In the second part of the test requires us to transform five sentences in the present tense Irish to future tense. I feel good when the hour is up. As I hand in my answer sheet. I am confident of getting a pass.

On Monday afternoon we meet one of my favorite teachers, Mr. Breen. He hands out our test, which contains questions in both Physics and Chemistry. Since I enjoy the class and keep up with Mr. Breen's lectures, doing my homework, memorizing the formulas and reviewing our weekly lab experiments, I feel confident that I will ace this test. Mr. Breen will be happy that the bogman from Legaginney did so well.

I admit I am a little nervous on Tuesday morning, as the next test (i.e. Mathematics) covers both Algebra and Geometry. My idol and mentor Hubert Maultsby tells me, "Take a few deep breaths and say a prayer as you read through the questions on the test. Read all the questions on the test and answer the ones that seem easy to you first, this will give you the confidence to answer the questions that seem difficult to you."

I write my responses to questions 1, 3, and 5 first and take a chance on questions 2 and 4 later. I am relieved when the one-and-a-half hours are over and hope I have done well to score at least a forty, which is a passing grade for an in-school exam.

I am a little surprised at how difficult our English test is. The focus on the whole test is questions on English grammar, including the present and past tenses on several verbs. I am disappointed that there is not an essay question. My mammy, a trained teacher, has told me that I am a good storyteller who should write a book one day, so I feel confident I would excel in a writing portion of the test.

My forecast regarding the history test turned out to be correct. We are asked to write an essay on the positive and negative aspects of Patrick Pearse's leadership during the 1916 Rebellion in Dublin. Being the son of an IRA man, I am quite familiar with all that happened during that historical and tragic week in Dublin. Even though the majority of the people of Ireland supported the Irish rising and were anxious to achieve home rule rather than serve the British Crown for another 300 years, they disagreed with Pearse taking over the General Post Office in Dublin with such a small contingent of Irish rebels. Historians still wonder why such a small group of people tried to take on the military might of what was then one of the world's major powers. The end result was that Patrick Pearse and his fourteen companions were executed by the British soldiers at Kilmainham prison in Dublin. Pearse's error in judgment is reported as one of the saddest incidents in the history of our homeland.

I don't have to hear too many bells ringing on December 23rd to get me out of bed, as we are scheduled to go home for two weeks to celebrate Christmas with our families. I receive a letter from Mammy saying that P. Joe will be picking me up in our trap with Maggie, my favorite horse, between noon and 1 PM today. Poor cousin Brian has to wait to be picked up until his dad has finished taking care of his dental patients. Unfortunately, his mother Dr. Maura Corr does not drive.

After breakfast I pack a small canvas bag with the barest essentials, say goodbye to Brian and the Scott brothers across the corridor and go sit and wait with several other students by the college's front door. To my surprise my math teacher comes down the main staircase. He recognizes me on his way to his car and says, "Congratulations Mr. Corr, you passed your Algebra and Geometry test" I reply,

"Thank you Father, do you remember my score?"

"Since you are one of the few country boys to pass I remember you got a 49."

"Thank you Father." I reply. "I am going home today feeling good, even if I have to work hard get a 49." What I wanted to say but didn't was, "Father I plan to get an honors score in June."

As I watch Father Bob drive off, I recognize Maggie trotting in the college driveway. My brother P. Joe, the most introverted of my siblings, is all smiles as he guides Maggie to stop on the opposite side of where the priests park their cars. To my surprise, he jumps out of the trap and gives me a big hug. After I get over the shock I go over and pull Maggie's mane to make sure she knows it is me she is taking to Legaginney. I am as excited about going home as I was during the opening scene of the *Mikado*.

P. Joe asks, "How was your first semester at Saint Pat's?" as he guides Maggie's trot down the college avenue towards Cavan town.

I decide to tease him a little and reply, "Probably the same as you experienced when you were there five or six years ago."

He laughs and says, "I bet the food is still lousy and some boys supplement their food by raiding the bishop's orchard." I am dumbfounded. Does he really know that I am part of a team that raided the bishop's orchard? I change my tune and thank P. Joe for warning me about the food. Then he laughs when I tell him, "I am very lucky to have Uncle Jim's wooden trunk to hide the apples under my bed."

There is a lot of traffic in town, as many of the local farmers are in town with their wives, doing their last minute Christmas shopping. Maggie has to walk up Farnham Street and the Dublin Road before she can start trotting again on the Ballinagh Road. I am waiting for a quiet moment with little traffic to ask P. Joe some important questions.

Sitting across from him in the trap and looking directly into his face I begin, "I have been anxious to talk to you about something that happened during the student retreat at the beginning of the school year. The retreat master, a very tall Redemptorist by the name of Father Duggan, spoke to us in a very strong voice about avoiding sin and obeying Jesus's command to love and forgive one another. He discussed all of the Ten Commandments and told us that we would go to hell if we committed sins against the sixth and ninth commandments. Both cousin Brian and I were confused when he went on to say, 'There is another sin being committed in this college and other boys boarding schools in Ireland that nobody wants to talk about, but I am going to talk about it today. It is called mugging. Those of you who commit this sin know what I am talking about. It is a grave sin and I want you to cut it out' (he yelled the final phrase). Neither Brian nor I have a clue what sin he is talking about. We even went to the library, looked up the word in the dictionary but it didn't help. It defined mugging as "assaulting some one, with the intention to rob. P. Joe do you know what the priest was referring to, since you were also a student there for two or three years?"

P. Joe smiled at first and gave Maggie a whack of the whip to keep her trotting. I feel that he doesn't want to talk about it. However, he says, "First of all don't tell Mammy or Daddy about it, because they will take you out of the college to protect you. I admit I haven't thought about mugging since I left Saint Pat's seven years ago. The truth, Finbarr, is that some of the senior boys use younger boys from the first and second year as substitutes for sex, since there are no girl students at Saint Pat's. I cannot tell you anymore than that, except that none of the older boys tried to mug me, when I was in the first or second year."

I stopped staring at him and just said, "Thanks P. Joe." Meanwhile, Maggie trots down Main Street, Ballinagh.

Twenty minutes later she takes us up Legaginney lane, past McCusker's thatched house, and we are home. Everybody who is home at that moment comes out to greet me as I jump out of the trap. I do, of course, get a big hug from Mammy and a surprise hug from Daddy. Brendan and Eilish won't be home for Christmas, as they are busy working in Dublin. Jack has sent a Christmas letter to all of us from the seminary in New Jersey USA. The rest of us are looking forward to an enjoyable Christmas family celebration, facilitated by our wonderful mother Nell.

As usual, Mammy's helper, Mary Farrelly, is ready for the big day. She has killed three geese, stripped them of their feathers and intestines and hung them up in the chimney to smoke. This afternoon Mammy is polishing off her Christmas pudding and has it ready to be cooked slowly overnight on the hob beside the fire. Tomorrow I will help Mary peel the raw potatoes to have them ready to cook into colcannon for our annual Christmas fiesta. After breakfast on Christmas morning I will help my two younger brothers Colm and Fonsie enjoy their Christmas gifts, while we all wait for Father Lawrence to drive from his parish to Legaginney.

Tonight the weather is frosty, and the moon and stars burn brightly over Potahee Mountain. I am already looking forward to walking up the Legaginney Road with Daddy at 6:30 AM on Christmas morning, for the mass at St. Michaels Church, Potahee. There will still be stars in the sky as we walk, just as there were stars guiding the Wise men from the East to the crib in Bethlehem on the first Christmas.

Chapter XVIII

Stealing without Guilt

Christmas Day's celebration in Legaginney is just as enjoyable as ever. I tell Mammy that this is the best meal I have had in six months. She laughs and says, "I suppose that is meant to be a compliment."

I reply, "Mammy, I wish you could come into the college and teach the cook how to make turkey gravy like you just made for today's dinner." She knows I love her gravy, especially when it's served over colcannon potatoes!

Christmas Day is the only day the whole family joins Father Lawrence in the parlor for dinner. That is all of the family except P. Joe, who prefers to sit in the kitchen as Mary Beatty prepares the food, and carves the turkey for Mammy to serve in the parlor.

My twelve year-old sisters Marie is the only one in the family who feels comfortable teasing our uncle, Father Lawrence. After he finishes eating his Christmas pudding, he sits in the large armchair before the fire. Marie goes over and sits on his knee. Uncle just laughs and starts tickling her as she tries to remove the Roman collar from around his neck. I don't know if he is embarrassed or expects Mammy to rein in her aggressive daughter, but all of sudden he stands and says, "I better get on the road, as I am afraid I may run into a heavy fog, when I'm driving through Stradone after dark."

As he leaves the parlor I approach him to say thank you for supporting me at Saint Pat's. He surprises me by saying, "Finbarr, I ran into one of your professors at the college last week. He said you are working hard and will catch up with the townies by the end of the school year." He doesn't say which professor, or whether it was a priest teacher or one of the lay faculty.

Marie is disappointed that her playmate uncle has gone, but the rest of us get more relaxed and want to keep the party going. We talk Mammy into playing a few gigs, reels and hornpipes on her accordion, and we talk Daddy into taking Father Lawrence's chair. We all just settle in and enjoy the flames in the fireplace until Mammy notices that the clock on the mantelpiece chimes that it is 7 PM. She glances at Colm and Fonsie, sitting on two stools by the fire, and says, "I am sorry to be a spoilsport, but two boys know it is their bedtime. It has been a long day since you went up to Potahee for the early mass with Daddy. As a send-you-off I will play one of Colm's favorite tunes, "Come back Paddy Reilly to Ballyjamesduff.""

Mammy tells me that we are the only nation in the world that makes the celebration of the birth of the Christ child so special. The Christmas holiday lasts a whole week. All the stores in villages like Ballinagh are closed until New Year's Eve. Farmers, like Daddy, take the week off, except for feeding the calves and pigs, and milking the cows. The Wren Boys visit us on Saint Stephen's Day and some entertain us by playing their melodeons and fiddles. People feel free to visit their neighbors uninvited to wish them a "Happy Christmas." Daddy offers the men a shot of Irish whiskey, while Mammy offers the women and men a cup of tea and a slice of her special Christmas cake.

The bushes along Legaginney lane are covered with white frost. The weather is cold - too cold to play football in the garden. We children have the choice of sliding on the icy pond at the bottom of the white field or playing hide-and-seek in the hayshed.

Colm and Fonsie choose to go sliding, while my sister Dympna says she will join us later to play hide-and-seek. I first test the ice to see if it is strong enough to carry us. Colm does not wait for me to wave him onto the ice. Always ready to take a risk, he slides, left foot first, across the shiny ice. Fonsie, a couple of years younger and less secure than his older brothers, is reticent. I take his hand and teach him how to slide.

I visit Pat Lynch's home, which is next door to his country store. His wife Bridie, son Mel and daughter Bernadette give me a warm welcome home and ask me what college is like. Meanwhile Pat goes outside, opens his shop and returns with a fresh barn brick loaf, full of raisins, to send home with me to Mammy for her being a good customer. Mammy reminds Colm, Fonsie and me that all this sharing of gifts and visits by neighbors is in memory of the birth of Jesus the Christ child in the stable of Bethlehem.

On the Friday evening before New Year's Day several local musicians, friends of Mammy's, come to Legaginney. Jimmy Quinn, a middle-aged man and also the best musician in the area, rides his bicycle ten miles to our house with his fiddle strapped to his back. Since Mammy knows he is coming, she sends me out that afternoon to invite Michael King and three of his musician friends to come our home for a "Session", as it is called. Mammy sends Colm and Fonsie to bed at the usual time, 7 PM. Colm, who loves Irish music and has already tried playing on Mammy's melodeon, decides to sit at the top of the stairway and enjoy the music. He knows that

Mammy will be too focused on playing her melodeon and Jimmy Quinn's directions to notice if he and Fonsie went to bed. Meanwhile, since I am now fourteen and in college, I am not sent to bed. I sit on the hob by the warm turf fire, beside Daddy, enjoying Jimmy's interpretation of the "Siege of Ennis" and other tunes that he teaches the other budding musicians this evening.

The two weeks of Christmas vacation flow by quickly, like gentle breezes over Potahee Mountain. Along with playing hide-and-seek in the hayshed with Dympna and my two younger brothers, I make quickie visits to Uncle Jim Brady in Lacken. Aunt Nora, Jim's wife and also my daddy's sister, is sitting by the turf fire and smoking a cigarette. She asks me, "Finbarr have you started smoking yet?" while holding out a box of Players cigarettes for me to take one.

Hiding my surprise I respond, "Not yet Aunty. I am afraid Mammy would kill me if she heard that I was smoking at such a young age."

Lizzie Corr and her husband Eddie Brady give me a warm welcome. Lizzie calls me "the three-penny beggar-man" sometimes and other times "the Noogey-man". Today she wants to know what going to college is like, as she stopped going to school when she passed her Primary Certificate Exam at age fourteen. I tell her all about Mr. Breen calling those of us from the country Bog-men, while boys like my cousin Brian Corr are called Townies. She says, "He has one hell of a nerve." Lizzie does not mince her words.

I reply, "One of my professors at Saint Pat's told my uncle Father Lawrence that I will have caught up with the townies by the end of the school year, which you know is in mid-June. That is a compliment to Miss Gaffney and

Master McCarthy and Mammy, because they taught me how to study."

Lizzie gets teary-eyed and says, "You were always a great gossoon (a local name for a pre-teenage boy), whether you were catching turf in the bog, going to the creamery with the kicking pony or selling raffle tickets for Noogey."

Not wanting the conversation going in that goody-goody direction I say, "Lizzie, I will tell you something that you must not tell Mammy or Daddy." She is all ears as I proceed. "As you already know, the food the students get at the college is just awful. Most days we don't get enough to make one decent meal. A few of us, led by a second year student from Leitrim, have come up with a risky plan to supplement our stingy diet. On moonlit nights we sneak into the bishop's orchard next door to the college and fill our laundry bags with his apples. In the middle of November we got enough apples to fill Uncle Jim's trunk that I keep hidden underneath my bed. I don't know exactly what would happen to us if we get caught."

Lizzie roars with her contagious laugh. "I promise not to tell your Mammy or Daddy."

Miss Berrill is happy to see me and says she is praying daily that I do well in college. Her major regret in life is that her parents didn't have any extra money to pay for her to attend school to become a professional musician. As I expected, the only neighbor who gives me money is the old reliable Bridget McCusker. I don't think she tells her husband Phil about her generosity; she follows me out the door and slips a full shilling in my pocket.

Since Mammy needs to do some post-Christmas shopping and wants to take advantage of the seasonal sales in McDonalds clothier shop in Cavan, she comes along with Daddy as he drives me, with Maggie pulling the trap, back to college. I am not sad leaving home. I know this is absolutely necessary, if I am to get an education and become a priest. Daddy drops Mammy off outside McDonalds so that she can do her shopping while he drives me the extra two miles to the college. Mammy, as usual, has tears in her eyes as she gives me a big hug goodbye, as she does when any of her children are leaving home.

Daddy does not get emotional. As he stops Maggie in front of the College main door and hands me my small suitcase, he merely says, "Here are a couple of shillings to buy some food if you are going out to Breifne Park in the next few weeks." He hands me a half crown, which I put in my pocket along with Mrs McCusker's shilling. I feel pretty lucky, as I also have one of Mammy's currant cakes in my suitcase.

I cannot wait until classes begin the next morning when the teachers give us our grades and tell us what subjects we passed or failed. I am happy to report that all of my hard work pays off. I pass six subjects and get honors in Irish and Science. I fail Greek by just four points. Our Greek teacher, Father Carroll doesn't scream at the ten students, including me, who didn't reach the mandatory score of 40 to get a pass. He calmly says, "Gentlemen, I know you are very disappointed with the results of your first test in Greek. Please don't be discouraged. This is your first time studying the language handed down to us by the ancient and world renowned authors like Plato, Homer, Euripides and Aristotle. The Greek language is much more difficult to learn than Latin. It is mandatory that all students at this college take three years of Greek, because if you go on to become a Scripture scholar you will need to read and translate the Bible from its original language Greek to English."

I am excited as I wait to hear what Mr. Breen will say about me, the Bog-man, getting honors in my first science exam. As a matter of fact he is careful not to turn any of the students off science, particularly the three who failed, one of whom was a townie.

In my heart I admit to myself that I am proud to be among the four Bog-men to get honors. He gives me a high five, as I leave to go to my next class.

The college food has not improved over the Christmas holiday. Thank God I have Mammy's currant cake to share with Cousin Brian and Pat and Des Scott across the corridor. A few days later Alphie Gallogly says, "My friend Jim McDonnell and I want to meet with you and Des Scott to discuss ways in which we can supplement our meals by getting into the college kitchen and stealing some food."

"Alphie you can count on us. My cousin Pat Phillips, who is a senior and a prefect, has a master key that can get us into the kitchen and the science lab, if we decide we want to cook some of the food we steal from the kitchen."

"Are you crazy Finbarr? You cannot ask him for the key, he would have to report you to Father Gargan."

"Alphie," I reply, "I am thinking that I could stop in to visit him before we go to bed and find out where he hangs his pants. I am his cousin, so he won't get suspicious. Then, on the night we are going to make the raid, we can steal the master key from the brown corduroys he wears each day. My guess is that he, like most of us, hangs his pants on the bedpost at the end of his bed."

"Finbarr, you are a genius" says Alphie.

Chapter XIX

A Hooley in the Kitchen

The atmosphere around St. Patrick's College is different during the winter months. While the trees and bushes are white with frost and the temperature in the early morning is below freezing, we get very little snow in Ireland compared to our neighboring countries in Europe. My fellow students frequently refer back to the blizzard of 1947, which we all remember. We were in grammar school then. I describe how our Legaginney lane filled with snowdrifts up to the top of the hedges and how we played in the snow with Master McCarthy and Miss Joyce, as the school was closed for a whole week.

For recreation during this season I choose to play handball and try to avoid playing football. I am afraid of hurting myself running and kicking ball on a hard, frozen field. If someone trips you accidentally or otherwise, you fall and end up with scratched and bloody knees.

Starting this, our second semester, I am feeling more confident than I did the previous September. The results of my first exam were pretty good for a bogman. I do know that I obviously have to work harder at my Greek to bring it up to par with the other seven subjects.

The key to my moderate success seems to be that I developed a system for studying and keeping up with my homework. I owe a lot to Hubert Maultsby, the model student in our class, and to teachers like Mr. Breen who apparently take a personal interest in our educational progress.

My sharing Mammy's currant cake with Pat and Des Scott helps the three of us become good friends. We have a lot in common. We are avid football fans and enjoy cheering for our county football team of Cavan, known otherwise as the "Boys of Breifne." Another thing we have in common is that our mothers are good cooks. We both look forward to either parent coming to visit and bringing delicious cakes. Des, who is generally quieter than his older brother Pat, gets all excited when I tell him that Alphie Gallogly and his classmate Jim want to meet with us to plan a raid on the college kitchen. I explain that since I know how to "steal" the master key that gives us entrance to the kitchen, I will obviously be playing a bigger role in the kitchen heist than I did in robbing the bishop's orchard.

My cousin Pat Phillips happens to be one of the two senior prefects this year. He is more introverted than I, but he's a friendly chap. His family lives in the townland of Legaweel, which is less than two miles away from my home in Legaginney. Because his mother and mine are best friends, our families frequently socialize.

As a prefect, Cousin Pat has his own single room and a master key that allows him entrance to most rooms and offices in the college. I presume he carries the key in the corduroy pants he wears daily to study and classes. My job before we meet Alphie and Jim is to find out where Pat hangs his corduroy pants when he goes to bed at night. He's part of my extended family, so I'm certain my job will be easy. I just have to wait for an invitation to his room to find out where his desk and bed are situated and if the bed has posts where the average fellow would hang his pants at night.

A couple of weeks later I go up to Pat at the end of our first study period and say, "I believe I saw your sister Moya coming up the college avenue today."

"Yes, she is home from her job in Dublin for a week and came today by bus to Cavan and walked out here to the college. Why don't you come up to my room after study hall ends at 9:15 PM and I will give you some of Mammy's apple cake? You must remember how good they taste." Just as easy as that, I set up the inspection of Pat's room and get the information I need to borrow his master key.

Pat and I enter room 309 on the third floor, at the end of the corridor, just directly across the stairway leading up from the second floor. I need to remember all these details, as we won't be able to turn on lights on the night we come to steal (or borrow) his master key. The first thing I notice is that Pat does not make his bed. I of course don't comment, as I presume that the junior dean Father Gargan does not inspect the prefects' rooms like he inspects Brian's and mine weekly.

Pat's desk is covered with books. Whatever time he is not required to supervise us in the study hall, he studies up in this room. He is, of course, doing a lot of study, as he is due to take his final public exam, the Leaving Certificate exam, in just four months.

Pat's dirty laundry is on the floor behind his bed. His closet door is open, so that I can see his "good" suit with two ironed blue shirts on hangers. His bed is of the old style: there are four iron posts with a brass top at each corner of the bed. I am guessing at this point that he hangs his corduroys on the post closest to him at the end of the bed. While I am observing all this he uses a plastic knife to cut me a generous portion of his mother's (cousin

Maisie's) Apple Cake, which, needless to say, is delicious.

While all this effort to discover a way to borrow the key is underway, I don't allow any distraction from my educational goal to catch up with the Townies by the time we sit down for our mid-June exams. If I don't get all my homework completed or have not learned to recite the assigned English poetry by heart, I bring the unfinished homework or English text book up to my bedroom after study hall ends at 9:15 PM. When the lights in our rooms are turned off at 10 PM, I go out as usual in my pajamas and sit under the light in the hallway to finish the job.

Father Carroll, my Greek teacher, is very supportive because he knows learning classical Greek is very difficult for all of us first-year students. The language has nothing in common with English, Irish or Latin. The Greek letters are written differently and the article "the:" has twelve different expressions.

One morning after breakfast I run into Alphie. He asks me, "Finbarr have you done your research and are you ready for the meeting with Jim and myself?"

"Yes I am, Alphie," I reply. "Just tell me when you want to meet Des Scott and myself. I made a visit to "you know who's" room on Monday after study hall, and now I know the whole set-up of his bedroom."

"I will get a hold of Jim today in class to tell him. We will meet this evening in the locker room downstairs immediately after supper, and we will make our plan. Thank you, Finbarr, for all you have done so far. I am very sure we can pull it off, just as we did last fall in the orchard."

In the meantime my friend from Dublin, Michael Smyth, tells me that Father Gargan gave him permission to visit his uncle Tommy Smyth (who with his wife Minnie owns the Railway Hotel in Cavan) provided that another student walks into town with him. He asks, "Finbarr would you like to come along? I know you are good friends with both my uncle and my aunt."

"Of course, I love both of them." Then I add a little humor, "If you had invited cousin Brian instead of me, he would be even more excited, especially if their daughter Mary is home from college. He has a terrific crush on her."

Michael laughs and says, "Instead of going on the college walk on Wednesday we will go visit my uncle and aunt. You know that they will give us a good meal."

I am feeling a little guilt. I didn't invite Michael to be part of the team that is about to raid the college kitchen. As a matter of fact, I cannot even tell him about it. Maybe, down the road, I can share some of the spoils from our raid.

Alphie is already waiting for us, *the three partners in crime*, to come downstairs to the locker room. He starts the meeting by saying, "Thanks to Finbarr, who has done his homework and come up with a plan to take the master key from Prefect Phillip's trousers. When we get it, we will have access not only to the kitchen but also to the science lab, where we can cook some or all of what we take from the kitchen. Finbarr, tell them how you figured it out."

I reply, "As you know, Pat is my cousin. I managed to get an invitation to his room for a piece of his mother's apple cake. His oldest sister Moya, who works in Dublin, was in to visit Pat that afternoon and brought the cake. While Pat was cutting the cake, I busily surveyed the room, recording where his bed and desk are situated. I don't think we will have any problem finding his trousers on the bed post. We can take them outside the corridor temporarily, remove the master key and return the trousers to the bed post. Then we'll put the key back in the same pocket after our raid." Alphie initiates a little applause, while Jim and Des join him.

Jim asks the next question, "When do we plan on making the kitchen raid?"

Alphie replies, "I think we need to discuss first how we plan to carry it out without getting caught by any of the priests or prefects. I believe, Finbarr, you have a torch we can use without having to turn on any lights in the kitchen or the science lab, correct?"

"Yep," I reply.

Alphie continues, "I believe the safest way to get downstairs to the kitchen is to take the elevator from the second floor. None of the priests' rooms are close to the elevator, and going down the stairs would run the risk of meeting a priest who is coming in late to the college from a family engagement." All three of us signal our approval by nodding our heads towards Alphie.

Jim raises the question again, "When are we planning on doing this? Tonight, next week or next month?"

Alphie laughs and says, "We need to decide on this together. Raiding the bishop's orchard was an easy decision."

I speak up. "Fellows, since we have arranged how to borrow the master key, I don't see any reason to wait a month. I suggest that we pick a night next week, probably midweek is safer. Des and I can go to together to my cousin's room right after midnight, take the key from his trousers and meet both of you at the elevator outside

133

my room on the second floor. Then we'll all go down the elevator together."

"That looks like a good plan," replies Alphie. "Do you all agree?" Jim and Des nod in agreement.

Des adds, "I suggest that each of us think about bringing a box or some container to carry the food we get in the kitchen to the science lab."

Alphie replies, "Please leave that to me. I am good friends with our science teacher Mr. Breen. I will tell him I need to borrow a container for a party I am planning in my room, and I know he will give me his thumbs-up approval."

We pick Wednesday of the following week, March 16th, the eve of our national holiday in honor of our patron Saint Patrick. For some strange reason I am not nervous over our planned raid or distracted from my studies. I am getting a handle on how to study Greek, and I've learned to recite all twelve expressions of the Greek article "the."

Now that we are already ten weeks into our second semester I am enjoying the rhythm of the classes. Each weekend I make sure to be ready on Monday morning to decline the Latin verbs for our teacher, Father Noel Fay. Over the Christmas holidays Father Fay assumed the position of chairman of the Cavan County Senior Team over the Christmas holidays, and now his whole personality has changed. He is obsessed with winning the championship of Ulster. God help any student in our class who does not know his homework declensions on any Monday following a loss at the Sunday game by the Boys of Breifne. Father Fay takes the long cane hidden underneath his cassock, and gives that student three painful strikes on each hand. So far I have been lucky to escape this punishment.

March 16th arrives. Alphie checks with me at breakfast to make sure that Des and I are ready to pick up the master key in room 309 at midnight. We are lucky! There is a full moon that night, so Des and I don't need to turn on my torch to find cousin Pat's room. Des holds the torch while I grab the corduroys off the bed post. I find the key in the right-hand pocket, along with some pennies and a sixpenny piece. We take the key and quietly return the pants, with the change in the pocket, to the bed post. Cousin Pat is in a deep sleep.

Alphie and Jim are waiting for us in the shadows by the elevator door. Alphie gives Des and me a tap on the shoulder while Jim presses the button summoning the elevator to the second floor. As we enter the elevator I hand our leader Alphie the torch. I carry the master key. We are speechless during the short ride down to first floor. Alphie's hand is shaking a little as he holds the torch in front of the locked kitchen door. I insert the key and, with confidence, turn it to the right. We all relax as I push the door open and Alphie leads us in with the lighted torch. He carries the food container borrowed from Mr. Breen. It is a very large kitchen.

Alphie acts like he has been here before. "Follow me," he whispers. "I see the large fridge over in the corner."

As Alphie opens the fridge door the light goes on. There before us are shelves loaded with steaks, legs of lamb, sausages, and other tasty items to feed the priests and their guests. Alphie takes two packages of sausages and puts them in his container. We have a hard time finding the bacon, which is hidden in a small compartment in the door. There are no eggs in the fridge. We find them on a shelf over the sink.

I whisper to Alphie, "Lets just take what we can cook tonight and leave the rest as is, hoping that the chef or staff doesn't recognize that something was taken."

"Okay Finbarr," he nods.

At most we are just ten minutes in the kitchen. Jim takes the two packages of sausages and carries them in his hand. Des has four eggs; Alphie has the bacon and half a loaf of bread, while I go in front with the torch. The only fingerprints we leave are mine on the handle of the kitchen door and Alphie's on the door of the fridge.

Within ten minutes we are in the science lab on the same level as the study hall. Alphie has the Bunsen burner going, frying the bacon. Since the moon is shining brightly outside, we scarcely need the torch to find our way around the lab. As the bacon is frying, we find plastic paper for Alphie to use. Des slices the loaf and spreads the slices in a row on the same bench that Mr. Breen uses to conducts his experiments. As Alphie finishes cooking the sausages and eggs, he uses a science ladle to spread them over the bread slices. Jim finds four plastic cups and fills them with cold water from the tap.

After a gentle applause for chef Alphie, we sit on the bar stools that surround the experiment benches and enjoy gorging, even eating the crisp bacon with our bare hands.

In the midst of all this eating, Jim puts on a big smile and whispers, "Happy Saint Patrick's Day, fellows."

While Alphie and Jim are cleaning off the benches in the moonlight and making sure that everything is put back where it belongs, Des and I excuse ourselves, and head up the back stairs to room 309 to return the master key to cousin Pat's right pocket, where it rejoins the pennies and sixpence. I must admit that I get a momentary fright when Pat gives a big snore just as I'm placing the trousers back on the bed post.

Chapter XX

Year Two at Saint Patrick's

Michael Smyth and I have an enjoyable visit with his Uncle Tommy and Aunt Minnie. They hadn't known we were coming: because we don't have use of a phone at the college, we couldn't call ahead. Minnie is busy making lots of apple cakes because the next day is Fair Day in Cavan. Hundreds farmers will be in town to sell their cattle. Michael and I volunteer to help Aunt Minnie by offering to peel the apples. She jokingly asks, "Are you fellows expecting to get paid?"

We laugh as Michael responds, "Aunty we would be happy to receive a piece of the apple cake after it is baked."

She replies, "I can do better than that. After I give you a meal I will wrap up one of the cakes and you can take it back to the college with you."

As we say our thank you and prepare to leave, Tommy and Minnie's daughter Mary comes in from the local Loretta College. She gives Michael a big hug and waits for him to introduce me. He teases her a little, saying, "I should make you guess who this is. Rumor has it that you and his cousin have a big crush on each other."

She surprises Michael by blurting out, "This must be Finbarr Corr, Brian's cousin from Legaginney. Brian frequently talks about him."

Mary is gorgeous. She has a beautiful face, with a good figure and shapely breasts, which I find are attracting my attention. She comes over and gives me a hug.

"Finbarr welcome to our home. Tell your cousin Brian that he owes me a letter or a phone call."

"I will Mary." I say. What I really want to say is, "How about you and me getting together for a little fun?" Later that evening I feel guilty and say to myself I had better confess. I did take pleasure in that sexual fantasy. While it is a natural feeling for a young man approaching age sixteen, it isn't a good habit to nurture for a would-be candidate preparing to take a vow of celibacy.

Michael and I walk quickly back to the college with Aunt Minnie's apple cake between us. We make it back just in time for study hall at 5:15 PM. To help me focus on my studies I look over Hubert Maultsby's shoulder and see he is learning the Wordsworth poem *Daffodils,* which was assigned to us by our English teacher. As usual, I follow his example and study items that I have to learn by heart at the beginning of the study period. At the same time I am thinking that I probably will not be sitting behind him in the study hall when we return in September.

When I return to our room at the end of study, Cousin Brian is anxious to know how our visit to the Railway Hotel went and if we saw the love of his life Mary Smyth. I decide to play a joke on him. Pretending to kiss him on the cheek, I say, "Brian you owe Mary a letter or a phone call and she sent this to you.". Laughing, he runs away and says, "I don't want my older cousin mugging me."

That same week we have our usual one-and-a-half hour double class with Mr. Breen, our science teacher. It seems odd at first to be helping Mr. Breen set up an experiment in which we will attempt to pass dry hydrogen over heated copper oxide to create H_2O (water). My last lab experience was eating my fill of Alphie's cooked bacon, eggs and sausages. Standing across from me on the other side of the large science counter is Des Scott, who has a big smile from ear to ear. My wink to him is meant to confirm that we are probably thinking the same thoughts today. The rest of our classmates are focused one hundred percent on the experiment.

Mr. Breen prepares the dry hydrogen, careful not to expose it to the air, which might cause an explosion. He carefully attaches a foot=long glass tube to the flask of hydrogen so as to allow it to flow gently over the heated copper oxide in a tube. In what seems like a miracle to us neophyte scientists, the gentle flow of hydrogen assimilates the oxygen from the heated oxide bar; and water begins to drip into the drinking glass held by Mr. Breen. We applaud while Mr. Breen smiles and says that's it real water and takes a sip. ($H2+CuO -H2O$)

Phil Lawlor, one of the more extroverted students in our class, asks, "Mr. Breen, is it possible to do the experiment in reverse, splitting the $H2O$ into hydrogen and oxygen?"

"Aren't you the smart Townie?" says Mr. Breen. "My plan is to reverse the procedure next week, using electrolysis."

Before the semester ends in mid-June we celebrate one more Hooley in the Kitchen, borrowing the master key from Prefect Pat's trousers. This time, with Alphie's, Jim's and Des's permission, we add my Dublin friend Michael Smyth to the *Team of thieves*. At breakfast he shares with me that he was very anxious as he held the torch while I "borrowed" the master key from my cousin's pants.

I don't allow any distractions from my studies during the two weeks before the year-ending exams. My goal, as I have already stated, is to catch up with the townies.

This time I have to pass every subject, including Greek. I take advantage of every extra moment to keep on top of the subjects I am anxious about. This time I am looking forward to getting honors in Science, Irish, Algebra and Geometry.

Since my brother P. Joe is busy helping Jack Murtagh cut the turf in Legaginney bog, Daddy has to come to the college with our mare Maggie and trap (wheel cart) to take me home for the summer holidays. In the letter I receive from Mammy, she says Daddy will not pick me up until around 3 PM, as he has to attend a meeting of the Cavan County Council at 12 noon on his way to the college. I am not disappointed. I feel I have done pretty well in all the exams, and I am looking forward to a fun summer in the bog, where I'll help make hay both at our farm at home and our second farm down by the lakes in Kilmore. Since Daddy didn't have lunch at his meeting and the college does not serve anything but breakfast on the day we begin our holidays, Daddy stops at a food store in Cavan town and buys two sandwiches and two bottles of Coca Cola for us to have on our way home.

As we ride through Cavan town and the village of Ballinagh the weather is sunny. We meet loads of people riding their bicycles to and from Cavan. Many of them say hello to Daddy, as he is well known in the area, where he was a politician for ten years and now has been recently elected to membership on the Cavan County Council. I am just as happy that he is not talking to me, as I cannot talk as freely to him as I can to P. Joe. I cannot wait to tell P. Joe about borrowing the master key from Pat's trousers and having a feast in the science lab.

It is usual for farm boys like me, who are in boarding school, to get the first day at home or at least half of it off,

141

before we are expected to join the workers in the bog or the meadows. Working in the bog is fun. We meet a lot of other teenagers to fool around with, and there are lots of picnic dinners and teas. Many of the families travel ten or twelve miles to cut their turf in our bog each year. Daddy does not mind us spending time with them because he feels it helps build his business of leasing part of the bog to their daddies each year.

Our typical work day in the bog or in the hay field is from 9 AM to 5 PM. Since it is bright here in Ireland until 10:30 PM during the summer months, boys my age and older usually play handball at the Lacken ball alley after work or join other young fellows kicking and catching a football. If I am feeling tired after working all day, I frequently join other boys and go for a relaxing, cooling swim in the river Eireann, which runs through my Uncle Jim's farm in Lacken.. We boys are very casual on these evenings, dropping our pants, jumping into the river nude, swimming downstream with the current, out of the view of prying eyes. All I have to remember at the end of the evening is to make sure I am home in time to participate in the family rosary before bedtime.

Chapter XXI

Cavan versus Mayo

The summer is whizzing by. One of the jobs assigned to me for the season is taking the milk from our farm in Legaginney to the creamery in the village of Crossdoney, almost three miles away. Some farmers hire an individual who picks up milk from several customers each morning from Monday to Saturday and transports it to the creamery. Daddy chooses to have me drive our pony and two-wheeled cart to do the job. I am accustomed to getting up early in college, so I have no trouble waking up at 7, saying my morning prayers, eating a good breakfast of porridge and fresh milk, and harnessing our pony by 8:15.

My brother P. Joe and Mary Farrelly milk the eight cows. When they finish, P. Joe puts the two cans of milk in the cart. I am soon on my way up the lane, stopping at our neighbors the McCusker's to pick up their can of milk. The cart's two springs, which sit on top of the axles, allow the pony to trot down Legaginney Bog Road without spilling the milk.

I often pass other vehicles on their way to the same creamery. For people like me going to the creamery is a social as well as a business event. I am proud to help my Daddy and neighbor Phildy McCusker make a financial profit. When I pass through the village of Crossdoney and turn right on the road to Cavan, I join the queue of farmers with horse and carts loaded with their cans of milk. Over time I get to know these fellows' names, and we chat about politics, the weather and Gaelic football. Some are great storytellers and enjoy trying to get some younger folks

143

like me rattled with ghost stories, or tales of the Banshee wailing to alert the community that somebody significant in the community is about to die.

The creamery manager recognizes our pony and says, "You must be one of the Corrs of Legaginney. Are you the boy who is in college, that your dad talks about?"

"Yes that's me. I am Finbarr," I say.

He sighs. "You wouldn't know by looking at me that I was a day-boy at Saint Pat's for three years and quit after I did my Inter-Cert exam. I shouldn't complain, as I got this good job after I quit." After a slight pause he continues, "I don't want you to quit as you will get a much better job if you complete the five years and pass your Leaving Certificate Exam."

"That is my plan sir," I reply.

After he records the volume of milk in gallons, I head to the queue at the back of the creamery where another employee will fill our three cans with skim milk, which we use to feed the calves and pigs on the farm. My daddy gets a check on the 15th of each month, in payment for the cream they separate from our milk. Mary Farrelly helps me unload the cans when I get home. I remove the pony's harness, give him a drink in the fresh stream that runs underneath the lane, and let him run free to graze in the orchard in front of our home.

Because the weather is unusually warm this summer, the bog turf has dried early and is already packed in the turf shed by July 1st. This guarantees that Mammy and Daddy and my siblings who are still at home will have enough fuel to stay warm the whole winter.

We're busy making hay the whole month of July. By my sixteenth birthday I am tall enough to operate the wheel-rake and drive our mare Maggie around the meadows, putting the dry hay in rows, ready for cocking. What I don't tell Daddy is that I push Maggie to go as fast as possible so that the whole field of hay is in cocks by 5. If that happens as planned, I am free to go up to the football field in Garrymore and play football until it gets dark at 10 PM.

I feel excited when Daddy invites me to go with him to Breifne Park in Cavan to see our senior county team play the Mayo county team. He knows that I love football, and he remembers how, before we owned a radio, I went to the McCusker's on Sunday afternoons to listen to the All-Ireland football final on their radio.

Later that evening Daddy shares with me that he has an ulterior motive for going to the game on Sunday. He says, "Michael Kelly, one of the Mayo footballers, is the son of Sean Kelly, who served with me in the IRA. Sean and I became good friends when we were imprisoned together for several months in Portumna, County Galway. Like me, he believed that England should give Ireland its freedom after all these years, and he was prepared to give his life, if necessary, to achieve that goal. I am looking forward to meeting his son, even if I will be cheering for Cavan."

I don't comment, as ordinarily Daddy does not discuss anything about his days or years in the IRA and forbids any of us, his six sons, to join the present IRA. Thanks to Michael Kelly, I am going to see my favorite athletes play a full hour of Gaelic Football.

Since Daddy and I will be riding two bicycles on Sunday to the game, rather than taking Maggie and the trap, I will go over to Uncle Jim's on Saturday and borrow his bicycle for Sunday. Fortunately, Sunday is a fine sunny day. Riding a bicycle six miles to Breifne Park is easy compared to riding sixteen miles to visit Uncle Father Lawrence.

We meet several fellow Breifne fans on the way to Cavan. Our cousin Thomas Francis Corr from Wateraughey, who himself is a very good club footballer, joins us as we walk with our bicycles up the hill past the house of other cousins who are known as the "Corrs of the Sandpit." Ten or twelve more cyclists join us in Ballinagh. Daddy knows some of them and says they are from the parish of Mullahoran, the home of Phil the "Gunner" Brady, Cavan's center full back. I don't have to worry about being in time for the game, as everybody who knows Daddy will tell you that he is always fifteen minutes early for any appointment.

As we park our bicycles in a secure parking lot, we notice that both teams are already suited up and walking down the driveway to the football pitch (field). The County has not built a dressing room for the players yet, as the football field is only a year and half old. One of the Mayo players points out Michael Kelly to Daddy, who walks over and taps Michael on the shoulder. I shake Michael's hand but, not wanting to be hypocritical, I don't wish him a good game. I am an ardent Breifne fan. Daddy and Michael keep chatting and smiling. I presume that Michael is sharing how his dad is doing thirty years later, and Daddy is probably telling him about his political career as a member of the Fianna Fail party.

The stands are almost filled by the time we pay our entrance fee and take our seats about midfield, five rows back from the sideline. The DeLasalle marching band is tuning up, preparing to lead the two teams who will walk side by side around half the playing field. Both teams are stretching and taking practice frees. Peter Donahue, the popular forward, is taking frees from 14, 21 and then 50 yards from the goal. I am bursting with excitement as I watch Phil "the Gunner" Brady, our center full back, kicking the ball out to his teammates Tony Tighe and center fielders Mick Higgins and John Joe Reilly.

P. J. Duke, Bill Doonan and Paul Fitzsimmons are lying on the grass and stretching their muscles. I remember that Higgins, Duke and Donahue were stars of the game three years earlier (1947) when, for the first and only time, the All-Ireland Football final was played in New York's Polo Grounds. The boys of Breifne defeated the boys from the "Kingdom" of Kerry by three points.

The parade ends and the referee from County Meath tosses a half crown in the air as he calls "Heads or Hearts" to give the winner the right to choose which end of the field they wish to defend for the first half. All of the players and everyone in the stands face the Irish flag of green white and gold while the band plays our national anthem. The players take their positions on the field. The four center fielders, two from each team, stand in the middle and wait for the referee to throw the football up for the tip off.

Mick Higgins of Cavan catches the tip off from John Joe Reilly and kicks it to full forward Peter Donahue, who is immediately fouled by the Mayo full back. Peter takes the free kick of the ground and puts it over the bar for the first Cavan point. (*For those unfamiliar with Gaelic football, a ball kicked over the bar is one point and three points are equal to a goal. A goal is scored by kicking or punching the ball between the goal sticks and under the bar.*)

The Mayo goalie kicks the ball out to midfield, where one of his teammates catches it and takes off on a solo run down along the sideline, careful to tip the ball on his right foot or bounce it every other step to avoid being whistled at for fouling. He attempts to pass it to Mayo's full forward, probably with the intention of scoring a goal. Fortunately for Cavan, Brady intercepts the pass. Two of the Mayo forwards, totally unaware of Brady's strength, attack to recover the ball. When he bursts out between them they understand why he is called "the Gunner Brady."

Chapter XXII

Preparing for the Inter-cert Exam

Excuse me for not telling you that Cavan beat Mayo by a score of 3 goals and 10 points to 2 goals and 8 points. My older sister Marie, who coaches me as I write my story, says,

"Finbarr you are going to turn off too many of your avid readers by going into too much detail about the football game. While I enjoy watching Gaelic football, I don't give a damn whether Peter Donahue scores six points versus five points from the fourteenth yard line. Not everybody is as crazy about Gaelic football as you are. Why don't you tell your readers about you and me cycling all the way to Longford to visit Aunt Sheila and Aunt Bridget."

Marie is a college student, boarding at Saint Louis School in Monaghan. She is preparing to do her Leaving Certificate Exam about eleven months from now, while I am gearing up for my Intermediate-Certificate Exam in June. She is very athletic. She runs track and plays Camogie, the ladies version of Hurley played by men. (*Whether it is Hurling or Camogie the game is played by two teams of fifteen players on a field that is 150 yards long and 90 yards wide. The players use a stick three and a half feet long with a curved blade that is three inches wide, called a Hurley. At each end of the pitch (field) is a goal formed by two posts about 21 feet high and connected by a crossbar eight feet above the ground. The players catch the small ball, which is cork centered, covered with leather and hit it towards the goal using their Hurley stick. The scores are counted like Gaelic Football, below the bar a goal and over the bar between the posts a point.*) Marie tells me,

"That's enough. They all know that you are a sports addict."

Marie borrows her sister Dympna's bicycle that she uses to ride five days a week to the technical school in Cavan. I borrow Daddy's. I dress comfortably for the thirteen mile ride, canvas sandals, short pants and a sleeveless pullover over a short sleeved shirt. Once we ride out Legaginney Lane and turn left, going past Potahee Chapel on our left, we ride up hill for three miles to Carryduff Cross. We turn right and follow the signs to Gowna. It is lovely town with several lakes. We stop there for a mineral (a soda). We spend half of the six pence that Mammy gave each of us as spending money for the trip.

As we pass by one of the lakes, about five yards from the road, I see four or five young boys about my age swimming in the lake. I jokingly say to Marie,

"Would you mind if we stop for about ten minutes and let me jump into the lake with them for a quick swim?" With an unusual aggravated attitude she replies,

"First of all Finbarr, you don't have swimming togs with you and notice that all the swimmers you see there have a lot more modesty than you and your friends swimming at Scarvey."

"Excuse me big sister," I reply "Can't you see that I'm just pulling your leg?"

We ride in silence for the next fifteen minutes.

We know the directions for the trip very well, as we frequently accompanied Daddy, when he drove our mare Maggie with Mammy aboard and whoever of our siblings wanted to come along for the drive to Aughnacliffe. Aunt Sheila and Uncle Chris have only one child, a red haired girl named Agatha. Her parents are teachers with Uncle Chris being principal of the local parish school. Aunt Sheila likes to tell the story of when I was a baby and came to visit them while Agatha was about five years old. I was laid down for a midday nap on her parents' bed upstairs. While the adults were having a meal down stairs, without their knowledge, Agatha comes up stairs and, according to the story I was told years later, Agatha thought I was getting cold in the bed. She spreads a blanket on the floor, pulls me off the bed and lays me on the blanket. She rolls me up in the blanket, covering me from head to toe and pushes me under the crib that had been used by her when she was a baby. As the story goes, Mammy goes up the stairs to check on me and possibly breast feed me and discovers that I am missing. After a slight panic and her calling for help downstairs, Aunt Sheila, accompanied by Agatha, comes up and Agatha points out where she hid me for warmth. I cannot confirm the authenticity of the end of the story, but here is how Aunt Sheila tells it,

"Finbarr, when we get you out of the blanket you are almost suffocated."

Since that story happened Uncle Chris died (R.I.P.), probably because of his dependency on alcohol. Aunt Sheila and Agatha give Marie and me a warm welcome. Aunt Sheila is retired from teaching and since this is the month of July Agatha is home from college for a holiday from studying Radiography. They are surprised by our visit, Aunt Sheila sends Agatha up the road to the local country shop to buy something special to serve us a nice meal. Meanwhile, she asks me several questions about my progress at Saint Patrick's College. She laughs heartily

151

when I tell her that Mr Breen christened us the boys from the countryside the "Bogmen", while the students from Cavan town who were educated by the Christian Brothers he calls "Townies." She is happy to hear that me, her nephew, is catching up with the "Townies."

After an appetizing lunch Agatha joins Marie and me as we ride over two miles to visit Mammy's spinster sister Bridget, who still lives alone in the home where Mammy was born and raised i.e. Mollyglass. Bridget is the oldest of the Doyle clan. I don't understand, why she nor her younger brother James, who lives on a farm in Belleville, never married. Bridget is a very devout Catholic, who not only walks the two miles every Sunday over hilly roads to Church beside her sister Sheila, but like Mammy recites the Rosary at least three times a day. Even though she lives quite a distance from Legaginney, she is always looking for ways to help Mammy, who she, Bridget, feels is overly burdened raising nine children in the same home. She actually takes P. Joe to live with her in Mollyglass for four years, as Mammy is busy rearing my two older sisters, my two younger brothers and me.

Marie and I leave Mollyglass for the ride home to Legaginney at 6:00 PM. Mammy is anxious to hear all the news from Aunt Sheila, Agatha and Aunt Bridget. I get a good laugh out of Mammy when I say,

"Agatha doesn't try to smother me anymore."

The summer always seems to end fast. I spend two weeks making hay on our Kilmore farm. It is a different experience than working at home on our farm in Legaginney. While Daddy owns both the house in Kilmore and Legaginney house, we cannot sleep overnight in Kilmore, since Jim McCaul. who herds our cattle, lives with his family in the home, as compensation for herding our cattle and taking care of it. We are, however, treated as family, as Mrs. McCaul cooks dinner for us and serves us evening tea before we take the ride home four miles to Legaginney. I wish that we could switch the orchard on the Kilmore farm to Legaginney, as the orchard in Legaginney is an orchard in name only. When we take apples home to Legaginney from Kilmore we cannot be accused of stealing, as unfortunately we could be, if our gang of thieves are caught stealing from the bishop's orchard beside the college.

Today is September 5th 1952. Daddy has a good summer on the farm. He sells twelve three year old bullocks for a good price at the Cavan Fair in August and then surprises all of us, including Mammy, by announcing at our evening tea, that he is buying a second hand van for himself and the family. He learns how to drive in a few days and tells me that he will be taking me back to college in his new purchase, instead of driving our beloved Maggie and trap. I wish I could draw a picture of the shock on Cousin Brian's face when I tell him Maggie's role of transporting me to Saint Patrick's is being replaced by a 1950 two-door Austin van.

Cousin Brian and I are still assigned to the same room across the corridor from Pat and Des Scott. As third-year students our seats in the study hall are half way back to the big desk occupied by the priest on duty, who supervises study hall. I can no longer look over my idol Hubert Maultsby's shoulder, but I do plan to follow his study habits I assimilated over two years of tackling the learning of poetry and the difficult subjects, like Greek and Geometry, during the first study period. I am determined to keep my grades up to par by organizing my study habits to do all my assignments during the regular study periods, without having to sit outside our bedroom finishing my assignments after the lights are turned off in our rooms.

We still have my favorite teacher Mr. Breen as our teacher for Physics and Chemistry. I enjoy his classes and in particular the relaxed atmosphere he creates in the special one and a half classes he conducts doing experiments in the lab. He almost makes me want to become a scientist. Father Carroll, my Greek teacher, greets me warmly during the first class, complimenting me for getting my best score in Greek in the two years I have been studying it. Since my Latin teacher is one of the two priests transferred permanently out of the college for allegedly 'mugging' first and second year students, Father Patrick Mallon, a big jovial man, takes over teaching us Latin in preparation for our Intermediate-Certificate Exam in June.

Father Bob McCabe, our English teacher, gives an extended introduction during the first class of this semester. He tells us that by studying English and developing our writing skills we are following in the footsteps of some of the most distinguished Irish playwrights, poets and literary scholars. He speaks of William Butler Yeats, the first Irishman to win the Nobel Prize for Literature. Sonja Massie author of Irish Pride says that Yeats's *"plays, poetry and prose defined the Irish people and their Celtic heritage."* Father Bob tells us that because we are Irish we have been given the gift of being natural story tellers by the Almighty. He encourages all of us to relax and think creatively as we write our essays this semester.

"I have no doubt", he says, "There is possibly a James Joyce or a George Bernard Shaw in this class." We all just smiled.

He finished his introduction by saying that most people think of Shakespeare as the greatest playwright in the English language, but his choice for greatest playwright is John Millington Synge, a Dublin man, who wrote *The Shadow of the Glen.* The Irish Catholic hierarchy didn't canonize Synge, since the principal character in the play is an adulterer.

The school year is getting off to a brilliant start. I'm enjoying being a student. My academic goals are to work hard and get as many honors as I can in my first governmental exam, since I passed the primary certificate exam in Legaginney School several years ago. My spiritual goal of developing a personal relationship with Jesus is happening. I know I will need of His help in discerning my vocation in life three years hence. My physical goal is to continue to exercise playing handball and some football. I realize already that I do not have the passion to become a footballer like John Joe Reilly, the captain of the Cavan Senior team. I honestly don't see the sense of killing myself at practice four or five days a week and risk being maimed, for what? When there is some honor at stake, like winning something as unimportant as a street league in Ballinagh, I can play football with the best of them. I do however feel more of an attraction to middle distance running. Maybe one day I will be the mile champion of County Cavan.

Chapter XXIII

My Godfather's Wake

The news of my godfather Frank Corr's impending death reaches Legaginney. I am feeling sad. Because all four of my grandparents died before I made my first Holy Communion, Frank, my daddy's cousin, has served as both a godfather and grandfather for as long as I can remember. I want to see him one more time to tell him I love him and say goodbye. I go up Legaginney Road alone, past my old school. Father McGauran's car is parked in front of Frank's kitchen. I am thinking that Father is in there, either administering Frank the Last Rites of Holy Anointing or giving him a final blessing as he passes to eternal life.

The kitchen is full of people. Francie, Philip, Elizabeth, Peggy and Nancy, all of Frank's living children, are present. Elizabeth greets me with a whisper as she points to the bedroom off the kitchen. My dear godfather is breathing very loudly, struggling to live. I stand with my back to the kitchen door, looking into the bedroom. Father McGauran is sprinkling Frank with holy water, while he reads from his prayer book. "Muddy" Corr, as her offspring, Frank's children, call their mother, is sitting on a short stool by the bed holding a blessed candle in Frank's right hand. I learn later, from my mother, that this is a custom among Irish Catholics to keep away the evil spirits from the dying person. I turn my eyes towards the kitchen fire, away from the bedroom. I don't want to watch him die.

Suddenly there is silence in the bedroom, except for Muddy's prayers leading the Rosary. Elizabeth opens the bedroom window to let her father's soul ascend to Heaven. Father McGauran exits, waving to the family without saying a word. Muddy recites the first half of the Apostles Creed and we all respond. She leads us in the first Sorrowful Decade of the Rosary, *The Agony in the Garden*. Peggy, the oldest sibling, leads the second, *The Scourging of Jesus at the Pillar*. Francie leads the third, *The Crowning of Jesus with Thorns*; Elizabeth, the fourth, *Jesus Carries his Cross to Calvary*; and Philip, the fifth, *Jesus is Crucified on Calvary*.

I walk home, forgetting what time it is. Mammy can tell by my eyes that Godfather Frank has passed, R.I. P. (May he rest in Peace) I am late for the Family Rosary. I recite my own prayers and cry myself to sleep. It is Tuesday night.

The following evening I go with Daddy to Frank's wake. The house is full of people from the neighborhood and a few cousins, like Thomas Francis Corr, from outside the parish. Phillip hands out the customary clay pipes to those who smoke, while Francie follows him carrying a dish of shredded tobacco. I don't take any, of course. My Daddy surprises me by taking a pipe, filling it with tobacco and lighting up. My whole family knows that he is so addicted to cigarettes, that he lights his first one when he gets out of bed in the morning. Nancy comes around with toffee sweets for me and two teenage girls who are not from our parish.

Some couples and individuals come in and go straight to the bedroom where Frank is laid out on white sheets on a single bed. Mammy tells me that some neighbors, like Joe McCusker, volunteer to bathe Frank, shave his

157

face, and dress him in a brown Franciscan habit. His feet remain bare, and his eyes are closed. A white sheet covers is put over Frank from his feet up to his chest, where his folded hands hold his Rosary beads. Most of the visitors kneel by the deceased and say a prayer. They return to the kitchen, shake hands with "Muddy," offer her their condolences and leave.

The rest of us, committed to "Watching the Whole Night," as part of our tradition, sit and drink Guinness or minerals, smoke pipes, and tell stories about the deceased. As expected, many of the stories about my humorous godfather get a laugh, not only from his family but also from those sitting in the kitchen and the overflow crowd sitting on the stairway going up to the other bedrooms. One local farmer tells us that his sons adored Frank, because he taught them a lot about growing lettuce, scallions and beets. But his two daughters were frightened of Frank, who had an ugly black mustache. When they were little girls going home from Legaginney School, he would try to hug and kiss them.

The night passes quickly as the men drink beer and smoke their pipes. Some men choose to sing a sad Irish melody rather than tell a story. Miss Berrill, a good singer, gets all of us engaged in singing the song "Come back Paddy Reilly to Ballyjamesduff" that was written by Percy French, one of Ireland's most famous songwriters and entertainers in his day. My daddy, who travels the whole County of Cavan, as a councilor, leans over and tells me that there is a statue of Percy French in Ballyjamesduff square.

Although I am tired, I am determined not to give in and ask Daddy to take me home. At midnight Muddy leads us in saying the Rosary, this time using the Glorious

Mysteries instead of the Sorrowful. She surprises me when she says, "Finbarr, his godson, will lead the second decade, commemorating Jesus's Ascension into Heaven."

Fortunately, I have my Rosary beads in my pocket. I lead off by reciting the first half of the Our Father. The "congregation" responds, "Give us this day our daily bread and forgive us our trespasses as we forgive those who trespass against us and lead us not into temptation but deliver us from evil. Amen." As Muddy finishes the Rosary by leading us in the recitation of the prayer *Salve Regina*, several of the older people leave and go home.

Francie continues to serve Guinness Stout all night. Some of the men get a little tipsy and look like they are ready to get up and dance an Irish jig. Muddy gives a No-No signal and tells Francie to stop serving any more Guinness. Around 4:30, the morning light comes in through the open kitchen door, which faces east. Elizabeth puts more turf on the kitchen fire and pushes the two pots on the crook to the side, leaving space on the fire for Nancy to place a large metal pan. Meanwhile Peggy takes a slab of homemade bacon, cuts it and places ten thin slices on the hot pan. In about twenty minutes the three daughters have prepared a full breakfast of bacon, eggs and homemade Irish bread for their eighteen or twenty overnight guests.

On Thursday evening Daddy, Mammy, P. Joe, Colm, Fonsie and I go to the ceremony, traditionally called "The Removal." The body of the deceased is placed in a coffin and taken to church. With help from two neighbors, Pat Lynch, the owner of the grocery store next door places Frank's body in the coffin. Eight young men, including my brother P. Joe, take turns carrying the coffin up the hill to Potahee chapel.

159

For some strange reason I don't understand, neighbors, Joe McCusker and Toddy Maguire place straw on the steep hill going up to the chapel. Daddy explains later that they fear the coffin carriers will slip on the steep hill. Ordinarily a hearse drawn by two horses takes the body to the church but, because of the proximity of the Corr residence to the chapel, the eight young men volunteer to do it, saving the family the cost of hiring a hearse.

Father McGauran, vested in soutane, surplice and purple stole, greets us as we enter the church graveyard. He blesses the coffin with holy water, reads a prayer from his ritual and leads the coffin bearers into the church. He guides them to lay the coffin on a stand before the main altar, where it will remain until burial the next day.

Since I am now in boarding school, I am no longer officially an altar boy at Potahee chapel. I go to Father McGauran and ask, "Father, since Frank was my godfather, may I serve the funeral mass tomorrow?"

As I expect, he is gracious and says, "Yes of course. You and your brother Colm can serve."

The chapel is almost full the next day when Colm and I vest in the sacristy and go out on the altar to light the candles and place the cruets with wine and water on the credence table. Father McGauran says, "Finbarr, your godfather must be very popular. Where did all these people come from?

"My godfather is very funny. I will always remember the kids in our Legaginney School talking to him during our recess period while he planted onions, lettuce, potatoes and beets in his little garden. While he planted he told us funny stories and answered our silly questions like, why do you spread cow manure in the furrow before you put the seed potato down? I am going to miss him, Father."

160

"I know. Finbarr, but isn't your godfather in a better place? He is already up with God in heaven, praying for you and all of us."

Father McGauran begins the mass with the prayer "Introibo ad Altare Dei" [I will go unto the altar of God]. He reads the Epistle and Gospel in Latin but delivers the eulogy in English. I cry on the altar as Father McGauran says, "The children of Legaginney School and our altar server Finbarr, Frank's godson, will miss Frank."

As is the custom throughout the Diocese of Kilmore, a funeral offering is collected before the offertory of the mass. Father McGauran invites the deceased's two sons Francie and Phillip to stand beside him at an offering table inside the altar railing. Most of the male attendees come forward and place their offerings on the table. Since Daddy is a cousin and a weekly visitor to the Corr home each Sunday morning after 10 A.M. mass, he places a ten-shilling bill on the table, while most of the others place a half crown or fifty pence.

The procession to the graveside is led by four of Frank's relatives, (including P. Joe) carrying the coffin. Colm carries the thurible, while I, walking beside Father McGauran, carry the holy water. Josie Beatty has already dug the grave, moving the bones of Frank's ancestors to the side, to be put back in the grave beside Frank as he is lowered into the grave. Father McGauran takes a shovel full of clay and throws it on the coffin as he says in Latin, "Remember man that thou art dust and unto dust thou shall return."

Chapter XXIV

My Fourth Year 1952-53

Passing the Intercert Exam and getting five honors out of seven subjects has given me confidence when Daddy drops me off at the college on September 4, 1952, the beginning of my Fourth Year. I am now 17 years old. I have less than two years to prepare for my Leaving Certificate Exam and to discern what career is in God's will for me.

Three years ago it seemed clear that He was calling me to follow in the footsteps of my uncle Father Michael Corr and become a priest. Today, I am not so sure, as I find myself attracted to a girl in Ballinagh and also to a young lady in Potahee who attended Legaginney School with me three years ago. If God is calling me to be a celibate priest, why is He allowing sexual feelings to distract me from that vocation?

Cousin Brian is making his bed in the same room we have shared for three years. I am breathless after hauling my heavy suitcase up the steep flight of stairs to our second-floor residence. Brian turns away from making the bed and teases me, "Why don't you use the elevator? You know how it works, since you and your buddies used it at midnight last year to get down to the basement and raid the kitchen."

I tease him back, "Brian, if you wish, you can take my place on the 'band of thieves' team this semester. You may borrow my torch if you don't have a light to guide you around in the dark. You may also borrow my trunk to hide the apples on the nights you go out to raid the bishop's orchard."

He replies sarcastically, "Cousin Finbarr, you are awfully generous."

Instead of the usual monologue we receive annually from Father Gargan at the beginning of the school year, this year we get a surprise. The college president, Father Gaffney, calls us all to the chapel and gives us what he intends to be an inspirational lecture, although we students are not impressed. Father Gaffney visits the U.S. frequently and is infatuated by life in America. He tells us that when he was there over the summer to study how the administrators of Catholic schools run their schools. He says that all secondary schools in the U.S. are called high schools and that the majority of the students are day students, most of who travel to and from school by bus.

Raising his voice, Father further reports that education in Catholic high schools in the U.S. focuses on educating the total person. The formula used is called P.I.E.S., where "P" stands for Physical Development, "I" for Intellectual Stimulation, "E" for Emotional Development, and "S" for Spiritual Development. Each student is encouraged to develop a physical fitness program and play one of the team sports sponsored by their school. The U.S. schools encourage their students to be creative writers, ask teachers questions in class and volunteer to be editors or reporters for their school newspapers.

These U.S. programs for emotional growth are something that we here in Ireland could emulate. The schools in Ireland often punish or suspend the students from troubled homes because of their behavior problems or emotional problems. In the U.S. the schools routinely provide in-house weekly counseling for such students and, if necessary, for their parents as well.

The spiritual program in the U.S. is similar to ours. Students attend masses on Sunday and holy days of obligation and confess their sins to a priest monthly. One advantage we have over the U.S. is our practice of saying the Rosary at home with our families at the end of the day, a practice that the U.S. administrators admire. Father explains that, because of all the after-school sports activities in the U.S., families there find it practically impossible to gather for an evening meal, much less for the family Rosary.

Father Gaffney pauses at this point and asks, "Will the students here please raise their hands if your family kneels each evening and prays the family Rosary?" About 80% of the students raise their hands.

Father Gaffney continues, "The Catholic schools in the U.S. have annual retreats for the students, just like we do here each October. While we match the U.S. in fulfilling the requirements for P, I and S, I do feel we need to put more emphasis here at St, Patrick's on your emotional development."

"Does anybody have any questions?" he asks.

After a moment's silence, a hand goes up near the back of the chapel. It is Alphie Gallogly, who asks, "Father wouldn't it help our physical development if all us of got three solid meals per day?" A few students smother their giggles, amazed at Alphie's courage.

Father Gaffney smiles and says, "I am glad you ask that question, Alphie. I plan to take up this question with our bursar, Father Duffy, who will discuss it with the food coordinator."

Classes begin on the following day as usual. Father Carroll, our Greek teacher, smiles at me and says, "You just made it, didn't you?" I smile back and say nothing. I know what he means. I barely pass the Greek exam with a score of 40%, while I get honors (over 60%) on five other subjects. Our class, the Fourth-Year students, has a new teacher as a replacement for Father Gaffney, who will be too busy with his responsibilities as president.

We are going to have a very good football team this year, not that I contribute to its success, except that my presence on the field during the practices makes their sessions feel more real. I greatly admire Jim McDonnell and James (Sticky) Brady. Jim is in his fifth year and due to make his Leaving Certificate Exam in June. James is a dayboy in our class and cycles eight miles one way to the college from Cormore five days a week. Although he is five inches shorter than I am, he can jump one foot higher to catch the ball. Some of the smart alecks in our class have christened him "Sticky" because of how he tackles any opponent in possession of the football. The real test of how good our team is will happen a month from now when we face our perennial nemesis, Saint Patrick's College, Armagh.

Since we are now in our fourth year, with less than two years from graduating with a Leaving Certificate, our class has the choice of registering for honor courses. If we are insecure about our competence in one or two subjects, we settle for a pass score. My confidence in getting five honors in my Intercert Exam helps me decide to take honors in Irish, math, physics, and chemistry and to aim for passes in English and Greek.

Our president's promise to speak to the college bursar about improvements in our quality and quantity of food doesn't change our menu one iota during the first month of the new school year. We still get only two slices of pan bread and jam for lunch. At dinner we get just the usual eight potatoes for a table of eight students. If you are unlucky to be student number eight to choose your potato on a particular day, you can be stuck with a half-rotten potato. Putting that potato together with an overcooked pork chop and a spoonful of cabbage doesn't fill the stomach of the average sixteen-year-old boy. As a result, the captain of our band of thieves, Alphie, has no trouble in persuading all five team members to join him in organizing a midnight raid on the bishop's orchard behind the college ball alley.

Once again we choose a Wednesday night. The moon is full. Laundry bags in tow, we meet Alphie at midnight in the basement locker-room. We sneak up the hill, careful to stay between the two football fields and the ball alley. I bring my torch just in case the moon disappears behind a cloud and we cannot see the apples on the trees. The only team member who is nervous is my friend from Dublin, Michael Smyth.

Within ten or fifteen minutes we are climbing the apple trees. We work in teams of two. One goes up the tree, tosses apples down to a colleague, who fills his bag and then his partner's bag. For some strange reason, the bishop's dog does not visit us and we don't need my lamp, as the moon is shining very brightly.

Alphie is not shy about challenging the president to improve the quality and quantity of our food in the dining room, but he does not want to push his luck by getting caught stealing from his lordship's orchard in the middle of the night. He goes around to all of us and says, "Fellows, it is time to wrap it up, let's go."

Back in my room, I am careful not to wake Brian as I empty my bag of apples into the now famous black trunk. I wait until the bell wakes us all up at 7 A.M. before I push it back under my bed.

The school year proceeds as usual. We do have a Gilbert and Sullivan opera directed by a new music professor, a layman. He chooses the *Pirates of Penzance.* This time I am able to persuade Daddy to drive Mammy in on parents' night to experience the opera, since she loves music.

Winter is not one of my favorite seasons. I frequently get colds that last several weeks. The winter of 1953 is particularly bad for me, as I contract the flu. When the religious sister in the infirmary takes my temperature, she is shocked to see it read 108 degrees. She anxiously looks at me, "Mr. Corr, you are not going back to the study hall. You are going to go to your room to get your pajamas. I am admitting you immediately to the infirmary."

I want to say, "Sister, you cannot do it this week. I am going to raid the kitchen with the band of thief's tomorrow night." That flu turns out to be a personal benefit (or salvation) to me. Alphie and his gang decide to go ahead without me. Alphie knows one of the senior prefects well enough to borrow his master key with the excuse that he wants to cook some eggs and bacon in the science lab. Alphie also goes to Cousin Brian and borrows my torch.

We don't know who does it, but somebody tips off the authorities in the college. The gang of thieves, minus yours truly, goes down the elevator at midnight and opens the kitchen door with the borrowed master key. Apparently, they all touch the door handle on the way in, not realizing it is covered with a purple dye that sticks to their hands.

When they return to their bedrooms, they wash their hands in the basins in their rooms. They don't realize that this purple stuff on their hands is dye that sticks to their basins. All that Father Gargan has to do is go around all of the 150 bedrooms while the students are at mass, list the ones that have the purple dye in their basins. The gang of thieves has no defense.

Later in the week, a priest science teacher, Father Travers, admits to the students in his class that he is the detective who applied the purple dye to entrap the gang of thieves. My torch is returned to me with a slight touch of purple dye on the knob.

Thanks to the awful flu I suffer for several days, I don't have the energy to feel bad about missing the kitchen raid. The only negative consequence for any of the thieves is that Des Scott's parents decide to move Des to a boy's school in Monaghan, rather than run the risk of having the phrase "Expelled from boarding school" included in his bio for future careers. We all miss Des.

I get a nice letter from Mammy telling me how proud she is that I am doing well at Saint Pat's. She adds a nice item at the end of the letter, saying she and Daddy are going to take a drive in to see me Easter Sunday afternoon. She adds, "We have a nice surprise. I will wait until Sunday to tell you, as an Easter gift for you."

I reflect on the surprise over and over. It cannot be another baby; she is too old for that. If they have won a million pounds in the Hospital Sweepstakes, I would see the announcement in the Irish Press or Independent newspaper. Cousin Brian guesses that something good that has happened to one of my brothers or sisters.

He is partly right, as Mammy tells me with all the enthusiasm of an Irish Catholic mother, "Your sister

Marie has decided to enter the convent in Saint Louis in Monaghan to become a nun."

I am shocked, as Marie has been dating boys for several years. We love to tease her about the night she sat and chatted with Terry McKiernan from Corlesmore near the railroad bridge at the end of our lane. Our daddy comes walking down the tracks with a gun he uses to shoot rabbits. Whenever we want to tease Marie, we ask, "Did you think Daddy was going to shoot Terry?"

After the play, my parents head home to Legaginney. When I say my prayers that night, I decide that, if Marie can give up sex and become a nun, I should be able to forgo sex and become a priest.

Chapter XXV

A Pilgrimage to Lough Derg

Pat Scott comes to our room the morning we are to leave the college for our summer holidays in June 1953. He announces, "Finbarr, my mother is taking Des and me on a pilgrimage this summer to a place called Lough Derg in County Donegal, and she is inviting you to come along with us." I am familiar with the pilgrimage, but have never been there. According to some parishioners from St. Michael's Potahee who have gone, it is the toughest pilgrimage in the world.

I reply to Pat, "I will ask my parents permission; I would love to go."

When I raise the question with Mammy and Daddy during our first evening tea together, Daddy speaks up first, saying, "I climbed the 2,500 feet of Croagh Patrick in County Mayo and attended mass on its peak. I believe spending three days fasting on Lough Derg is a lot more challenging than climbing the Croagh" He adds jokingly, "It is more difficult than catching turf in the bog or pitching hay in the hayshed."

Mammy adds, "I would love to go sometime, but I am too busy feeding you all to go this summer. My sister Sheila made the pilgrimage and says the place is also called Saint Patrick's Purgatory. I have no problem, Finbarr, with you going with Mrs. Scott and her two boys. She is a very responsible person." She looks over at Daddy and says, "Can you give him two or three days off from farming at the end of July?" Daddy nods his head. What

I don't say to them is that maybe making the pilgrimage will help me decide what vocation or career to choose after I pass my Leaving Certificate in June next year.

Next day I join my brother P. Joe and Jack Murtagh to cut and catch turf in our bog. At almost eighteen years of age, I like catching turf, placing them on a wheelbarrow and wheeling them out twenty yards to dry on a bank of heather. It's good exercise, especially for someone like me who has been cooped up in classrooms and study halls for several months. In the bog I run into the usual characters, who come from far and near to rent a bank of turf from my father. We have fun catching up on family gossip and sports news. They want to know how well I am doing in college.

Besides attending Sunday mass and joining the family each evening for the rosary, each day I also pray an extra rosary as part of The Novena Rosary. Using a little booklet my mother gave me, I offer this Rosary for twenty-eight consecutive days for one special intention. This month I am offering it up for the grace to make the right career decision next June.

Our daily schedule in the bog is more regular than when making hay, either at home in Legaginney or at our second farm in Kilmore. We come to the bog at 9 A.M. and leave at 5 P.M. I can easily make plans with friends to either go for a swim over at Scarvey or go up the hill to Garrymore to play football until it gets dark. By the end of June we have finished all of our cutting and catching of turf. We pile the dry turf into stacks called "reeks" up to five feet in height before we transport them home to the turf-shed about ten yards from the kitchen back door.

We are about halfway through saving the hay when I receive a letter from Pat Scott about the trip. He is asking if I Daddy can drop me off on Friday morning July 25th at Uncle Barney's office, beside the bus station on Farnham Street Cavan. He also writes that his Mammy has made reservations for all four of us to take the bus that will carry all the pilgrims from our diocese to Lough Derg on that day. The bus is scheduled to leave Cavan at 9 AM. Daddy drops me off at 8:30. I am excited and anxious.

The bus is full of people who are more Mrs. Scott's age than teenagers like Pat, Des and me. The trip is uneventful until we have to cross the border into Northern Ireland for a few miles before we reenter the free-state into County Donegal. Our bus driver explains to the British soldier who enters the bus that we are all pilgrims on our way to Lough Derg. As he soldier exits the bus, he salutes and waves us on.

Arriving at the river Shannon, we get off the bus, our small suitcases in hand. It is windy, causing the waves to be choppy and about one foot high. We can see the Island of Lough Derg and the steeple of St. Patrick's Basilica in the skyline about half a mile are taking their seats on one of the three boats at the water's edge. I immediately reflect on how this sacred sanctuary has become an integral part of our Irish Christian heritage drawing millions of pilgrims over the centuries. I am excited and have no fears as I await my turn to enter one of the boats.

Des says, "I am glad we all wore warm overcoats; it is going to be pretty chilly out there on the lake." Mrs. Scott smiles and says, "Dessie, it is going to be a lot colder tonight, when we are going around the rocky beds in our bare feet, making the Stations."

A veteran of two previous pilgrimages, Mrs. Scott is trying to prepare us for what's ahead.

Our busload from Cavan fills the third boat; two

workers push the boat off the sand and onto the lake. Pat, Des and I cuddle to keep warm. Mrs. Scott laughs and says nothing.

As we leave land, the driver pilot in the back guides the boat to the left, into the wind and waves rather than directly towards the island. I am guessing that he does not want to take any risk of the boat keeling over from all the wind and waves hitting at its side. We arrive at the island twenty minutes later. Mrs. Scott explains that Monsignor Eamonn Conway will welcome us and will give us a brief outline of the behavior expected by all pilgrims during their three days on the island.

Monsignor is a tall man with a wind-blown, ruddy face and is wearing warm leather boots. He welcomes us and, with a stern voice, adds, "No pilgrims will be allowed to stay on the island, if they refuse to remove their shoes and stockings." As kids in Legaginney we went barefooted to school from May 1 until the end of October, so I'm not concerned.

Monsignor Conway adds that in the century since the pilgrimage began hundreds of pilgrims left their shoes at home to walk barefooted from their homes in Northern Ireland to the lakeside and, after the pilgrimage, back again. Monsignor finishes his instructions, saying, "Each day you will be served one meal consisting of black tea and toast without butter. If you prefer, you can request wheaten bread toasted. You may choose whatever time of the day you wish to have your meal. May our Heavenly Father, his Blessed Mother and Saint Patrick bless you with abundant graces during this pilgrimage on Lough Derg."

Pat, Des and I remove our shoes and socks, putting them and our suitcases upstairs in a locker room off the

173

large male dormitory. We make sure to bring our warm jackets and caps to survive the windy night on this island on the lake. Even though we are hungry, we decide to wait a few hours before eating. With the booklet in hand that Monsignor Conway gave to each of us as we left the boat, we begin the prayerful part of our pilgrimage.

The booklet welcomes us to Lough Derg, a place of peace and personal challenge. It tells us we are just among millions of people of all faiths who have come to Lough Derg during the past 1,000 years. It states, "*There are no outsiders here: barefooted we are all equal. We are called to share each other's joy, feel each other's pain.*" The staff of volunteer priests and nuns is committed to hear our story, help us get in touch with our authentic selves and so find forgiveness, healing and strength.

The directions we receive call for us to make nine Stations during the three-day pilgrimage. To get started we each make a personal visit to Jesus in the Blessed Sacrament in Saint Patrick's Basilica. We then go to St. Patrick's Cross, outside the Cathedral, and recite one Our Father, one Holy Mary and the Apostles Creed. We then proceed to kneel at one of the several beds, this time standing at St. Brigid's Cross and recite three Our Fathers, three Hail Mary's and one Creed. We walk around the outside and then inside of St. Brigid's bed and say three Our Fathers, three Hail Mary's and one Creed. Kneeling at the cross in the center, we repeat the same prayers again. We then walk four times around the basilica outside, reciting seven decades of the Rosary and one creed.

By this time I am starving and suggest to Pat and Des that we stop praying and walking and have our one promised meal. Pat says, "We should, as Mammy has already eaten her meal."

We sit at a table in the dining room with two girls our age from County Donegal.

We learn later that they are twins, boarders at Saint Columb's College in Londonderry. They are both shy girls, but that does not stop Des and me from flirting with them. Pat says later, "Even on a pilgrimage you two cannot leave girls alone."

All three of us laugh when the meal promised by Monsignor Conway arrives. Pat and I ask for wheaten bread toasted, Des takes the toasted loaf slices. We laugh because the meal reminds us of the miserable lunches we get back at St. Patrick's College, with one exception – at least we get jam on our sandwiches back at the college. I enjoy my cup of warm black tea and put a full spoon of sugar in it. I am surprised that the young volunteer server brings me an extra slice of toasted wheaten bread and fills my cup again with hot tea. I feel warm and full as we walk back to the basilica to begin making our Second Station.

The warm feeling lasts only while we are in the basilica. As the sun begins to set, the temperature outside is now about ten degrees cooler. As I walk on the cobbled stones in my bare feet inside Saint Brigid's bed, I remember that Daddy's compared working in the bog to this ritual. This is one time I thank God for being a "bogman" versus a "townie" with soft-soled feet. I am bothered more by the coldness of the flagstones than by the uncomfortable feeling of walking on jagged rocks.

As I complete my visits to St. Brendan's bed, St. Catherine's, St, Columba's and walk four times around the basilica completing my second station, I come across Des performing one of the Corporal Works of Mercy on Maureen, one of the twins. Apparently, after kneeling at the crucifix inside St. Brigid's bed, Maureen fell and gave herself a gash in her right knee.

Knowing that his mother always carries adhesive bandages in her handbag, Des takes Maureen over to where Mrs. Scott is, sitting outside the basilica.

Mrs. Scott applies an adhesive to Maureen's bleeding knee and then sends both Maureen and her sister over to the First Aid Station to get the appropriate medical attention.

Des, Pat and I sit in a corner outside the basilica that is sheltered from the cold wind. Maureen and her twin Patricia join us after Maureen's knee is cleaned and bandaged. We have a good time sharing college stories until Mrs Scott, who has already finished her Third Station, comes and says, "Boys, it is too early to relax. It will take you over an hour to make your Third Station. Monsignor Conway will be calling all of us into the basilica at 10 P.M. to make the next four stations. Remember we don't get any sleep tonight."

We leave the comfort of sitting cozily in the corner beside two shy but attractive girls to start the Third Station. First we visit the basilica and then walk around it four times saying the assigned prayers, followed by stops at the four beds dedicated to Saints Bridget, Brenda, Catherine and Columba. We are not the only pilgrims trying to get our Third Station completed before 10 P.M. The beds are crowded, causing several people to slip and fall like Maureen. Getting up from kneeling at St. Brigid's cross, I lose my balance, but a big fellow, with a strong County Antrim accent, grabs me before I too gash my knee.

As Mrs. Scott warned us, we are all called into the basilica at 10 P.M. by the tolling of the basilica's bells.

A pilgrim priest is standing at the pulpit. With a strong County Cork accent, he leads the prayers for the Fourth Station. The crowded basilica makes me feel warm and sleepy, but the continuous alternating kneeling and standing keeps me awake. Without a break, another pilgrim priest, this time with a foreign accent, leads the fifth station, followed by two more pilgrim priests leading Stations six and seven. It must be 2 A.M. by the time we finish all the stations and are free to go back out in the chilly air.

Des encourages Pat and me to join him in a race to our favorite sheltered spot outside the sacred walls of the basilica. A young couple from Dublin beat us to our favorite spot. Seeing the disappointment on our faces, they invite us to cuddle up beside them, which we do. They initiate the conversation by asking us why as teenagers we were motivated to make the pilgrimage.

Des replies, "Our Mammy, a very devout Catholic, made the pilgrimage years ago and invited us to come along. I didn't want to disappoint her." Both Des and Pat look at me. I feel obligated to be honest. "I am graduating from St. Patrick's College in Cavan next June, and I am uncertain about what vocation or career to choose for the rest of my life."

The lady smiles at her husband and says, "Jim and I had a similar situation ten years ago. We were both single with a desire to marry and have children. Jim is from Navan, County Meath; I am a Dublin "Jackeen." She laughingly says, "We met here ten years ago, shared our story, became attracted to each other and ended up getting married on May 1, 1944. We come back here almost each year to renew our vows and thank God for the grace of having found each other."

Pat, Des and I survive the chilly night without sleep. For some reason that none of us can understand, the temperature the next morning is about twenty degrees warmer than yesterday. We don't need our warm overcoats. The day goes by quickly as we make the Eighth Station and then have our daily meal a little earlier.

Perhaps because of the warmer weather, people seem to be friendlier. We meet nice people who have come from Boston and New York in the United States. I tell the New York couple that I have a brother named Father Jack Corr stationed in St. Patrick's Church, Chatham N.J., about thirty miles outside of New York City. They don't know him, but they do know the town of Chatham and find it a lovely place.

Because we are allowed to go to bed tonight, Mrs. Scott encourages us to make the Ninth Station so that we can go to bed early enough to be rested for departure on the first boat tomorrow morning. The next morning we rise to another lovely day and go to mass in the basilica at 8. The celebrant is Monsignor Conway. He wishes us a safe trip home and hopes we will come back to St. Patrick's Purgatory at some future time in our lives.

Participating in the pilgrimage was the most challenging experience in my life. Having Mrs Scott, her two sons Pat and Des with me made it bearable. Spiritually I am becoming more aware of how much Jesus loves me, when he accepted his crucifixion and death on Calvary in reparation for my sins. The question that I ask myself is, am I prepared to accept his call to become a priest and forgo all of the pleasures of having a wife and family.

Chapter XXVI

My Last School Year at Saint Patrick's Cavan

I am disappointed that my good friend Des Scott is no longer at our college. As reported earlier, his dad, the principal at Cootehill Technical School, transferred him to a boys school in County Monaghan. He didn't want to take the risk of having Des expelled from St. Patrick's. Des was one of the 'Gang of Thieves' who got caught in the purple dye trap when Father Gargan went around to all the rooms and found the dye on their basins. His brother Pat is back again in the room across the corridor from ours. Instead of having his brother as a roommate, he has a classmate from County Leitrim.

Our annual retreat begins the first week after we return to the college. I tell the Jesuit retreat master that I am confused. I confess that while I am contemplating entering the seminary to be ordained a priest, I have been dating a nice girl named Dympna from the local village. He shocks me by asking "Did you have sex with her?"

"Off course not, I am dating her but have no intention of marrying her."

"Tell me what happened."

"I have an old friend named May Daly, who agreed to "play gooseberry" *(one who escorts a young couple dating)* by walking Dympna from her home on Main Street to the bottom of the village, where I meet them. I take Dympna by the hand; walk out Tuberorra Lane, which should in fact be called Lovers Lane, because that is where young couples go for a walk while courting."

My Jesuit confessor seems unsatisfied with my report and asks, "What actually happened on the date?"

I hesitate, "We hold hands, walk and talk for about half a mile. When we come to a place in the lane where we could easily climb over the ditch I invite Dympna to come into the field, telling her to avoid all of the thorny bushes. We find a mossy bank and sit and cuddle."

"What then," he asks."

"We hug and kiss passionately; I touch her breasts outside her blouse."

He looks away from me and says in a low voice, "You know this is a sin against the sixth commandment. For your penance say one Our Father and ten Hail Mary's."

I feel like screaming, "You bastard, I come to you expecting help in resolving my confusion. I am glad you are leaving Friday. I will find a more empathetic spiritual guide."

I go to the chapel, say my penance and have supper.

Alphie is already studying at the University College, Dublin (UCD) and Des Scott is at another boarding school, none of the 'Gang of Thieves' wants to attempt raiding the college kitchen. We are waiting to see if the college menu improves before we decide to raid the bishop's orchard during October.

My football skills are not improving enough for me to be considered being a sub on the college football team; I decide to switch to middle distance running. Frank McBrien, a classmate, is practicing sprinting. We agree to run together during the fall and winter and are ready to participate in track meets at Cootehill and in other towns that sponsor such meets. We plan to use the walk around the football field, which is four hundred and forty yards in the perimeter. My athletic hero is a fellow Irishman Ron Delaney, who recently won a gold medal for the 1,500 meters race at the Olympics in Melbourne. Here in County Cavan we have Matt Rudden, who lives fifteen miles from our college. He is a member of the Laragh Harriers and wins races ranging in distances from four hundred and forty yards up to five miles at meets all over Ireland. I can use him as a guide and motivator as I continue my training.

It is only eight months until our class sits for our final public exam the Leaving Certificate Exam. I have registered to take honor courses in four subjects: Irish, Mathematics, Physics and Chemistry. I am well aware of how much to study and how to schedule my time over the next eight months to achieve the best results the second week of June 1954.

I'm making good progress with arithmetic and algebra; I still have a lot of catching up to do with geometry and trigonometry. In regard to trigonometry, I find myself creating my own mental blocks to learning this branch of Mathematics. As a child I remember saying to myself, "Since I never plan to leave Ireland, why should I study which city is the capital of France and how many states are in the United States." Similarly, if I am thinking of following my calling to be a priest why should I study the relations between the sides and angles of triangles? Why do I need to know the methods mathematicians use in applying these relations in solving problems involving triangles which are used in navigation at sea, surveying property or building houses? I have to face the block head on, if I am going to achieve honors in Math next June.

Becoming a neophyte in Trigonometry won't prevent me from being ordained a Catholic priest.

I still enjoy Physics and Chemistry. The double class sessions in the science lab with Mr. Breen are stimulating and fun, as they have been for four years. He sometimes talks about retiring, while some of us, who feel close to him, joke back saying, "Mr. Breen you cannot desert us 'bogmen', after all you helped us not only catch up with the 'townies' but helped us pass a few of them in scoring a higher grade."

Our new Irish teacher, Mr. O'Reilly who replaced Father Gaffney, our college president, gets us honor students involved in writing Gaelic poetry in mid-October. He uses, as a model, the Irish patriot, Patrick Pearse's poem *Mise E^ire* (*I am Ireland*) written in 1912. For over one hundred years the British government forbade Irish poets to write poems directly honoring Ireland. The poets ignored the unjust rule and wrote about a fair lady, who everybody knew represented our native country. I plan to write my first poem in Gaelic about the lady I respect most in the whole world, my Mom. Her habit of welcoming the stranger at our doorstep, her devotion to Jesus present in the Blessed Sacrament and her respect for his Blessed Mother Mary in her daily recitation of the Rosary, exemplifies all the positive characteristics and spirit of our Catholic homeland.

The days, weeks and months are flying. The food in the dining room is just as miserable as last year. What is left of our 'band of thieves' is three students, all in our fifth year. We decide, under my leadership, to make our final raid on the bishop's orchard on a moonlit Wednesday night in mid October. We fill our three laundry bags with apples and store them in the black trunk underneath my

182

bed. We don't raid the college kitchen, as the risk of getting caught is higher and the possible punishment more severe. Eating a couple of apples after our light lunch is a good supplement to help us survive until dinner at 5:30.

Our senior football team does well, beating St McCartan's in Monaghan and St Columb's, but unfortunately lose to St Patrick's Armagh, in spite of three of our players, James 'Sticky' Brady, Bernie Doyle and Pat Delaney playing a great game. We have another Gilbert and Sullivan Opera. This year the director chooses my favorite opera *Mikado*. This is one time I regret not being a singer, as I would enjoy being in the chorus.

Daddy picks me up in his van two days before Christmas and this time drives directly me home. Celebrating Christmas in Legaginney is always special and a busy time. Mammy makes her usual Christmas plum pudding. Having watched her for several years I know the recipe by heart. She prepares the fruits first, mixing sliced apples, sultanas, raisins, almonds in a big bowl, adds self raising flour, brown sugar and three table spoons of Irish whiskey. She leaves the mixed ingredients in the bowl, covers it with plastic and puts it in the cool parlor overnight. The following morning she takes the bowl to the kitchen and adds bread crumbs. If it is too stiff, she will add half a cup of milk and stir it around. She places the plastic back on the bowl and then places the bowl into a large pot of boiling water, with the hot water reaching three quarters of the way up the side of the bowl. The pot of boiling water is placed on hot coals on the hob by the turf fire and allowed to simmer for four or five hours.

Since Brendan is no longer living at home, I help Mary Farrelly prepare the geese for our Christmas dinner. Dad kills the two geese by breaking their necks, Mary and I take over stripping the geese of their feathers and singeing the light down that remains over a small fire of twigs we light in the garden. After the innards are removed, Mary hangs the two geese in the kitchen chimney to be smoked in preparation for our Christmas dinner. When finished Mary gives me a big hug adding,

"You are a great gossan, Finbarr."

I go to the movies in the local village of Ballinagh just once during my Christmas holiday. I stand for a few minutes in the shadows watching people walk in. I want to see my girl Dympna, who I have not contacted since the end of August. She comes down the street to the theatre, walking hand in hand with a fellow at least ten years older than I am. He has a serious limp on his left side. I follow them into the theatre, paying the entrance fee on the way. I am not feeling any jealousy towards the fellow with the limp. I sit close enough for Dympna to see me. She sees me but ignores me. This is how my brief romance with Dympna ends.

When we return to the college on January 6th I tell Father Gargan, the dean, I would like to have a priest spiritual director who is not a member of the college faculty. He replies, "I will call Father O'Neill at the Cathedral. You will like him a lot, as he is used to working with teenagers at the Cathedral. I will make an appointment for you to see him in the visitor's parlor next Wednesday evening before he goes to the chapel to hear confessions."

"Thanks Father" I reply. I am a little anxious waiting in the study hall for someone to tell me that Father O'Neill is waiting for me in the visitor's parlor.

At 5:15 PM the prefect of the study hall taps me on the shoulder and says, "Finbarr you have a visitor waiting for you in the parlor."

Father O'Neill is a young man, probably the same age as my brother Jack, who was ordained a priest in 1951 and is serving in New Jersey, USA.

Father greets me with a smile and says, "Father Gargan tells me that you want to speak to me. How can I help you Finbarr?" I reply calmly, "Thank you father for seeing me. As Father Gargan probably told you, I am doing my Leaving Cert Exam in June. What he doesn't know is that I am having a serious problem figuring out what to do with my life after I leave Saint Patrick's. I had a bad experience last September when I sought spiritual guidance from the retreat master. When I told him I was confused between following a call to the priesthood like my brother Jack and three uncle priests and my attraction to a young lady in our local village, he proceeded to condemn me as a sinner for touching a lady's breasts outside her blouse and left me more confused and angry than when I first entered the confessional."

Father O'Neill smiled as he responded, "Finbarr you ran into an old-school priest, who focuses too much on sexual sins, rather than first of all helping young men like you understand that sexual attraction to a person of the opposite sex is a gift from our creator. Secondly, those men who forgo sexual pleasure to become priests do so because of the Catholic Church's long standing discipline of requiring celibacy of its priests and religious brothers. Your situation of being attracted to women, yet experiencing a calling from God to become a priest, like your brother and uncles, is very common among young Catholic men. My job over the next few months is to help you discern the voice of God calling you and your ability to observe celibacy from the time you are ordained a sub-deacon, a year before ordination." I just wish it was that simple. The good news is that I like Father O'Neill, he is non judgmental and after my first experience with him I feel he will help me clear up this awful confusion I am experiencing.

Chapter XXVII

The Decision

At least once a year my uncle Father Michael Corr sends Mammy a letter from the U.S. His correspondence is always friendly, and he always asks about everyone in the family. He doesn't have to ask about my brother Jack, because Jack is an associate pastor in Saint Patrick's Church, Chatham, New Jersey, less than fifteen miles from my uncle's rectory in East Orange.

Mammy always invites my uncle to come back for a visit his homestead Legaginney, which he last saw before he left to serve as chaplain in the Second World War. His reply is always the same, "Thanks, Nell, for your thoughtful invitation. I don't travel too much anymore except for my annual winter vacation in Florida. I fear that most of the people I knew around Legaginney are dead, and I don't want to come over just to visit cemeteries." My hope is to visit him in the U.S. some day.

For some unknown reason, my brother Jack has stopped writing home to my parents. During the first two months they are not too upset. As the silence stretches to three months, Mammy cries each day that Peter the postmaster comes by without a letter from Jack. Daddy is angry and disappointed. When Mammy is out of earshot, he says to whoever is listening, "We may never hear from him again." I have my own suspicions about what is going on with Jack, as I know he likes women a lot. I decide to keep my mouth shut, even though I am angry at him for hurting my parents.

About the same time, a letter arrives from the Chancery Office in Paterson, New Jersey. Its news is that Paterson's bishop James A. McNulty and his brother Monsignor John McNulty, president of Seton Hall University, are coming for a week-long visit to County Meath, their mother's birthplace. The letter includes an invitation for Mammy, Daddy and me to meet them for lunch at the Headfort Arms Hotel in Kells. My uncle Father Lawrence arranges for me to be absent from the college for the event. I am excited at the prospect of meeting the distinguished clergymen from America!

The two reverends are busy chatting with some of their mother's relatives when we reach the Headfort Arms. Monsignor John escorts us into the dining room, giving each of us a handshake and warm embrace. He says jokingly, "My brother will join us in a few minutes; you know bishops like to talk a lot more than monsignors or simple priests."

We all laugh. The bishop and his brother are both tall, but Monsignor John has a larger waistline than his older brother. Looking at Daddy, Bishop McNulty smiles and says, "John Frank, I would recognize you anywhere as a brother of Father Michael Corr, pastor of Blessed Sacrament Parish in East Orange. He had a distinguished career as a chaplain in the last war, but never wants to talk about it. We had a hard time getting him to accept the title of Monsignor."

Mammy speaks up, "We have invited him to come home many times, but he keeps refusing."

The bishop replies, "I don't know if he has shared his latest medical news with you. He has cancer behind his left eye and will probably need an operation." I am sad; I don't want him to die before I get a chance to meet him.

188

At lunch I order chicken. My parents choose fish. The bishop and Mammy do most of the talking. When we finish eating, the bishop looks at me and says, "Young man what plans do you have for yourself, when you finish boarding school?" To my surprise I reply, "Your Excellency, I and my wonderful spiritual director meet regularly at the college. He is helping me discern my vocation."

"Finbarr, you are more than welcome to join your brother John as a priest in the Diocese of Paterson. I know you may prefer to join your uncle as a priest in the Archdiocese of Newark, but that is impossible. They have so many seminarians from within the Archdiocese that they can't accept any outside candidates right now. If you choose to be adopted by the Paterson Diocese, we will pay for your tuition at any Irish seminary you elect to attend; and we will welcome you to our diocese after your ordination.

Since Bishop McNulty has mentioned Jack, my mom takes advantage of the moment and, without a tear in her eyes, asks, "Your Excellency, are you sure our son Jack is okay? He hasn't written a letter to us in six months."

The bishop appears shocked and replies firmly, "Mrs. Corr, I will see to it that your son writes to you before the end of the month." For my mother's sake, I am relieved. I have no sympathy for Jack. He deserves whatever chastisement Bishop McNulty gives him.

Pat Scott and I share our feelings about wanting to be priests. Pat is not surprised to hear me confess my struggle with the thought of lifelong celibacy. He reminds me of his brother Des and of my flirtation with the attractive twin girls on Lough Derg. But then he surprises me by saying, "Finbarr I am thinking of signing up for the Diocese of Miami in Florida."

Not wanting to distract him from following God's call, I ask gently, "Pat, have you given much thought to your decision? I am thinking of going to the Diocese of Paterson. I have recently met their bishop, Bishop McNulty, who gave me a warm invitation to join my brother Jack as a priest in his diocese. He also told me that the Diocese of Paterson will pay my tuition at any seminary in Ireland I choose, and then will welcome me as a priest of the diocese after I finish my studies. You are welcome to join me, Pat, if you wish. Bishop McNulty told me to bring a colleague along if I wanted to." Pat decides to think about it for a day.

My studies are going well. I am confident that I will earn honors in Irish and science. I enjoy studying mathematics, but trigonometry is still a challenge. I am enjoying the spiritual direction with Father O'Neill. I tell him that I'm confident that the grace of the Sacrament of Ordination will help me forego sex with women. When I mention my plan to apply to the Diocese of Paterson, he is disappointed,

"Finbarr, you don't have to go to America. Your grades are good; you could attend Saint Patrick's College Maynooth and be ordained for the home Diocese of Kilmore, like your uncle Father Lawrence Corr."

"I am sorry to disappoint you, Father. After thinking and praying about it for a couple of months, I feel that, with my extrovert personality, I am more suited for priestly ministry in the United States than Ireland."

As June 4th, the day of our Leaving Certificate Exam, approaches, I and my classmates spend more time sharing our dreams and aspirations. I am not surprised at Dan Gallogly's announcement that he will apply for acceptance at Saint Patrick's College Maynooth and be ordained for the Diocese of Kilmore. Dan ranks second in our class academically, after Hubert Maultsby. I can imagine Dan following in the footsteps of Father Robert McCabe, our popular English teacher at Saint Patrick's Cavan. Hubert shares the news that he is applying for a scholarship at University College Dublin and Trinity College, also in Dublin. Frank McBrien says he feels he has a call to the priesthood, but is not ready to decide.

When Pat Scott and I announce together that we are applying for Saint Patrick's College, Carlow, with both of us waiting for acceptance into the priesthood of the Diocese of Paterson in New Jersey, there is silence in the room. My cousin Brian tells me later that they expected Pat Scott's decision, but were surprised by mine.

Dan Gallogly looks directly into my eyes and like my spiritual director, says, "Finbarr, your grades should be good enough for you to be accepted in Maynooth; you don't have to go to the foreign missions."

During the final week in mid-June before we take the Leaving Certificate Exam, I am feeling lonely. We all say we will keep in touch, but common sense tells me otherwise. I tell my Dublin buddy Michael Smyth that I will probably be seeing his Uncle Tommy and Aunt Minnie and their children, Paddy and Mary, from the Railway Hotel more often than I will see him.

He replies, "Whenever you are going through Dublin on the way to the seminary in Carlow, you can give me a call and I will take you for a ride on my motorcycle. I will be attending University College Dublin, until I qualify as a grammar school teacher."

I tell Jim "Sticky" Brady that I will see him play football for our county team.

He tells us, "Playing football is not a living, it is recreation; I will be going to Veterinary College, as I enjoy working with animals."

Most of our class expects Phil Lawlor to become a professional golfer like his dad. At age eighteen he is already an accomplished golfer, with a handicap of nine. But Phil shares a different aspiration with us, saying "Phil Cullivan, who graduated from St. Pat's four years ago, is completing architectural school this month. He has offered to mentor me, if I wish to become an architect."

My cousin Brian Corr has no intention of following in his three uncles' footsteps and becoming a priest. He has no desire to be a dentist, like his dad or a medical doctor like his mother. He tells us, "From the time I was in grammar school with the Christian Brothers, I have been attracted to the Air Force. I am fascinated with learning how to fly and do radar detection. Since Ireland is not one of the world powers, I feel it is going to be a safe career, provided I pass all of the physical and emotional tests to become an Air Force pilot."

We sit for the Leaving Certificate Exam next week, which begins with our test in Irish on Tuesday morning at 9.

Chapter XXVIII

On To the Seminary

Jack writes home two weeks after Bishop McNulty verbalizes the edict to my mother, "Mrs Corr, I will see to it that your son writes to you by the end of the month."

I am still in college when the letter arrives.

During Dympna's next visit to the college, the week before my final exam, she reports,

"Mammy cried tears of joy when our postman Peter handed her the letter." And then she adds, "I don't understand Jack, why would a priest be so mean to his parents?

I try to make a joke, "Dympna, maybe he has a girlfriend, you remember him being very friendly with Carmel Ryan, Sergeant Ryan's daughter?"

"Finbarr, I don't think that's funny. Marie gave up boyfriends when she went into the convent, Jack should do the same, give up women."

The Leaving Certificate exam was easy. Some of my classmates, especially my friend Michael Smyth, were distracted by the thirty or so fifth-year female students from the Loretto School across the road, who sat in our study hall with us to take their Leaving Cert. I decide to repress my usual behavior of flirting with sexually attractive girls. If I am going to pursue my studies in the seminary to become a celibate priest, I better begin now to curb my sexual appetite.

This week I learn a lot about how my classmates deal with stress. James 'sticky' Brady's behavior is the most traumatic. He gets fits of hysterical laughing, before we enter the study hall to sit for each exam. I have learned that taking deep breaths through the nose and going for a walks with either Michael Smyth or Pat Scott relaxes me.

I have one final session with my spiritual director. I feel satisfied with the discerning process we have done together. He is getting more accepting of my decision to pursue my studies for the priesthood in a U.S. diocese, rather than my own home Diocese of Kilmore. I say I am waiting for an acceptance letter from St. Patrick's College, the seminary in Carlow. He nods.

Since childhood, I have followed the example of my devout mother who prays the Rosary three times a day. My dad says the Rosary once a day, even if he comes home late from a political meeting, too late to participate in the family rosary. Neither of them misses Sunday mass, except when they are sick, or have an infectious cold or flu.

I enjoy saying the Rosary and try my best to meditate and picture in my mind the several spiritual moments celebrated in each of the five decades of the Rosary. The Descent of the Holy Spirit on the apostles in the Upper Room in Jerusalem, the third decade of Glorious Mysteries, is a good example to demonstrate. The eleven anxious apostles are huddled together with Mary the mother of Jesus and some other close friends. They know that Jesus, while on earth, promised to send a comforter, the third person of the Blessed Trinity. They are nervous, as they miss Jesus and don't know what to do next. They are literally too scared to go out and preach Jesus's message of love, forgiveness and healing. All of a sudden a bright light encompasses the whole room. They know something powerful is about to happen. The Holy Spirit appears in the lighted room, in the form of a dove, who circles the room touching the heads of the frightened people. The immediate effect is that these cowardly witnesses to Jesus become strong and are motivated to go out on the streets of Jerusalem and preach as their master Jesus did. The remarkable miracle that followed was that each recipient heard their message in their own tongue.

Mammy asks me what kind of cake I would like to celebrate my 19th birthday on July 25th.

I reply "You know I love your boiled cake."

She smiles and says, "Finbarr you will have to go into Murray's shop in Ballinagh to buy the fruit. Pat Lynch does not carry all the different currants and raisins I need."

Eilish, my oldest sister, who is home on holidays from her job at the Spa View Hotel in Lisdoonvarna, volunteers to walk into town with me to do the shopping. Mammy asks Dympna to come home early from her secretarial job in Cavan.

She tells her,

"Finbarr has a special announcement to make after he cuts his birthday cake."

Dympna replies,

"Is he really going to join the Palestine police, as he has been telling several girl friends over the past two years?"

Mammy pretends she doesn't hear the question.

Mary Farrelly leaves Legaginney and goes back to Clones, County Monaghan to take care of her ailing brother. Her boyfriend Josie Beatty, determined not to lose the love of his life, rides his bicycle the twenty one miles from Legaginney to Clones every weekend to visit her. We all know that it just a matter of time before they decide to marry and they will be living together in the little house at the bottom of the steps leading up to St. Michaels Church in Potahee. I will miss having Mary present for my birthday party and to be present for my dramatic announcement. I do know that once the news becomes public Josie will bring the news to her. I can guess what she will say, "Finbarr was always a good gossan, a loyal altar boy and a good partner with me in fleecing the geese of their feathers for the Christmas dinner. He will make a friendly priest."

When P. Joe has finished milking the cows, using the new milking machine, Daddy is in from the fields, with no plans this evening for a political meeting; we all sit around the oval table in the kitchen. The three siblings who don't know what the dramatic announcement is all about are Dympna, Colm and baby brother Fonsie. Mammy and Eilish serve us tea and her favorite currant cake. Dympna is in her usual teasing mood.

She says, "I pedaled like hell up the hill from Ballinagh and coming down the hill from Legaweel, I almost rode into gate at the railroad crossing as Miss Berrill was clearing the railroad tracks for a special train she was expecting. I hope that whatever announcement my younger brother is going to make is worth all the risks I took to be here for it."

Everybody laughs except me. Eilish goes to the parlor and puts nineteen tiny candles on the boiled cake. She lights the candles and walks into the kitchen while Mammy begins singing "Happy Birthday to you."

As I blow out the candles I say a silent prayer to

myself. I pray to our Blessed Mother Mary that my decision to become a priest is the right decision and that she will protect me for whatever years her divine son Jesus wants me to serve him.

When I raise my head the whole family, who are present, including P. Joe, who usually skips emotional moments like this, are staring at me.

I am surprisingly calm as I begin my prepared revelation, "As Mammy knows I have great respect for Uncle Father Michael in America. Since she told me about all the good he has done as a priest in New Jersey and a chaplain in the last war, I feel a call from God to follow him and become a priest in New Jersey."

I pause for a moment and notice that Dympna has lowered her head and may be crying.

Eilish speaks up to break the tension, saying, "Finbarr tell us the rest of the story."

"Since I began serving mass with Father McEntee I have been thinking about becoming a priest. I have said novena Rosaries to our Blessed Mother Mary asking for guidance. During the past year at the college I had my own spiritual director who helped me discern what plans God has in mind for me. When Daddy, Mammy and I met Bishop McNulty a couple of months ago he invited me to join Jack and become a priest in his diocese of Paterson New Jersey. I will start my studies at Saint Patrick's College in Carlow the first week in September. I plan to spend six years studying there and be ordained in Ireland, so that Mammy, Daddy and all of you can be at my ordination. I remember that both Mammy and Daddy were disappointed when they couldn't be at Jack's ordination in 1951, since it took place in America.

This time Daddy breaks the tension in the kitchen saying,

"Finbarr we will all be praying for you each night when we say the Rosary."

Mammy asks all of my siblings not to talk about this disclosure to their friends, as she expects me to live a normal life until I go to Carlow. Once again my mother reveals that she knows me better than I know myself.

I continue to hang out with local guys at the Lacken crossroads, I play handball at the Lacken ball alley, I practice football and go swimming in the river Eireann at Scarvey. If somebody asks me what I am planning to do, now that I am finished college, I tell a little lie saying I am thinking of joining the Palestine police. That works nine times out of ten.

The tenth time it didn't work with my cousin, Pat Phillips, a constant reader who replies with,

"Nice try Finbarr, the Palestine Police haven't existed for the past ten years."

I enjoy the summer going to dances at the local parish hall accompanied by Barney Brady, Phil Smith of Legaweel and Mel Lynch, who has taken over organizing and operating his dad's traveling shop. He buys eggs from the housewives of local small farmers and instead of giving them money he gives them groceries i.e. tea, bread and butter. One of the humorous things that happened, with all of them watching me, was when I was dancing with this lady at the local parish dance. I like to dance, particularly with good dancers. This lady is a fine stepper on the dance floor. To my knowledge, she is not a local girl. I notice as I dance with her a second or third time that our pastor Father McGauran, who sits at the dance hall entrance collecting entrance fee, is staring at me and not smiling. I notice Barney Brady is laughing and telling something to Phil Smith. I go over to Barney and ask what is so funny?

He replies,

"Are you planning on going to the parochial house tonight?" I ask why and he replies. "Finbarr, you are dancing with Father McGauran's new housekeeper."

Meanwhile Barney is dancing with a nice tall dark-haired girl named Dolores Coyle from Ahaloora, which is at the other end of the parish. He comes over to me and whispers,

"Finbarr would you like me to introduce you to her younger sister Maggie; she is that beautiful shorter red haired girl standing beside Dolores. If she likes you, we could take both of them home this evening to Ahaloora."

I take advantage of the question and shock Barney as I say,

"Barney for two reasons I cannot do that tonight, I don't have a bicycle with me to cycle to Ahaloora and secondly, I feel I need to stop dating girls, as I am going to a seminary in Carlow in two weeks, to begin studies to become a priest."

"Tell me Finbarr, you are joking, aren't you", he blurts back.

"No Barney, it is true, I have been thinking about if for a couple of years."

"My God it will be awful if you are ever ordained a priest."

The next day I go into McDonald's shop in Cavan with Mammy and order a black suit and black tie, the customary dress for seminarians. The instructions I get from the seminary were to enter on September 4th wearing that outfit. The instructions also added that tailors from Cleary's Department store in Dublin would be visiting the seminary to measure us for the clerical soutanes.

Upon returning home I am greeted by my brother Fonsie, who himself is preparing to become a boarder at the college I just left,

"Finbarr you received a letter from the Department of Education in Dublin, this must be your Leaving Certificate results." I passed all five subjects and got honors in Irish and science, and that darn trigonometry prevented me getting honors in three.

Finbarr with classmates, Leo Dolan and John Connelly, gardening at the St. Patrick's College Carlow during the Fall of 1955

Chapter XXIX

Welcome to Saint Patrick's College Carlow

I rise early on September 4 and get dressed in my clerical black suit, white shirt and black tie. I walk up the road to St. Michael's Church, Potahee, to make a visit to Jesus present in the Blessed Sacrament. I then walk down the hill to say goodbye to my godfather Frank Corr and his wife, and also to Jimmy Beatty and his charming wife.

Mrs Beatty, being her usual generous self, takes a half crown out of her purse and puts it in my pocket. She points up to the Church on the hill and says, "Finbarr, I hope we are both still around and not planted in the graveyard up there when you come home for Christmas."

I earnestly reply, "I want you both to live until I am ordained a priest six years from now."

She smiles. "I hope so. Keep Jimmy and me in your prayers."

Our neighbors Phil and Bridget McCusker are surprised to see me in clerical garb. Like Barney Brady, Bridget believes I am too fond of girls to have a vocation to the priesthood. I just smile and say, "Mrs. McCusker, please pray that I am making the right decision." In spite of all her anxious feelings she goes up to her bedroom, finds her purse and comes down with a ten-shilling note. I thank her for the gift and her promise of prayers.

I can tell that Mammy has mixed feelings, as I kiss her goodbye. She is probably thinking, "I am going to eventually lose Finbarr, when he goes to America." Daddy has tears in his eyes as he watches the two of us exchange a long hug. He is driving me to Cavan to meet Mr. Scott, who has volunteered to drive Pat and me the 150 miles south to the seminary in Carlow.

As we are driving past Miss Berrill's house at the railroad crossing, Dad surprises me by stopping and blowing the horn. He rolls down the window and calls to Miss Berrill, "Don't you want to say goodbye to your friend Finbarr?"

Daddy returns to his silent, reflective mode as we drive through Ballinagh. I want to have a conversation. I ask, "Daddy, are you going to miss me?"

After a moment's silence he replies, "Yes I will. You are a hard worker. I am glad that you are not going off to America like Jack. I don't think you are going to forget us like Jack did last year."

Knowing that it is hard for Daddy to share his feelings, I now understand how very hurt he was by Jack's silence of over six months. I don't want him to worry that he is now losing another son. "I will never forget you Daddy. Your hard work and your dedication to helping people find jobs have inspired me to follow your brother Father Michael's example."

We arrive about fifteen minutes early on Farnham Street, which is typical for Daddy. He never wants to have anybody waiting for him. I ask him to stay there to meet the Scotts while I go down the road thirty yards to say goodbye to Tommy and Minnie Smyth at the Railway Hotel. To my surprise, I recognize a girl from Wateraughey walking towards me on the opposite sidewalk. I remember that I kissed her passionately after a football game three years ago, and I quickly assess that she is even more attractive now. I can tell by her facial expression that she is in shock at seeing Finbarr Corr in clerical clothes. She does not speak, and neither can I.

The Scotts arrive on Farnham Street at twelve noon as planned. Pat's Mom sits in the passenger seat, while Pat and I sit in the back. After a few words of gratitude from Daddy for their taking me the rest of the way to Carlow, we start the three-hours-plus drive. To make the journey easier, we avoid Dublin and go through smaller towns that I am not familiar with like Naas in County Kildare and Port Arlington in County Laois. The fall weather is very pleasant, making the driving for Mr. Scott more enjoyable. We stop at a candy store in Naas, where Mr. Scott treats us to biscuits and a mineral drink.

The college is easy to find, as it is situated next door to the Cathedral of the Assumption, in the center of Carlow. All that Mr. Scott has to do is find the street with the big Cathedral spire. As we drive through the big gates, opened by the gatekeeper, and continue up the avenue to the front door of the college, Mrs. Scott laughs and says "I didn't think we were committing you both to a prison."

I jokingly reply, "The gates are not to keep us in Mrs. Scott, but to keep girls out." Pat laughs "Finbarr, leave it to you to bring girls into the discussion."

There are seven or eight cars parked in front of the main door to the seminary. I learn later that they belong to the priests who teach there. A priest in his mid-fifties, wearing a black soutane with a cape, greets Pat and me with his deep monotone voice. He explains, "Welcome to St. Patrick's, gentlemen. I am Father Kinsella, the junior dean. The janitor will show you to the freshmen's dormitory on the second floor. The bell will ring in about one hour to summon you to supper."

He turns and walks away without even a smile. While Mr. Scott is removing our suitcases from the trunk, I go over to him and say in a joking manner, "Don't leave. Pat and I have not decided if we are staying." He looks at me with a curious expression. I respond, "I am just teasing you. Thank you for driving us here."

Before we take our cases upstairs, I notice two students playing handball on the alley about twenty yards from the front door. They are in shorts and tee shirts, and I can tell even from this distance that they are both good players. Seeing two students playing a game I love makes me feel a lot more comfortable than the unfriendly welcome from Father Kinsella.

Having had a private room with plenty of space at St. Patrick's Cavan for five years and now being ushered into a dormitory in Carlow with about thirty mates is quite a let down. My favorite trunk, inherited from Uncle Jim, barely fits under the bed. Each student has his own cubicle, which contains a single bed with just three or four feet between the bed and the wooden divider that separates one cubicle from the next. If I was a fat guy, I would have trouble turning around in the cubicle. My friend Pat and I both laugh. Pat says, "I can see we were both spoiled by having private rooms for five years in Cavan."

We go over the ball alley to watch the two fellows play. They stop their game to introduce themselves. The shorter guy says, "I am Des Fitzgerald and this is Mike Hayes, we are both from Saint Flannan's in Clare."

I reply, "I'm Finbarr Corr, from Saint Patrick's Cavan. My buddy Pat Scott is from Cootehill, County Cavan. We both play handball, but not as good as you guys."

The bell rings, calling us for our first meal in this seminary. Pat and I are wondering, as we walk into the dining room, if the food will be better or worse than we experienced in Cavan. We don't have to wonder for too long. The meal consists of toasted loaf bread, sliced ham and hot tea. Jim Finain, the sub deacon who sits at the top of the table serving as our prefect tells us with a smile, "This is going to be one of the best meals you are going to receive until you go home to your mother's cooking for Christmas. You better enjoy it."

Coincidently, Des Fitzgerald is assigned the cubicle next to mine. Besides being a good handball player, he tells me, "I prefer to play hurling, a game you guys from Cavan don't know much about."

I tease him back, "Only girls play that silly game in Cavan - and we call it camogie. Real men like Phil "the Gunner" Brady and John Joe Reilly play football."

"I know, I know, you Cavan guys haven't gotten over beating Kerry in the only All-Ireland final held outside of Ireland at the Polo Grounds New York in 1947."

I already feel a bond with Des and his friend Mike Hayes.

The bell rings again at 7 PM to call us to the Junior Chapel for night prayers. The junior prefect Deacon Jim Finain reads the prayers. Father Kinsella, who is kneeling beside him, asks us to be seated as he begins to make an announcement in the same monotone voice with which he greeted Pat and me four hours earlier,

"Gentlemen, welcome to the seminary of Saint Patrick's. You may as well know from the beginning that the rules of the seminary are stricter than those you experienced in your past five years of boarding school. Becoming a successful priest to serve almighty God in a country like the USA involves living a disciplined life. Tomorrow when the rest of the seminarians join us you will not be allowed to communicate with the senior seminarians who are studying Theology. You will be free, however, to socialize and play Gaelic football and soccer with the second-year philosophy students. The first and second year philosophy students make up Junior House, Deacon James Finain is your prefect, and I am dean of Junior House."

After a momentary pause he continues, "The third, fourth, fifth and sixth-year students make up the Senior House. You will join them each morning in the Senior Chapel for Mass. Finally solemn silence is observed from after the last study period until after breakfast the next morning. You don't have to observe solemn silence this evening. That rule comes into effect tomorrow evening when the rest of the seminarians arrive. Good night. We will have Mass here in this chapel at 8 AM tomorrow."

The last thing Des says to me before we go to sleep is, "Finbarr, do you believe that you and I can keep solemn silence each night from now until we go home for Christmas?"

At breakfast the next morning I quickly notice that, while all of us students are from the one island of Ireland, we have very different accents. Pat Duggan from Donegal asks Paddy O'Shea for the milk. With his heavy northern accent, Pat says, "Pawdy will you pass me up the 'mulk'?"

"Is it the 'meelk' you are looking for Pat?" Paddy replies in his Kerry accent.

I am sure that some of my classmates will be surprised by my flat Cavan accent. However, I also expect that these accents will be tamed when we all take elocution classes.

Even though there are a lot more rules in the seminary than at St. Pat's in Cavan, I adjust more easily than I did five years ago when I entered the boarding school. I no longer feel inferior to my classmates. I make good friends and am relieved to learn that nobody in the seminary, professor or student, is going to refer to me as "the bogman from Legaginney."

Chapter XXX

Life in the Seminary

Deacon Jim sticks his head into the dormitory and rings the brass hand bell at 7:00 AM. The washroom, containing twenty basins, is crowded as we all wash our faces. Most of us make it on time (7:30 AM) to the junior chapel, as our prefect Jim reads Morning Prayer, followed by twenty minutes of silence. We learn later, that during the twenty minutes we were supposed to be meditating. Fr. Kinsella leads us in celebrating our first mass in the seminary. He uses the gospel reading for the day as basis for teaching us how to meditate. The passage is from the gospel of Luke Chapter 10,

"Behold I send you forth as lambs in the midst of wolves. Carry neither purse, nor wallet, nor sandals, and greet no one on the way. Whatever house you enter first say, "Peace to this house!" And if the son of peace be there, your peace will rest upon him; if not it will return to you."

Father Kinsella comments,

"Sit back and listen to God's Holy Spirit speak to you. As first year seminarians you are young lambs, spiritually speaking, discerning the voice of God. Pick a theme for your meditation today." The theme I choose is 'Peace'.

I get a nice surprise for breakfast, hot oatmeal with milk. I realize, by watching how some of my classmates eat it, that they are not as excited about the meal as I am.

They were not raised like me in a family of nine children, where the corn to make the porridge was grown on our own farm. Our prefect Deacon Jim tells us all that this is the first time in his five years in the seminary that he has porridge for breakfast and he hopes this not just a one time menu. He adds,

"Believe me this breakfast is much better than the serving of sliced bread and jam that we usually have."

Classes don't start until tomorrow, when the rest of the seminarians are here, Des Fitz (as he prefers to be called) invites Pat and me to play handball with Mike Hayes and himself. Since they are better players than either of us, I ask them to make up a game of Mike and Pat versus Des and me. They agree. While Mike moves more slowly on the alley than Pat does, his accuracy in returning the ball to the bottom of the wall makes up for his tardiness. Des and I give them a good challenge and win one of the three games we play.

Matt McInerny, the senior member of our class and a graduate of Saint Columba's College in Derry, decides to run around the college track several times, continuing his training as a middle-distance runner. Dan Gould and Dennis Dulia, both from County Cork, go out onto the football field with their hurling sticks and hit their small leather coated ball up and down the field. I am already impressed by the athleticism of my new classmates and the prospect of having several different sports and competitive games in the seminary.

As the rest of the students arrive that afternoon I am surprised that one of them recognizes me. His name is John A. Clarke from Blenacup, County Cavan, and a second year philosophy student. He says,

"I know the Corrs of Legaginney. Your brother Jack, who is now a priest in America, used to play for Cornafean, a team I play with during my summer holidays. My brother Tom, who owns a car dealership in Cavan, knows Dympna Corr, isn't she your sister?"

"That right." I say.

The dining room is full for the evening meal. Another priest with a much more welcoming attitude introduces himself to our table,

"Welcome to the seminary fellows." With a wink to our prefect Jim, at the head of the table, he goes on,

"I am Father Dowling, the senior dean. If you make it through the first two years of philosophy, you will have to put up with me for four years, while you study theology before you are ordained priests in 1960."

As he leaves to go on to the next table, prefect Jim fills us in on his role in the college.

"Fr Ned, as we call him, is going to be your Latin teacher. You will like him, as he is usually friendly, probably the most friendly professor in the college. He is very athletic and will be accompanying you on the Wednesday afternoon walks, three of four miles out the Dublin road. Both he and the Vice President Fr. Robert McCabe play golf."

As expected, classes begin the following morning for all of the students.

Our first class is elocution, with Professor Father Richard Dwyer. He is a short man, prematurely grey, with an articulate voice. As Fathers Kinsella and Dowling did, he welcomes us to the seminary and immediately adds,

"My job is to begin the six year process of creating twenty four first class priest preachers to go as 'missionaries' to the United States, Australia, England or to a home diocese here in Ireland. Please raise your hands and introduce yourselves if you are going to be ordained

210

for a diocese here in Ireland."

Dan Gould is the first to raise his hand,

"My name is Dan Gould; my plan is to be ordained for the Diocese of Cloyne. I must add that since our diocese has plenty of priests, I expect to be sent to a diocese in England for four or five years, until I am needed in the Diocese of Cloyne."

Michael McManus, a classmate of mine from St Patrick's, Cavan says,

"My name is Michael McManus. I have been accepted as a candidate for my home Diocese of Kilmore" A third student, a shy person, with an apparent introvert personality, raises his hand.

"I'm Mick McLaughlin. If I complete my six years of study and still want to be a priest, I will be ordained for the Diocese of Killaloe."

The fourth and final member due to serve the Catholics of his native diocese raises his right hand and stands.

"My name is Des Fitzgerald; I have applied for acceptance in the Diocese of Killaloe, but have not had a reply so far."

At the request of Father Dwyer all the rest of us, destined for foreign dioceses raise our hands and announce the dioceses who have adopted us as their prospective priests. Pat Scott and I are the only candidates for the Diocese of Paterson, New Jersey. When the smallest student, of the twenty four in our class, Joe Hynan raises his hand saying,

"I am Joe Hynan I am scheduled to be ordained the Diocese of Melbourne, Australia," Father Dwyer cannot resist teasing him saying,

"How come, the smallest student in the class volunteers to go the furthest away to serve our Lord as a priest, all the way in Australia?"

He continues his lecture,

"The fact that all of you have plans to serve the people of God in dioceses all over the world, does not excuse you from being the best explicit speakers of the English language and the most organized and intelligible preachers of the gospel. To give you an example this morning I will read one of my favorite passages from Shakespeare's *"Julius Caesar"*. And will ask for a volunteer to read it after me."

"Friends, Romans and Country men lend me your ears.

I come to bury Caesar, not to praise him.

The evil that men do lives after them,

The good is oft interred with their bones

So let it be with Caesar."

All of us are very impressed with his articulation and the spacing of the words and sentences.

"Who will volunteer to read it again?"

He says and waits. Several students look down and put their head in their hands. To me the long silence is embarrassing. I think of Josie Beatty practicing his acting in Legaginney parish hall before it is dramatized to the whole parish and say to myself, "what the heck?' I raise my hand and go to the podium, imagining that I am on stage, mimicking Brutus, eulogizing his deceased friend Caesar. Imitating Josie I speak slowly in deep voice, from the depths of my stomach. Looking out at my audience I can see that I have caught the attention of my twenty three

Anthony

classmates. Father Dwyer just smiles with approval. The bells rings, signifying class is over.

A short heavy-set priest enters the classroom carrying a copy of the bible. He doesn't welcome us to the seminary. He introduces himself instead,

"I am Father Robert Prendergast, your Scripture professor for this semester. I wish I could say I am an expert on the Holy Bible. I am not. I will however share my love of Sacred Scripture with you and introduce you to the most recent research and understanding of both the Old and New Testament. While most Christian Churches interpret the bible literally and base their beliefs on the literal interpretation of the bible, our Catholic Faith is based on both the bible and tradition. We do however join other Christian Churches in believing that the bible is the Word of God."

The most interesting professor to introduce himself to us today is Father PJ Brophy, popularly known by the students as "Pa" Brophy. He is very personable and likes to tell stories about his travels in the United States, Europe and the Holy Land.

He is teaching a subject that is new to all of us first year Philosophers, i.e. *Introduction to Philosophy*. Unlike Father McCabe 'Pa' admits his expertise is philosophy. When finished studying at St. Patrick's College, Maynooth and after being ordained a priest for the Diocese of Kildare and Leighlin he returned to University College in Dublin and achieved his Ph. D in Philosophy. The text book he is using for class is written in both Latin and English.

At 5:00 PM all the students go the study hall. Father Kinsella, who supervises us during this evening study, announces that if any first year students wish to meet Father Tom Brophy, the spiritual director of the college, please raise your hands and go up to his office. I raise my hand and go to Father Kinsella's desk and say,

"I am Finbarr Corr." For the first time I see a smile and he responds,

"Your name is easy to remember Mr. Corr; you are presently the only Finbarr in the seminary."

I go up to the second floor and knock on Father Tom's door. A pleasant, inviting voice responds,

"Who do we have here?"

"I am Finbarr Corr, a student from St Patrick's College, Cavan, and a student for the Diocese of Paterson, New Jersey."

"Welcome Finbarr, that is a very distinct name. Saint Finbarr is patron saint of Cork. I believe you had a brother Jack here, who went on to finish his theological studies in NJ."

"That is correct Father." I reply.

"How can I help you Finbarr?"

"First of all Father, I come from a family of priests. My dad had three brother priests, one in the home Diocese of Kilmore, Father Lawrence, two in New Jersey, one of whom, Father Tom is deceased, who died as a young priest in the sacristy, from an appendix attack after saying mass. The other brother Monsignor Michael, who I have not met, is still active as a priest in NJ. He is a former chaplain, serving in the US army during World War II. He was the one who motivated me to become a priest."

"The Corr clan has quite a history of having priests in the family" says Fr Tom.

I reply, "That is not all. I have been told that I not only have an Uncle Fr. Tom, I also have a grand Uncle Father

214

Tom and a great uncle Father Tom."

"That is almost unbelievable. Would you like to tell me how you decided to become a priest?"

After a brief sigh, I begin,

"From the time I started serving mass as an eight years old I have had the desire to become a priest like Father Michael. Just like most teenage boys I became attracted to girls at school and in the neighborhood. I did some passionate kissing and petting outside the clothes, but never had intercourse. While in boarding school I was introduced to a priest from the Diocese of Kilmore, who became my spiritual director. He was very helpful in discerning God's invitation to me. Now I am asking your help on my spiritual journey over the next six years."

"Are you also signed up to be a priest in the Paterson Diocese, NJ just like Jack?"

"That's right" Then he shocks me with his final comment for the interview.

"Finbarr, you will regret the fact that you are a good-looking man, the women in the US will go crazy when they meet you."

Chapter XXXI

What's next?

At the seminary I enjoy the challenge of getting to know my new class, twenty-four fellow students from different parts of Ireland. Some students come from families similar to mine. Pat Duggan has two brother priests; Paddy O'Shea, from Kerry, has several cousins who are priests.

One student, Dan Kelleher is different from the rest of us. Although Dan is generally friendly, when he is not in class or study hall, he spends every free moment kneeling and praying in the chapel. His cubicle in the dormitory is next to Des Fitz's, two spaces away from mine. While Des and I cheat on solemn silence, whispering to each other before we go to sleep, Dan faithfully observes the rule for silence and does not even smile or look at us during this period.

I sign up to play Gaelic football and soccer. The fellows from Donegal and Derry are much better at soccer than those of us born south of the border. At age five, they started playing soccer and continue every week at St. Columba's College. To my surprise I like playing soccer much more than Gaelic football. Soccer is a less violent game with less physical contact, and it gives a definite advantage to young men like me who are adept at using both feet to dribble the ball past a competitor.

In fact, I don't enjoy playing Gaelic football at all. Where is the sense in getting bumped and bruised in a game when nothing is at stake and you're playing just to develop your skills? But for one week I have no excuses. I have been selected to play Gaelic football for my province of Ulster, versus the students from the western providence of Connaught. I volunteer to play halfback, which involves less running than the positions in forward and center field.

I am competing against John Connelly, a good footballer from Galway. Kevin Flanagan, one of John's teammates, kicks the ball towards us; I jump higher than Connelly and catch the ball. As I am coming down and getting ready to kick it back past Flanagan, Connelly jumps and hits me under the chin with his shoulder. Shocked and angered, I drop the ball. As I fall backwards, I kick both my feet in the air, to knock the ball out of his reach. I miss him altogether. Any spectator and that includes Father Ned, can see that I've lost my temper and am attempting to hurt John. But Father Ned, a sports enthusiast himself, doesn't interfere in the game. He probably excuses the behavior, chalking it up to a tough competitive game, between rival provinces.

Thanks to Pat Duggan and Kieran Doherty from Donegal and to John A. Clarke from Cavan, we give the guys from Connaught quite a game. The score is all square at halftime, with each team scoring one goal and three points each. The second half is not good news for us fellows from Ulster. I allow Connelly to score three points on me, while Colman Brady, playing center half-forward, scores two goals.

Later I feel guilty. I realize I am not going to be an effective priest is if I routinely lose my temper, like my dad, every time someone confronts me physically or emotionally. I decide that I must come up with a plan to manage my temper. I cannot wait and expect a miracle cure on my ordination day. Whatever plan I create, I will discuss with my new spiritual director "Holy Tom."

I come up with a plan that involves controlling my curiosity as a first step to controlling my temper. All of senior and juniors sit in choir for daily mass in the senior chapel. We face our classmates across the aisle.. I pledge not to look across the aisle for six months. I know this will be difficult for me, as I am a curious individual.

When I tell Holy Tom about it, he just smiles and says, "Finbarr, I believe you are on to something here. By resisting the urge to see and hear activity across the aisle, you are learning to control all your impulses, including the impulse to be angry. That immediate interruption, consciously made, will give you that split second you need to decide against doing something stupid."

After breakfast each day we have fifteen minutes to go upstairs and make our beds. One morning, when Des Fitz and I go up to make our beds, we experience a real shock. Dan Kelleher, the model seminarian in our eyes, has packed all his personal belongings and folded the used sheets and blankets in a neat pile on the bare mattress. My first thought is that there has been a death in the Kelleher family.

But Dan has other news. He invites Des and me to stand inside his cubicle. In a solemn tone he announces, "Finbarr and Des, I am thankful for your friendship over our last couple of months in the seminary. After prayerful reflection and discussions with our spiritual director Father Brophy, I have decided to leave the seminary and pursue another career. I don't feel I am good enough of a person to be ordained a priest. I am taking the bus today to my home in Cork. I didn't want to leave without saying goodbye to both of you."

Des and I are in total shock. Before we shake his hand, I say, "Good luck, Dan. You are a great guy, and will be successful in whatever career you follow in life." Dan lifts his big suitcase and walks down the stairs, leaving Des and I rattled. I feel like crying. and am thinking, there goes Dan Kelleher, a very religious fellow, who decided he is not good enough to be a priest, while I am still here struggling to manage my impulsive temper and forget several girlfriends.

Later, in class, I look over at Des. I know he, like me, is incapable of focusing on the lecture. As we go to bed that night Des taps the side of his cubicle and whispers, "Corr, I think we are in luck. The good holy guys are leaving first. You and I will be the last to leave."

Chapter XXXII

A Promise Kept

To my own surprise, I keep my commitment not to look across the aisle of the senior chapel for a total of six months. People who know me well as a curious individual, like Pat Scott and Michael McManus, are in shock. Pat, who sits and kneels beside me in the chapel, nudges me to look, when someone across the aisle is doing something humorous. It is tough, but I resist.

When visiting Holy Tom for spiritual direction during Lent, I tell him about my success. He exclaims, "Congratulations Finbarr, I honestly didn't believe you could keep your commitment."

The food in the seminary is a little better than the food we ate in the boarding school in Cavan. My friend Pat and I don't have the luxury of receiving food packages from our parents, as the long trip to Carlow from Cavan is too much to expect, even from devoted parents like ours. I confess to having a bigger appetite than Pat. If his brother Des was with me here, we would probably be planning to raid the college orchard. Pat and I laugh when we recall the raids on the bishop's orchard in Cavan and my theft of the master key from my cousin Pat's pants, for our raid on the college kitchen. I don't want to risk being expelled from the seminary.

Fortunately, we come up with two more practical solutions to deal with our hunger problems. We get friendly with Michael, the headwaiter, who coordinates delivery of the food from the kitchen to the dining room.

With the help of another staff member, Michael cleans up all the tables after the students have their dinner. I say to Michael, "My friend Pat and I would be happy to help you two clean up the tables if you would agree to give us some of the food left over from the priests' dining room."

Michael gets a little nervous at first and says, "In order to prevent either of us from getting into trouble I think you should ask your prefect, Mr. Finain, first. In the past some prefects have agreed, but others haven't." Fortunately, our prefect agrees.

Having learned how to clean tables at home in Legaginney, I have no trouble piling the dirty dishes into plastic basins and placing them on a table outside the kitchen. Pat is very good at wiping the plastic tablecloths. When we finish, Michael goes downstairs to the kitchen and soon returns with two plastic bags full of leftover chicken, slices of ham, and rolls with packages of butter.

We both shake Michael's hand. He says, "Thanks to you fellows for helping us clean up the dining room. You have earned your reward." We take the loot up to our dormitory. I share some of mine with Des Fitz and Mike Hayes. All of them eagerly offer to join us next week as part of the cleanup crew.

Our second source of extra food comes through the generosity of a wonderful family, whose dad "immigrated" from Cavan to the town of Carlow several years ago. Dan Shanaghy, a builder by trade, is a brother of Stephen Shanaghy, a postman from Lacken, who goes with my dad to political meetings all over the county. Dan's wife Kathleen, a native of Carlow is a charming, warm-hearted woman, just like my mom back in Legaginney. The Shanaghys own a cafe on Coal Market Street in Carlow.

Every other Sunday, when Kathleen and Dan come to visit me and bring a big basket of food, I feel the same warmth and support as if I was back in Legaginney. Dan regales me with stories of his youth in Lacken with two brothers and two sisters. I recall that, as a young boy, I witnessed his dad William riding his bicycle without a flashlight in semi-darkness and crashing into another cyclist in a dark lane. When a couple of us ran down from Lacken Crossroads to help after we heard the crash, William's only problem was that his pipe lid had been lost in the crash and he couldn't find it. One of Dan's sisters became a missionary nun in South Africa. The other sister immigrated to New York and is married to Pat Rafferty.

Each time I receive a basket of food I also share some of it with Pat, Des and Mike, who becomes my very good friend, as well as my role model for studying. Mike and I frequently go for walks around the grounds after breakfast, before we are summoned to the study hall. Mike, an introvert by nature, talks sparingly in the morning, while I want to discuss philosophy and logic, subjects that are new to us first-year students. I am surprised to learn on one of these morning walks that Mike has a photographic memory and remembers practically verbatim every word and sentence uttered by our philosophy professor Father "Pa:" Brophy.

As time progresses and final exams approach, I am studying very hard and holding bazz sessions with Mike as we circle the football field. (*A "bazz" session involves reviewing all of the semester's study material in the days just before the exams.*) Studying at the seminary and sharing with Mike, I feel a lot more confident about academics than I did during any of my five years in boarding school.

One of the gifts that Mike brings to all of us is an enthusiasm about learning to play golf. He tells us that he learned to play as a youth when he was a caddy at Lahinch Golf Course in County Clare. Both Vincent Maguire and Mike chip and putt on the grass behind the senior chapel. One day when Father Ned is out walking he sees Mike and Vincent chipping and putting. All of us spectators expect Mike and Vincent to get in trouble, but to our surprise Father Ned asks them if they would like to create a mini par-three course in the same area.

Mike smiles and looks at Vincent, who nods his head in assent as he says to Father Ned, "Thank you Father, I know there are several classmates like Finbarr and Pat Scott who want to learn the game."

Father Ned adds, "Just be careful in designing the course that none of the golf shots will be directed in any way close to the chapel." I am very happy at how all of this is turning out. As a future priest, I know I am joining a group where many of its members, like my uncle Father Lawrence, are avid golfers.

The end of the school year arrives with examinations in all five subjects. I believe I have done very well and don't have any worry about my academic performance. I am a little worried that I haven't had a letter from my Mom since the beginning of May. I continue to write to her and Dad each week telling them that I will be home for the summer holidays on June 12th.

I feel very lucky that Tom Clarke has volunteered to take me home along with his brother John A. I pack a small suitcase so that I won't be carrying a heavy load when I walk the last four hundred yards down Legaginney Lane. I don't want to take advantage of Tom's generosity by asking him to drive his car over the rocky lane to our home.

Our trip home to Cavan takes almost an hour less than our trip down in September with Mr. Scott at the wheel. Since Tom travels a lot each week, related to his business of buying and selling cars, he is very comfortable driving at a speed of sixty to seventy miles per hour on good roads, only slowing down when he passes through towns and villages on the way.

Tom knows that his brother John and I are avid supporters of the Cavan Football team but that we are behind on the news of the team's successes and failures because we observed the seminary rule of not reading newspapers. On the trip he spends over an hour updating us on their record. He wraps up his report, saying, "Cavan plays Derry in the Ulster final on Sunday and, if they win, that they will need your prayers to beat Kerry in the All-Ireland seminal final the following week." I am looking forward to the freedom of being able to follow Phil "the Gunner" Brady and John Joe Reilly as they pursue wining another All-Ireland Football championship.

As we drive down Legaginney road I thank Tom and John A. for their kindness and ask Tom to drop me off at the entrance to our lane. Tom says, "Say hello to your sister Dympna for me. We will be in touch with you before September to arrange to take you and John back to Carlow."

I am excited walking up the lane, carrying my suitcase, looking at the familiar hedges and trees along the way. The sun is shining and the light breeze keeps me cool as I try to sneak unnoticed past McCusker's' thatched cottage. I don't want to stop into to see Mrs. McCusker just yet. I am anxious to see if everything is okay at home.

As I am walking quickly past McCusker's', I look to my right into the White Field, as we call it. I am totally surprised as my eyes behold a group of local farmers busy planting potatoes in our field, about one hundred yards from the lane. I stop and stare, but cannot see my Daddy. I run down the hill towards our home, fearful that something bad may have happened. Daddy's car is parked in the yard. Dropping my suitcase I run into the house and before I hug my Mom I say tearfully, "Where's Daddy?"

Mom replies, "We didn't want to distract you as we knew you were having exams before you came home. Daddy has been sick in bed for four weeks with a big swelling underneath his chin. Doctor Arnold has been out to see him several times."

I don't wait for any more excuses. I know that Mammy adores Dr. Arnold and puts him on a pedestal. I run up the stairs and can hardly believe what I see. Daddy, who is usually thin, now looks like a ghost. Propped up against a pillow, he smiles at me, but is unable to talk because his swollen throat won't allow it. I don't remember what I said. Looking back all I know at that moment is that I have to do something drastic, otherwise Daddy is dying. I immediately think of Surgeon McMullen, six miles away in the Surgical Hospital in Cavan.

I run down the stairs to the kitchen where Mammy is busy preparing dinner for her returning seminarian son. She can tell by my face and attitude that I am very disturbed. I restrain myself from yelling. I am, after all, supposed to be able now to manage my inordinate feelings. I grab her two hands and say, "Mammy, have you thought of telling Surgeon McMullen in Cavan? Dr. Arnold is going to let Daddy die. I am going to ride to the post office in Ballinagh on Daddy's bike and call McMullen to ask him to come out immediately to examine Daddy."

Mammy starts crying and says, "Maybe I am putting too much faith in Dr. Arnold. He has been very helpful to me fixing my varicose veins."

I quickly eat part of my dinner, then hop on Dad's bicycle and ride the mile to the post office as fast as I can. The postmaster Paddy Smith is most helpful. He knows my dad very well and appreciates my concern and the need to get Surgeon McMullen to come right away.

Addressing the surgeon's nurse on the phone he says, "Nurse, this is an emergency. Your boss knows John Frank Corr from Legaginney, a brother of Dentist Corr on Farnham Street. According to his son Finbarr, who just came home today from the seminary, his dad is choking because of a swelling underneath his chin. Dr. Arnold, the family doctor, has not been able to fix it. We need Surgeon McMullen to come out this evening to see him."

I am more relaxed as I cycle back home with the news "to expect Surgeon McMullen to come to our home between 6 and 7 PM." Mammy seems relieved. I go upstairs and tell Daddy that Surgeon McMullen is coming to check on him this evening. I add, "I am sure you agree with me that we need a second opinion." He nods in agreement.

Meanwhile, Colm and Fonsie are home from Legaginney School. Dympna arrives home about 5 PM after riding six miles from the technical school in Cavan. She agrees with my decision to have Surgeon McMullen come out and examine dad. She says, "I don't think that the swelling is going to go away from under his chin by taking medicine. I believe that the surgeon is going to take him into the hospital and operate."

Dympna's forecast is correct. Dr. McMullen arrives as promised at 6:30. I go upstairs with him and stay during the ten-minute examination. He is very cordial with Dad and addresses him directly, saying, "John Frank I can see you need an operation. This swelling is not going to disappear on its own. I will send an ambulance out for you early tomorrow morning, and I will operate on you tomorrow afternoon."

Chapter XXXIII

Thank you, Surgeon McMullen!

The next morning, an ambulance, almost too wide for our narrow rocky lane, drives up to our front door. Mammy has Daddy all cleaned up and dressed in new pajamas she has set aside for emergencies like this. The driver and the male nurse escort Daddy down the stairs, while Mammy and the rest of us watch tearfully. They place Daddy on a stretcher and lift him into the back of the ambulance. I offer to ride in the back with Daddy.

The male nurse looks kindly at me, saying, "Sir, that won't be necessary; your Dad won't be operated on until this afternoon. You will not be allowed into the operating room. I suggest that you or one of the family come into the recovery room about 3 or 3:30 this afternoon when your Dad should be awakening from the anesthesia."

Dympna speaks up, "Finbarr, I will be finished with classes at the Tech and can ride over and be there when Daddy wakes up."

My faith in Surgeon McMullen is rewarded when Dympna rides in our lane about 9 PM with the good news that Daddy is fine and that Surgeon McMullen had said, "The Corr family should thank the postmaster in Ballinagh who summoned me to Legaginney yesterday. If your father's cyst was not removed, he would have choked to death in two more days."

Dympna told us that she sat with Dad in the recovery room, saying her Rosary, until he woke up at 5 PM. She added, "He has a few stitches in his throat, but was able to talk to me. The nurse attending him says he will have the stitches removed in a few days and will be ready to go home then."

With Dad recovering and P. Joe already in England to start a non-farming career, Colm and I are the only Corrs available to work with Jack Murtagh at the bog, where he cuts the turf and tosses them out to us on the bank.

Even though I am working hard in the bog and on the farm, I enjoy a very happy summer. Dad is alive and getting physically stronger, faster than any of us had expected. Three weeks after his operation he drives down the half mile to the bog to bring evening tea and Mammy's currant cake to us. The farmers who rent our turf banks are delighted to see him.

Sad and depressing news travels quickly in Ireland. Because of his political career as a county councilor in County Cavan, Dad is well known and loved throughout the county. As farmers meet at the creamery or at fairs in town, they pass the news among themselves,: "John Frank almost choked to death, because his family doctor didn't realize that the cyst growing under his chin was slowly choking him."

The summer holidays fly by in what seems like only a couple of weeks versus what is really three months. On September 7th I find myself standing at the end of our lane on Legaginney Road with my suitcase, waiting for Tom Clarke to pick me up and drive me and his brother John A. back to Carlow. Because of Tom's heavy foot on the accelerator, we arrive in Carlow much earlier than expected. I want Tom to meet a fellow Cavan man, Dan Shanaghy. I persuade him to drive us down to Coal Market Street to visit Dan and his wife Kathleen instead of dropping us off too early at the seminary.

I am excited, as this is my first opportunity to meet their four children. Their only daughter Mary is a beautiful teenager, and their three happy sons Liam, Noel and D.J. are all excited to meet us. Dan and Tom share stories about individuals and families they both know from the County of Cavan. After an hour's visit, and biscuits and a cup of tea compliments of Kathleen, we bid the Shanaghys farewell. Tom drops us off at the seminary and heads back home to Cavan.

Since I am now a second-year philosophy student and John A. is a first-year theological student in Senior House we are not allowed to talk to each other except on days called "mixers." About four times a year the students from both houses meet for some rounds of competitive sports between the two groups. This evening we meet twenty five new students' first year philosophers who arrived yesterday. Pat Scott, Michael McManus and I are disappointed that none of them are from our alma mater, St. Patrick's Cavan. We can only notice one substantial change in the college over the summer; the local bishop has appointed Father Patrick Lennon, a reputable theologian, as president of St. Patrick's College Carlow.

I'm in the same cubicle in the dormitory as last year, beside Des Fitz. One of the new First Philosophers is assigned to Dan Kelleher's old cubicle. The opposite personality to Dan, he is an outgoing fellow, who describes his origin as "born in the Kingdom of Kerry."

I tease him, saying, "Paddy, you come from the county that our Cavan team whipped in the 1947 All-Ireland played in the Polo Grounds."

He doesn't think it is funny. "How many All-Ireland championships does Cavan have? We have sixteen."

We have a surprise the first night in the study hall. The new president, Father Lennon, is seated at a table at the front of the study hall. The table is loaded with new books that we realize later are prizes for us students. Father Kinsella, the junior dean climbs into the prefect's high desk and announces, "Gentlemen, this evening we are happy to reward students who worked hard last year. The names of students who scored first, second or third in each subject will be placed in this hat, and we will draw names to determine who wins the prize."

Speaking in Latin, he then switches to announcing the subject and then the names of the three students who scored first, second and third in the exam. Nobody is surprised at when Father Kinsella announced that Michael T. Hayes ranked first for philosophy. Most (especially me!) are very surprised when he announced "Finbarr Corr" as second. Mathew McInerny is third. After a moment's pause, Father Kinsella draws from our three names in the hat and reads that Michael Hayes is the winner. We all applaud as Mike walks up to shake the president's hand and receive a new book on the Bible as his prize.

Mike is listed as one of the top three students in all five subjects, while I am listed as among the top three in only three subjects. I win one prize and receive a biography of Blessed Oliver Plunkett as my prize. Mike and I tease each other later about being competitors for prizes, while inside I am feeling proud of being listed amongst the top students in the class. This is an accomplishment that I, a bogman from Legaginney, didn't achieve during my years of study at Saint Patrick's Cavan.

My self-confidence as a student is growing as I continue to attend classes and study daily. Playing soccer and Gaelic football two or three times a week keeps me in good physical condition. If somebody hits me hard or trips me up on the football field I don't overreact. Whenever that happens, I manage to find a split second before I explode. During that split second a voice within me seems to say, "Finbarr, let it go (or walk away) before you make a blooming idiot of yourself."

As the semester continues, I join Matt McInerny for runs around the circumference of the junior football field. I easily keep up with him during the first three laps around the field, but, whenever he decides to sprint around the track for the fourth and final lap, he leaves me twenty or thirty yards behind. He tells me that, to become a good middle-distance runner and champion miler, a person needs to be able to sprint the final three hundred or four hundred yards. This is another goal I set for myself.

Since several of the courses we study involve translating the texts from Latin into English, I feel I am becoming more literate in the Latin language. Father "Pa" Brophy tells us that we are fortunate to have studied Latin in our boarding schools, as Latin is the basic language from which Italian, Spanish and French have developed.

I continue to think about different accents, especially mine. I wonder how my County Cavan accent will sound when I am an active priest in New Jersey, USA? I will get a chance for feedback from my classmates next year when we, as theology students, we will each have a turn to do a spiritual reading during breakfast for three mornings.

In all honesty, I hear a slur in my speech when I listen to my recorded voice. Using my Irish humor, I sometimes say, "I get my good looks and brains from my mom, but my slurred speech and arthritis come from my father."

Mike Hayes takes me down a peg when he asks jokingly, "From whom do you inherit your humility, Finbarr?"

Chapter XXXIV

Rotten Row 1956-57

Tom Clarke drops his brother John A. and me off at the seminary at 3 PM on September 4 1956. Today is a milestone, of sorts, on my journey towards the priesthood. I am no longer a philosophy student in Junior House. I'm now a first year theological student in Senior House. I am excited to be taking another step towards ordination, which is scheduled for the second Saturday in June 1960. I am also relieved to be moving from the dormitory and the cramped cubicle to the spacious room I will share with two other classmates. Before we left for our summer holiday Mike Hayes, Des Fitz and I agreed to share a room on the third floor over the priests' dining room in a section nicknamed "Rotten Row."

My excitement is short-lived. When I meet Mike Hayes on the main corridor, inside the front door, he says, "Finbarr, I have disappointing news. Des decided, at the last minute yesterday, that he no longer wants to be a priest. He is looking for a job working in a bookie's office in Limerick."

"Oh my God, Mike, you must be joking," I respond.

"I wish I was," he replies. "He also asked me to give you his regrets and the message that he plans to attend our ordinations in a few years."

My first thought is that it will take some time for me to recover from this shock. Secondly, I am asking myself why, if Des is leaving, I am staying. With a heavy heart I take my suitcase past the priests' dining room and up the three flights of stairs to room 302 in Rotten Row.

Mike's suitcase is sitting unopened on one bed, while the second bed is already made up with clean sheets and pillow. I pull the suitcase from under the bed to find out who is rooming with Mike and me. It is a happy surprise. My classmate from St. Pat's in Cavan, Michael McManus, has decided to room with us.

Before we begin our new courses in moral theology, canon law, the Old and New Testament, elocution and rubrics, we have the annual distribution of prizes for the last school year by Father Lennon and Father Kinsella. Mike Hayes, as usual, tops the list in four of the five subjects. I get first prize in Scripture and have fun teasing Mike as to why I outscored him.

Besides graduating from the dormitory, as seniors we are now allowed to study in our bedrooms rather than in the college study hall. This is as an advantage for me. I look forward to discussing the topics presented in class and getting new insights from Mike. Michael McManus joins us in reviewing the theology classes. Like me, he envies Mike Hayes' photographic memory and the resulting ease of his quotes from Saint Thomas Aquinas, Saint Augustine, Irenaus or one of the other Fathers of the early Church.

Another advantage of life in the Senior Theological House is that we have better professors than we had in Junior House. The president, Father Lennon, is a very engaging teacher and gives us ample opportunity to raise questions if, for example, we don't grasp the difference between Aristotle's philosophy and Thomistic theology.

Father Ned is our new elocution professor, or more accurately, the teacher assigned to train us as good preachers. I have already learned a few significant things from Father Carroll in Junior House. He tells me not to worry about the slur in my speech because, if I speak slowly with a bass voice, my slur will not be recognizable.

It is easy for Father Ned to demonstrate a bass preaching voice, as his conversational voice sounds as if it is coming from the depth of his stomach. During the second week of classes he tells us that the best way to become good preachers is "Practice, Practice, and more Practice." He adds that he is going to give each of us the opportunity to preach a homily in the senior chapel in the presence of all the students in Senior House. He surprises us all, saying, "Who should be first, do we have any volunteers?"

My friend Mike raises his hand and says, "Father Dowling, I nominate Finbarr Corr." Several students giggle, and Mike adds, "According to Father Carroll, Finbarr was the best in our class at reading Shakespeare." Ned looks over at me and I nod my head signaling "I accept."

Father Ned then says. "Finbarr, take the Scripture readings for next Sunday, write a two-page homily and give it to me for review before you preach it next Monday evening at the beginning of night prayer."

I'm both excited and nervous. After class, I check on the readings for the following Sunday. I am relieved to discover that the topic of the gospel is The Good Shepherd (John X-verses. II ff) I spend a few hours creating the best homily I can, personalizing it so that I can preach it with passion on Monday evening. My two roommates review it for accuracy.

I take the homily to Father Dowling in his office on Friday afternoon. He smiles to himself, as he reads it. "I am looking forward to your presentation on Monday evening. I believe you have the potential to be a very dynamic preacher. If you feel like having a practice session in the senior chapel while it is empty, feel free to do so. You may bring your buddy Mike Hayes with you, since he was the one who volunteered you to do this."

"Thank you Father," I reply. "Mike and I are good friends and play a few tricks on each other, from time to time. This time he won. I do appreciate the opportunity to be able to rehearse in church, and I will give it my best shot on Monday evening."

My two roommates accompany me to the Senior Chapel for the rehearsal on Saturday afternoon. They sit on different sides of the church, each in the last seat. The pulpit is about three feet high. When I climb up, I stand for a moment and look out to become comfortable with the height and the view. At the start I speak slowly and with a deep voice. I direct my words to both Mike and Michael McManus, turning my head from side to side as if I am conversing directly with each of them. Michael gives me a signal to raise my voice, which I do. When I finish the homily, both of them are very complimentary. I become more relaxed and am actually looking forward to Monday evening.

Besides preparing to give my first homily, I am also preparing to run in the college sports in two weeks. I am feeling fit, having practiced my running in our meadow under Potahee Mountain during my summer holidays. While some of my classmates will choose to run sprints of 100 or 200 yards, I have learned over the years that I am more proficient in middle distance races of 800 yards or one mile.

At my classes on Monday I confess that my mind is more focused on delivering my first homily later that evening. My good friend Mike is very supportive. Referring to a new television program on RTE featuring the popular American preacher Bishop Fulton J. Sheen, he says, "Finbarr, remember that Bishop Sheen gave his first homily when he was a student like us in a seminary in the United States. He was probably anxious that first time, but see how he developed to become the best Catholic preacher in America, only a few years after his ordination."

"Thanks Mike," I say. "I have no desire to become a nationally recognized preacher when we both start our priestly ministry in the U.S. in 1960."

At 7:45 PM Father Ned introduces me from his seat in the choir. I will face him and the others from the pulpit in only a few minutes. He announces, "Our first student preacher for this year is Finbarr Corr, a graduate from another Saint Patrick's College that school is in Cavan. He didn't volunteer to preach this evening. His good friend Michael Hayes volunteered him." Most of the students laugh, which helps me relax as I mount the pulpit.

Father Ned continues, "As is our custom, I will ask three students to critique Finbarr's homily and preaching style when he finishes. I'm not going to announce who the critics are, as I want you all to listen carefully. You will learn something from this man from Cavan. Go ahead, Finbarr."

I repeat my behavior from the rehearsal: I take my notes with me to the pulpit and stand silently for four or five seconds as I look at the "congregation." Then I begin, saying, "I am the good shepherd. The good shepherd lays down his life for his sheep. I am the good shepherd, I know mine and mine know me." I pause before I go on. I am fascinated as I feel the gazes of 110 men in black cassocks. Their eyes are locked on me, the former bogman from Legaginney.

I finish with a passionate appeal," Jesus says in today's gospel, 'For this reason the Father loves me, because I lay down my life that I may take it up again.' Are you prepared to lay down your life for the sheep that God the Father will entrust to your care?"

Father Ned calls on John A. Clarke to critique me. John says, "Knowing that Finbarr comes from a family of priests, I am not surprised to see that he already has the qualities and personality to hold our attention here this evening. I give Finbarr a B+ for content and an A for his presentation."

Father Ned calls on a second student from John A's class, Alan Malone. I have never met Alan. He stands up and hesitates for a moment and with a wry smile says,

"Father Dowling, do you know you picked another Cavan man - Mr. Clarke - to critique Finbarr? I am sorry I cannot second Mr. Clarke's comments. It is true, that while Finbarr is a very engaging preacher, I don't know if the native Yankees in the US will understand his flat Cavan accent. (*The people of Ireland call all U.S. citizens "Yankees."*) Most of the students in the chapel and Father Ned roar laughing.

Father Ned announces, "We are running out of time here. Let me ask any deacon who is not from Cavan to offer some insights to help Mr. Corr develop his preaching skills.

An older looking seminarian stands up and addresses the students. "My name is Seamus Trainor. I am from County Tyrone. I compliment Mr. Hayes for nominating Finbarr Corr to be the first in their class to give a homily.

Finbarr may speak with a Cavan accent, but I was very engaged during the ten-minute homily he gave this evening. The content was perfect, he looked very relaxed in the pulpit, and his passionate ending came across as a natural part of his personality."

With a thank you to the three critics, Father Ned announces that the preacher next week will be Michael T. Hayes, as nominated by Finbarr Corr.

Several students from our class laugh, while Mike puts his head down, smiling to himself. Before we go to sleep, Mike says "Fair play to you Finbarr, you now have one up on me."

Chapter XXXV

A meeting in the Priests' Dining Room

We were disappointed before Christmas. Our head waiter and friend, Michael, tells us he is offered a new job, which involves better wages and benefits at The Seven Oaks Hotel in Carlow. Instead of telling him we are upset, we congratulate him and wish him good luck in his new career. We will miss him, because of his kindness in providing leftovers from the priests' dining room, when we cleaned the tables. When we ask him who is going to take his place in the student dining room, he says,

"Miss Garcia, the kitchen manager, says Father Duffy, the new bursar at the college, wants to save money on employee salaries, in order to improve the quality of the food for the seminarians. My job is not going to be filled. I don't know who is going to be in charge of setting up and cleaning the dining room tables."

This means that our source of getting extra food by helping Michael after meals is no longer possible. We're not going to approach Miss Garcia. She has the reputation of being a strict witch with the kitchen staff and servers. We'll depend solely on the generosity of our friends, the Shanaghys, to bring us extra food.

My training with Mom tells me, saying good luck and thank you Michael is not enough gratitude to Michael, after getting leftovers from the priests' dining room for over two and a half years. I decide I'm going to take up a collection from my classmates. Since I have been a fundraiser from age eight, selling three penny raffle tickets for the Irish missionary nicknamed 'Noogey,' I'm not afraid to ask my friends and classmates for a couple of shillings. I decide to ask one of my rich classmates, whose name will remain anonymous, for five pounds. He's an only child, born into a rich family. After a slight hesitation he donates the five pounds.

"Corr, you have over three years to go before you will be ordained a priest and you are already practicing taking up Sunday collections," he says.

"Thank you, good friend," I say. "Michael will appreciate your generosity."

I contact several of my classmates and collect 19 pounds and 10 shillings. I add ten shillings from my meager account, making our thank you gift to Michael a 20 pound note.

Michael says, "When I get established as a waiter at the Seven Oaks I will ask the manager to allow me to invite you, Mike and Pat Scott to come out for a free dinner."

The weather this winter is milder than usual. I enjoy being home for Christmas. Dad has recovered almost as well as anybody could expect. During a quiet moment, when we are alone, he tells me how appreciative he is of me intervening and summoning Surgeon McMullen out to Legaginney. I tell him thank you.

Because of the weather being so mild I keep up my running exercises around the meadow in Legaginney. First I jog a half mile to warm up, and then run four quarter miles in about one minute and fifteen seconds each. I then jog a half mile to cool off. I am determined to be able to challenge Matt McInerny in the mile race on March Ist, during the annual sports day at the college.

I feel good that my desire to become a priest in the U.S. is not a financial burden on my parents. They have paid for four of my siblings going through college and are paying for Dympna and Colm, who are attending a technical school in Cavan town. Thanks to Tom Clarke's kindness, I don't have to worry about paying bus or train fare to and from Carlow several times a year. I don't have to burden my parents to pay my tuition at the seminary, as they would have to do if I was attending St Patrick's College Maynooth, to be ordained for the home Diocese of Kilmore. Since the Diocese of Paterson adopted me as a future priest they pay my annual tuition at Saint Patrick's. I'm sure I will have to pay some of it back in future years, while serving as a priest in New Jersey. When everything is going so well for me, both financially and educationally, passing all my subjects with honors, I wonder when the axe is going to fall.

Along with training for the College sports on March 1st, which is a Wednesday, I also volunteer with several other garden enthusiasts, i.e., John Connelly, Leo Dolan and my friend Mike, helping Father Pa Brophy beautify the grounds around the college. (See picture attached). Gardening with Father Pa on Wednesdays makes more sense to me than walking four or five boring miles out a country road with fellow seminarians. I learned from Mom, an ardent gardener, how to plant seeds and bulbs in our flower garden at our home. Dad taught me how to plant and fertilize potatoes, lettuce, beets, brussel sprouts and cabbage. Father Pa is now teaching all of us, volunteer gardeners, how to pick plants that fits into his ambience to present an attractive picture for visitors to the college.

March 1st is here. I'm ready to run a fast mile. I watch the other athletes run sprints and cheer my own class running relays. I know that my principal opponent in the mile is Matt, a six-foot-two athlete from Saint Columba's in Derry. Unfortunately, the mile race is scheduled as the last event of the day.

When the sprint races are finished I borrow a pair of track shoes with metal spikes from a colleague, who is a speedster and runs track at the Santry Track in Dublin.

Six of us line up to run the mile. At the start, Matt takes off, leaving the rest of us ten or twenty yards behind. I decide after the first lap to run faster and get in behind Matt. I find a rhythm, running step by step with him. I am running very comfortably, almost on Matt's shoulder. By the third lap I can see from the corner of my eye that Matt and I are about forty yards ahead of the rest. When the bell goes for the final lap I take off passing Matt. He does what I did for half the race, he runs by my right shoulder. Thirty yards from the finish line Matt makes a burst to the front that I cannot match. I try my best but it is not enough. Matt touches the tape while I am still ten yards behind. I congratulate him.

"Finbarr you gave me quite a challenge; Congrats for being a good second."

The following Wednesday is Ash Wednesday, when we all receive ashes on our foreheads. "Holy Tom" addresses all of us in the Senior Chapel.

"I don't have to emphasize fasting for Lent here in the seminary, as most of you believe that the normal amount of food you receive is already meeting the standard for fasting. What I would like to ask you to do is observe the regular periods of silence, which is part of the seminary's discipline and use the silent moments to reflect on God's presence in your life."

My two roommates and I agree to keep the solemn silence from the end of the evening study period until after breakfast the following morning, as our penance for Lent. I have no trouble observing our resolution for the first two weeks. During that period John Connelly, who rooms next door to us in room 301 informs me that his roommate Chris Taylor, a third year theology student, goes down early on Monday mornings about 6:00 to the priests' dining room and brings up several slices of fruitcakes that have been left over from the priests' dinner the evening before. I tell my two roommates about Taylor's activity and neither of them is interested in following his behavior, even though all three of us would like some additional food. I decide to give it a go next Monday morning.

I get up about 5:30, wash my face in the portable basin, and get dressed without turning the lights on. I don't want to wake up my roommates or talk to anybody as we are keeping solemn silence for Lent. I get a box of matches so that I can have a light to see the cakes on the table. I leave our room, without noticing that Michael McManus's bed is empty. I walk down three floors of carpeted steps to the door of the priests' dining room. The door is ajar. In spite of the night light behind me, I cannot see a thing inside the dining room. I have the matches in my hand, ready to light one, when I feel I am close to the dining room table. I'm figuring on touching a high chair, as I go in past the open door. Instead of the back of a chair I almost die of fright, as I touch a man's head. It feels like a dead man's head. Instead of lighting a match I start to run out the door.

A deep voice from the other side of the table says, "Sit down sir."

The next thing I remember is standing at the first Station of the Cross, forty yards away in the Senior Chapel, pretending to be making the Stations for Lent.

Starting the First Station, Jesus is condemned to death.

I genuflect and say, "We adore thee of Christ and we praise you because by your holy cross you have redeemed the world." I'm wondering about my possible punishment.

As I am walking to the second Station I see Fr Ned coming in the door of the chapel. Now I know it was his deep voice who said "Sit down sir."

He must have been sitting on the other side of the table waiting for each 'thief' to come in and line them up in the dark dining room. He'd followed me to the chapel as he didn't know who the mystery student who bolted from the dining room and ran down the corridor. The next question I needed to answer was who the student was sitting in the dark, whose head I touched. Was it Taylor or somebody else?

When I finish the fourteen stations, I nervously step outside the chapel to make a toilet stop. Father Ned follows me and says in a gruff voice,

"You better pack your bags sir, you are finished."

Chapter XXXVI

Redemption

After breakfast, Michael McManus 'confesses' to me that he was the "dead body" sitting at the table, whose head I touched in the priests' dining room, when I panicked and ran to Church. He didn't know who it was who got scared and ran out of the dining room. At first, he thought it was Chris Taylor who touched his head. Later he discovers it was me, when he goes upstairs and sees my empty bed.

He makes a good suggestion, which I totally agree with, that we don't tell anybody except our roommate Mike what happened to us this morning. Knowing Father Ned as we do, he is already gloating to his fellow faculty members and will be gloating to students, who he is particularly friendly with, about what a good detective he is. We both agree that if I hadn't run from the dining room his plan was not just to have us lined up, but to include the worst offender, Chris Taylor.

I admit to Michael McManus that I am nervous, even though both of us have, up to this point, a clean record in the seminary. Michael responds with,

"What pisses me off is that Ned was tipped off about Chris Taylor raiding the dining room and we two dopes get caught, instead of him, making our first raid."

(*The punishments for breaking rules in the seminary are twofold, for a more serious offense, like leaving the college grounds without official permission, the guilty student would receive a penalty called a 'Caveat' (a warning) or as it is called colloquially a "Cat". The penalty for a less grievous offense is called a P.W. i.e. President's Warning. The seminary rules say, if you receive three 'Cats', you are automatically expelled from the seminary. The bottom line is both of us are nervous and hoping for just a P.W.)*

On Wednesday we overheard a conversation where Father Ned was inquiring from one of the students he befriends, Alan Malone, saying,

"Alan what's happening among the students recently, is anybody in serious trouble?" Alan replies,

"I haven't heard of any of my classmates getting in trouble, what are you referring to?" "Never mind, it is not that important." He replies.

We go to classes as usual on Monday and Tuesday. The professors or students don't treat us differently, since they don't know about the 'crime' we committed. By Thursday both Michael and I are more relaxed. At the end of Father Ned's elocution class he asks Michael and I to remain behind in the classroom, as the other students leave for lunch.

He addresses us,

"Gentlemen, going into the Priests' dining room without permission or an invitation is breaking the college boundaries for students. I have discussed your transgression with the president Dr. Lennon. He has decided that, since neither of you has a history of breaking the rules; he will issue you both a P.W. Please go to his office this afternoon at 4:15 PM, before you begin your studies."

We both sit nervously, waiting for Dr. Lennon to open his door and are wondering will he see us together or individually. We could hear him speaking on the phone and when he hangs up he comes immediately and opens the door with a friendly greeting.

"Come in gentlemen or should I say mini-thieves."

He asks us to sit on the couch opposite him, while he sits in a plush armchair.

"I know that the food you fellows get daily in the dining room needs to be improved. The new bursar, I appointed recently, Father Duffy, has promised me that it will; he is working on it. Part of your training here in the seminary, as future priests, is to learn to respect the laws of the Church. You are never allowed to take the law into your own hands. The reason you both are getting a President's Warning instead of a Caveat is because, up until this time, you both have clean slates, free of any missteps. You may go on to your studies now. I don't want to have to discipline you again."

We both responded together "Thank you Dr. Lennon."

Our roommate Mike can tell by our faces, as we walk in our bedroom door, that the news is good. I have such a sense of relief; I can hardly focus on the study I need to do for a Canon Law test, being given by Father Ned next week.

During my next meeting with 'Holy Tom', I share with him both the bad news and good news about our visit to the Priests' Dining room. He laughs heartily saying,

"Father Dowling announced to all of us that evening at dinner. He was bragging about being a good detective. He didn't tell us your names at first, but made a slip saying,

"The second fellow, Finbarr, ran scared, as he thought he touched a dead man's head at the table and ran like a frightened rabbit to the Senior Chapel.' We all applauded him and he was very happy."

249

I don't know what is causing my change of attitude; I feel a new sense of freedom and confidence in being a seminarian. I am on my way to become a devoted priest like my heroic uncle Father Michael Corr, who went to serve God and his people in the State of New Jersey. I am thinking that getting caught, attempting to steal food from the priests' dining room makes me feel normal. I am human; I can and do make mistakes. I also can handle being disciplined. I am learning how to control my quick temper. I am no longer obsessed thinking about girls.

At the end of the school year I receive the Order of Tonsure with my classmates.

I am now an official cleric of the Holy Roman Catholic Church, looking forward in a few months to taking a vow of celibacy, as all of our class are ordained sub deacons. I will be then reciting the Divine Office daily of Matins and Lauds, containing a series of Psalms, prayers and readings.

When I go home as a sub deacon, I now wear my black suit and Roman collar, whether attending mass in Potahee or going out formally. I continue to help Daddy working in the bog and in the fields, making hay and cutting the oats. I obviously don't wear clerical clothes while working in the bog, the hayfield, practicing running or playing football.

During this period I am fortunate to meet the best middle and long distance runners in the county. Matt Rudden is a member of the Laragh Harriers. He holds the record for our province of Ulster for the 400 yards, half mile, two miles and five mile races. He invites me to join his brother Vincent and compete in the Novice Mile Championship of Cavan and Monaghan at the Cootehill Sports. In the month leading up to the event I have the opportunity to practice running the mile with Matt. I learn a lot from him that day. He teaches me new stretching exercises before you do the quarter mile warm up. I think I surprised Matt, when I kept up with him for three quarters of the race. When he began his final sprint for the last 300 yards I kept pace with him finishing only five yards behind him. His comment afterwards is affirming,

"I may be looking at the Novice Champion of Cavan and Monaghan here."

Daddy drives me to Cootehill on Sunday August 5th. The track on which we are due to run is in the shape of a football field, about 440 yards in circumference. Dad says,

"Finbarr you should do well here, as this field has the same surface as our meadow where you have been practicing for the past couple of years."

"You are right dad. I don't do well running on hard track surfaces or in road races."

The sports event begins with a three mile road race from the center of Cootehill out to Tullyvin, where the all of the sprints, the mile race and jumping take place. One of the students, Brian O'Reilly, who I know from St Pat's in Cavan, is in the race. I cheer him as he enters the field to make one final lap of the track. I am ready for my race. I put on my new track shoes and start doing the warm up exercises I learned from Matt.

I greet my five competitors, including Vincent Rudden, at the starting line. At the sound of the gun I take off pretty quickly, as I don't want to get blocked at the corners or have to go around other runners to begin my final 300 yard sprint. Without planning it, I became the pacesetter in the race. Vincent is running on my shoulder for the first 200 yards. While the Laragh harriers are all cheering their member Vincent, his big brother Matt is cheering for both of us. At about half way in the race, I'm feeling great; I pick up my speed a notch. I know Vincent is not a strong finisher like his brother, but I don't know the capacity of the other four runners. I am about ten yards ahead of Vincent, as the committee rings the bell for the last lap. I don't go all out until I am about 200 yards from the finish. With Vincent right on my shoulder I take off sprinting with long strides and consistent breathing through my mouth. Vincent's club members yell,

"Go Vincent, you can do it"

I beat an exhausted Vincent and the other four runners by several yards. Dad is at the finish line and is there to see me accept the silver colored cup as the Novice Champion Miler for the counties of Cavan and Monaghan.

Once again John A. and I get chauffeured back to the seminary, compliments of his older brother Tom. This would be the last time for me to enjoy this privilege, as John A. is scheduled to be ordained in June and would be leaving Ireland in the summer of

Finbarr admiring the silver cup he won as Novice Mile Champion of Counties Cavan and Monaghan, July 1959

1959, to begin his ministry in the Diocese of Camden New Jersey.

As third year theology students we don't have to room on Rotten Row. Pat Scott, my fellow Cavan man, invites me to room with him. We get a comfortable double room on the third floor of the main building. My friend Mike and Michael McManus decide to room together. Instead of Mike and I taking walks together after breakfast Pat now joins us. I feel better about that, as the only conversations I get out of Mike are grunts up until midday.

Thanks to our bursar Father Duffy, the food in the dining room is better than last year. I tease Michael McManus saying,

"Do you think that you and I should get an award from the student body, because we dramatized the problem to President Lennon and Father Ned by attempting to raid their dining room?"

Michael replies,

"I would be satisfied if Chris Taylor apologized to both of us. All I get from him is a shitty grin, every time I meet him."

The school year goes well. For recreation, I enjoy gardening with my friends (Picture attached) I play in the soccer league, the interprovincial Gaelic football competition and enjoy pitch-and-putt golf with Mike and Vincent on the par three course behind the chapel. My studies are progressing as well as usual. I still have 'bazz" sessions with Mike before written exams. At this time I am preparing for my oral examination on Theology and Canon Law with Dr. Lennon. This is the final test we sub deacons have before we are ordained deacons of the Church. I'm not worried about it. I know I won't be as concerned as I was when Michael McManus and I received our P.W.'s

Chapter XXXVII

A Pleasant Surprise

My good friend and colleague from County Cavan now-Reverend John A. Clarke on his way to the U.S. to serve in the Diocese of Camden, New Jersey, which means that his brother Tom is no longer our chauffeur. I have no choice but to take the bus from Cavan to Dublin, and then switch to the bus for Carlow. Before I report to the seminary, I make a brief visit with Dan and Kathleen Shanaghy and their four children. They already know about my misfortune of getting caught attempting to raid the priests' dining room and are now relieved to find that I just received a P.W. (*President's Warning*) instead of a Caveat. Kathleen says, "Finbarr don't worry about food this coming year. Dan or I will come up to the seminary every couple of weeks with some goodies from our cafe here."

"Thank you Kathleen, you are very kind. We are all hoping that the new bursar keeps his promise of improving the quality and amount of food for us seminarians."

Kathleen laughs, saying, "You can believe that when you see it."

All of my classmates return and are preparing to be ordained as deacons, our final step before we become priests on June 11, 1960. We do have one more academic hurdle to cross before we become deacons. We each have to present ourselves to Doctor Lennon for an oral examination in moral theology. Since I have passed all of my written theological exams with honors, I am not anxious about the test. But I find that this is a misjudgment on my part: I learn that Dr. Lennon asks tougher questions of the more intelligent students. Knowing that I am in the top ten percentile in the class, he asks me to explain the difficult concept of "double effect," as well as when it applies and when it can't be used . I reply, "First of all, today's theologians and Catholic historians attribute the creation of the Double Effect principle to Saint Thomas Aquinas. He stated that four conditions need to be present for any act with both a good and bad effect to be legitimate. Firstly, the act being contemplated must be morally good or morally indifferent (e.g., removing a cancerous womb from a pregnant woman). Secondly, the bad effect cannot be intended (e.g., indirectly aborting a live fetus from the cancerous womb). Thirdly, the good effect cannot be the direct result of the bad effect. Fourthly, the good effect should be proportionate to the bad result."

"Well done, Mr. Corr. Can you tell me of a situation where the principle of Double Effect does not apply?"

I immediately think of a situation with my mom. During one of her eleven pregnancies, the doctors in the hospital told her that carrying that particular fetus to term could cause her death. My mom replied, "That is a risk I have to take. Abortion is against the practice of my faith." I am a very happy student as I leave Dr. Lennon's office.

While I am still rejoicing over passing my final oral exam, my classmate Joe Hynan approaches me with a big smile and says, "Congratulations, Finbarr."

"What for?" I ask.

"Ciaran Doherty, Padraig Farrell and you have been appointed prefects at Knockbeg boarding school for the next school year. The announcement is on the notice board outside the dining room."

What a pleasant surprise! I think to myself that this is my lucky day. On further reflection I realize that I am in shock. How can a college administration appoint me, a student who received a P.W. a mere two years ago, to such a responsible position in a boys' boarding school? An hour later, I experience another surprise. Father Dowling informs me that I am to move out to Knockbeg after Easter, two weeks hence, to learn from this year's prefects, Deacon Michael Kelly and Deacon Anthony McLaughlin, how they fulfill their function of supervising the students.

I discuss the appointment with my spiritual director Holy Tom. He simply says,

"Finbarr, your appointment is a tribute to your academic achievements and the leadership skills you demonstrate".

My next task is to obtain a bicycle for the final semester so that each school morning I can ride the three-and-a-half miles to the seminary and back to Knockbeg before the students begin their first study session at 5 PM. Deacon Jim, whom I am replacing, is kind enough to sell me his bicycle for two pounds. Since he will be living back in the seminary for the last semester before he is ordained, he won't need a bicycle.

Father Patrick Shine, the president, and his associate professors, Father James Kaye, Father Moling Lennon and Father Garrett Murphy, give me a warm welcome to Knockbeg. My two colleagues Michael and Tony tell me that being selected as a Knockbeg prefect is the best appointment a deacon can receive. Michael says, "Riding out the front seminary gate, all dressed up in your black suit, you feel a great sense of freedom. There is very little traffic on the road to Knockbeg. The only negative is occasional riding in the rain."

Tony cautions that it is important not to become too friendly with the students, because they will take advantage of a deacon's friendship and create havoc in the study hall. I relay the same message to Padraig and Ciaran when they join me in September. Unfortunately neither of them heeds me. Half way through the semester both of them ask why the students are afraid of me and not of them. I reply, "Because, for the first month, I insisted on absolute silence in the study hall. They see me as a mean S.O.B. and are afraid I am going to report them to Father Shine."

I also do one more thing to make my nine-month job easier. My semester of preparation at Knockbeg allows me to learn who "the tough gang" is among the school body. Bobby Fox and Colm Scanlon are the leaders. Two other, more passive guys hang out with them. After I finish supervising study hall the first evening in September, I call the gang of four aside and ask, "Now that we are starting new school year, I need to know who is going to run the show. Is it you four or me?"

Bobby replies for all of them, "You are, Mr. Corr. You are in charge."

"That settles that. I don't want to be competing with you for leadership. Whether you are aware of it or not, you walk around the study hall and campus as if you are the leaders. Since you admit I am the leader, I am going to ask for your help. If I have to leave the study hall for any reason, I want you four to take a stand and see to it that silence is observed in my absence. In return for your help I promise not to attack your gang or humiliate any of you in public. I will respect your leadership skills as long as you respect my leadership role."

A few days later, while supervising the students, I experiment by leaving the study hall for ten minutes. When I return, the students are absolutely quiet, heads lowered, studying at their desks. Bobby Fox swings around in his desk and looks at me as if to say, "Shazam (their knick name for me), we are keeping our commitment."

Another benefit of being a prefect at Knockbeg is that I can ride past the Shanaghy cafe about once a week to have a cup of tea and a raisin bun, compliments of Kathleen. On Sunday morning when we ride into the seminary for a second Mass at 10:30, we stop at the cafe and buy the *Sunday Irish Press* and *Independent*, stuff them inside our clerical shirts, and deliver them secretly to the students who ordered them.

When I go home for Christmas, both Daddy and Mammy are anxious to know what plans, if any, we can make for my ordination at The Cathedral of the Assumption, Carlow, on June 11. They are not familiar with what happens at the ordination of a son, because they couldn't afford to fly to New Jersey nine years ago for my brother Jack's ordination. To save their money I do not propose printing invitations to either the ordination or the first Mass the following morning in Potahee.

I tell my parents that I will be happy to send simple cards, including an invitation to ordination, to whomever they wish to invite. Each priest being ordained is allowed to invite ten lay people to occupy a reserved seat in the cathedral. All invited priests will be seated on the altar with Bishop Keogh.

Mammy gets emotional and says, "I don't think Marie (*now called Sister Dolora*) will be given permission to leave her convent in Los Angeles and fly to Ireland."

"If that is true, Mammy," I say, "the very first holiday

I get in New Jersey I will fly to Los Angeles and visit her in the convent."

"She will love that," Mammy replies.

Daddy speaks up, saying, "I have a feeling from one of Jack's recent letters that he is coming over on the Queen Mary with a priest friend Father Daly and that both will be at the ordination. I know that my two brothers, Father Larry and Barney the dentist, will be there. I add, "In addition to my brothers and sisters, I would like to invite my cousin Nuala Phillips and her new husband Harry Nally to Carlow. My running companion Matt Rudden has told me already that he plans to be there."

Dad announces that, since there will be eight cows to milk on that Saturday morning, he plans to do the milking early with the electric milking machine, and then drive the three hours to Carlow for the ceremony. I marvel that this is the same daddy who almost died four years ago, because of an invasive cyst on his throat. Mammy plans to travel the evening before with Uncle Barney and Aunt Maura.

The following semester at Knockbeg goes very well. Both of my colleagues, Pat and Ciaran, learn to balance strictness with the students in the study hall but friendliness with them at other times. Father Kaye becomes very friendly with the three of us and invites us to his room to watch sports events or movies on his TV. Since I can't play soccer or Gaelic Football at the seminary, I decide to continue my running around the football field at Knockbeg for exercise.

After Easter, when my replacement prefect moved to Knockbeg, I switch back to living full time at the seminary. The "gang of four" surprise me by thanking me for how I treated them during the school year. For the next few weeks the emphasis for my classmates and me is on preparing spiritually and emotionally for our life-altering change. Holy Tom reminds us that the sacrament of ordination leaves an indelible mark on the soul: *"Tu es Sacerdos in Aeternum secundum ordinem de Melchisedech"* [You are a priest forever according to the order of Melchisedech].

Following our five-day retreat, Father Ned takes all of us and the seminarians who will serve at the ordination to the cathedral next door to the seminary for a thorough rehearsal. He asks our class president, Matt McInerny, to do the first reading and Vincent Maguire the second. As usual, Father Ned cannot resist being humorous and says as we finish, "Gentlemen, this is your last chance to change your minds; making a decision this time tomorrow will be too late." Only a few people laugh.

The day arrives. Twenty four in all, we dress in our white cassocks, each with a deacon stole over the right shoulder. Bishop Keogh greets each of us as we process past him into the cathedral. The cathedral choir, accompanied by violins and saxophones, welcome us into the cathedral. I know that I will remember the prostration before the main altar forever. I accept the action as demonstrating my willingness to serve the people of God for the rest of my life. The only distraction I entertain while lying prostrate on the floor is wondering if my dad made it on time. When I stand up to walk over to my seat, I looked towards the congregation. There he is, sitting beside Mom, in the fifth pew on the aisle.

The presiding bishops impose his hands on our heads. When the ordained priests approach to do the same, my brother Jack pinches my left cheek, to let me know it is he. The whole ceremony lasts an hour and a half. The congregation applauds, and the choir sings a recessional hymn as we process out of the cathedral to the college grounds. My Mom knows to drop to her knees as she receives my first priestly blessing. Dad looks a little exhausted, as I bless him and help him to his feet. Uncle Barney pushes the gift of a gold watch onto to my left wrist, as I finish blessing him and Aunt Maura.

At the reception afterwards, I introduce my friend Matt to my family and welcome Harry Nally, Nuala's husband, into the clan. Knowing we have a long drive home to Legaginney, I stand up and thank my family and friends for coming to my ordination. Daddy drives me back to the seminary to pick up my memorable suitcase, a gift from Uncle Jim that I have already packed. Mammy wants me, the new priest, to sit up front with Daddy, but I refuse, saying, "Thank you, Mom, you and Daddy are still the head of the Corr family. I can sit in the back and read my Divine Office for tomorrow, as it will be a busy day."

St. Michael's Church Potahee is already filled to capacity on Sunday at 9:30 AM when I arrive at the sacristy to prepare to say my first Mass at 10. Our old housekeeper from Legaginney, now Mary Beatty, is serving as sacristan. She is excited to call me "Father Finbarr" as she assists me in getting dressed in chasuble and stole. My brother and his friend Father Jim Daly concelebrate with me. There is absolute silence in church as I begin with "*Introibo ad Altare Dei*," the traditional antiphon in Latin.

My brother Father Jack preaches a short homily, most of it to welcome everyone to my first holy Mass.

As I finish the Mass, I invite the entire congregation to come to the altar rails so that I may administer my priestly blessing. Everybody, including Master McCarthy receives it in Latin. My high school friend Barney Brady from Potahee is the exception. I bless him in English and then ask, "Are you still shocked that I became a priest?" He just smiles.

The family and friends invited by my parents follow us to the Railway Hotel in Cavan for a lunch and speeches. My dad gives the shortest speech, saying in Gaelic, "I extend to all of you A Ce~ad Mile Failte [one hundred thousand welcomes]."

Personally, I confess I am overcome with emotions, when I thank my parents and my uncle Father Lawrence for supporting me during the long journey to the priesthood. The nice part of this lunch is that we are enjoying it in a hotel that belongs to my second family, the Smiths of the Railway Hotel.

The following morning our guest Father Daly is having breakfast with the Corr family in Legaginney. My dad, always the gracious host, says to Father Daly, "Because of Finbarr's ordination, we are taking a week off from farming. We are available to drive you wherever you wish to go, since this is your first time in Ireland."

Father Daly acts surprised but responds reflectively, "I would love to go to Portumna."

"I know it well." says Dad. "I was in prison there."

On the way to Ireland on the Queen Mary, Jack had joked with his colleague Father Jim, saying that if Dad had stayed in prison Mammy would have done a better job rearing us nine children. He learns the whole truth when I tell him, "Dad was in prison and went on a hunger strike while he was serving as a volunteer in the Irish

Republican Army's (the IRA's) fight for freedom." Since Jack and Father Daly are flying back to the U.S. from Shannon Airport, Dad and I drive both of them through Portumna on the way to the airport in Limerick.

I am scheduled to fly to New York on August 16, to begin my priestly ministry in New Jersey. With two months to spare before my departure, I use my ordination gift money to buy a second-hand "Austin 40" automobile to drive around. I enjoy driving the thirteen miles to Columcille in Longford to visit Aunt Sheila and her daughter Agatha. I have made this same trip so many times on a bicycle. Mammy is a little nervous, sitting in the front seat, as I continue driving up the hilly road to Mollyglass, the home where she was born. Mom's older sister Bridget, a spinster, lives there all alone.

During this busy time of visiting friends and family, I make a commitment to pick up a mutual friend in Cavan named Miriam Healy and take her to visit a mutual friend, Mary Berwick in Monaghan. Unfortunately, I am an hour late getting there. Unlike most of my relatives and friends, who are empathetic to a busy, newly ordained priest, Miriam is angry and lets me have it. This is the first time since my ordination a month earlier that I have to control my impulsive Irish temper. I say nothing as she yells at me and sits in the front seat. I decide I am going to drive quickly to make up for lost time and to avoid being rude back to her.

I drive out of town towards Monaghan at about twenty miles per hour, over the speed limit. The road is wet from a recent shower. As the car rounds a sharp bend in the road, it goes into reverse and we go backwards into ditch six-feet deep. A fellow driving past stops to help and sees this gentleman with a collar on, with his legs in the air, and sitting beside an attractive young woman in the ditch. The man is a Protestant!

Within a half hour we are pulled out of the ditch and on our way. I am unable to talk to Miriam, as the muffler is broken and the noise of the engine is horrendous. Mary Berwick is very empathetic, even though we arrive two hours late. I have the muffler repaired and buy new pantyhose to replace the ones Miriam tore in the ditch.

The custom in most Irish families is to have a going-away party for any members immigrating to the U.S. Mammy organizes mine for August 14, two days before I depart.

The neighbors all come. Women cry as they bid goodbye, while the men talk about football or fishing and ignore saying goodbye. Miss Berrill sings, "Good Bye Johnny Dear, when you're far away don't forget your dear old mother, far across the sea. Write a letter now and then, send her all you can, and don't forget where e'er you roam that you're an Irishman."

Eleven or twelve of the group join my parents at the airport as I prepare to embark on an Aer Lingus flight to Idlewild Airport in New York. I cannot wait to get on the plane, as the pain of seeing my mother cry her eyes out, is very hard for the "kid" leaving Legaginney forever.

Unfortunately, or maybe fortunately, the lights won't function and the plane cannot take off. Twenty minutes later the captain tells us all to get off the plane. I suddenly get the idea to pretend I am coming home ten years later. I get off the plane and say with a heavy Yankee accent, "Mammy, please tell me who all these folks are. I have been so long away I don't recognize anybody."

Twenty minutes later, while we are still teasing each other and laughing, the captain announces over the speakers, "Flight EI 114 is ready for departure. All aboard please." This time nobody is crying, not even me. Somebody yells "Finbarr, please go and let us go home." I wave my hand and reply, "Good Bye! America, here I come."

"That ill-spent life"

(Music: The Royal Loyal Lilly O)
By
James Brady

T'was early in the month of May
To this earth I forced my way.
Condemned to hardship and poor pay.
And they called me Jimmy Brady O.
Oh Ho, Ho Ho, Ho Ho
And they called me Jimmy Brady O

They wrapped me up in a snow white shawl
They held me up and let me fall
You should have heard the wretched squall
The first hard knock for Brady O
(Chorus)

When round the house I used to creep
They never got a wink of sleep
And now and then they'd take a peek
Saying, Where the devils Brady O?
(Chorus)

One day I scampered down the hall
And scraped the paper of the wall
When just about to hop my ball
Down came the rod on Brady O
(Chorus)

I remember when I went to school
I smashed the windows with a rule
And the teacher blared, "You blinking fool"
And insulted Jimmy Brady O
(Chorus)

Later on in quest of knowledge
The old man sent me off to college
But he might as well have cooled his porridge
They couldn't put brains in Brady O.
(Chorus)

Through Lacken's rocks I toiled for years
Muck and cow-dung to my ears
Subjected to such nasty jeers
As, "that's the stuff for Brady O "
(Chorus)

But now I live a life of ease
Taking things just as you please
And sometimes (never!) gets a little squeeze
And that goes hard on Brady O.
(Chorus)

Now after all why should I grouse?
Or envy little Mickey Mouse
They shout 'hello' from every house
Oh, there goes Jimmy Brady O.
(Chorus)

There is nothing more I can relate
And with St. Peter rests my fate
You may be sure he will bang the gate
And it is back to blazes Brady O.
(Chorus)

Good Bye 'Old Lamp'

(Electricity turned on in Lacken on 5/19/55)
By
James Brady

On many a wild and stormy night
Ere slumber chains had bound me
You cast your faint old glimmering light,
in patches all around me.

Still, you were all I had 'Old Lamp,"
From dusk to early morn.
You showed me light to read and write
And excavate a thorn.

Not often did I trim your wick
Or dust your dull reflector
And never did you let me down,
When I filled you with Bright Nectar.

Now I press the gentle switch
I hail the new arrival
Oh, the splendor of it dazzles me
No hope for your survival

The time has come to make your bow
Good bye 'Old Lamp' for ever
Till the darkening shadows cross my bow
Can I forget you? ....Never

Milking Song

(to the music of Ora Pro Nobis)
Jim Brady

Thrush, my poor old sucking cow,
Suckey, Suckey, Suckey cow
Some could milk but I know how
Ora Pro Nobis.

Milking ways have changed I fear
Buzzing motors, rubber gears
Times may be bad but milk is dear
Ora Pro Nobis.

Thrush my poor old Suckey pet
Now is no time to make your wet:
Ora Pro Nobis

See how those little gadgets fit
Just like gloves upon your teats
Now don't plaster me with shit
Ora Pro Nobis

Thrush my poor old Suckey Suck
Suckey, Suckey, Suckey Suck
Blast your skin, cant you stand up,
Ora Pro Nobis

So now the can is filling up
Soon won't hold another sup
So say good bye to Biddy Duff
And Ora Pro Nobis

The burial of Tom McGovern

In Memoriam
By
James Brady

Here lie the bones of honest Tom
In the mound we softly laid them
Mid the rugged scenes of the mountains wild
And the hovering clouds to share them

No pomp or splendor spoiled that scene
Since he sought no fame or glory
T'was the climax of a life serene
The burial of the lowly (R.I.P.)

Lowly indeed was that burial scene
Reflecting his wish to the letter.
He loved his God, he loved the Queen
And her sister Margaret better!

To an Irish nun in California

(Marie Corr)
By
James Brady

Down through the years I've watched her grow,
And her clear blue eyes like embers glow,
A Flower Fair came not to stay,
For 'ere it bloomed 'twas snatched away.

She leaves the world and friends behind.
Her motive's of the noblest kind.
She ploughs a furrow for seeds to grow
That Heaven may reap and she shall sow.

I see her now through a bright sunbeam
-but what's a memory just a dream-
And I hear her plead with Heaven's Queen
To bless and guard "Th. Old Isle of Green"

Lets set but a limit to the loss
With her must lasting peace abide
For she seeks the beam that's on the Cross
And "The Thorns that crown the Crucified"

....

An Appreciation by {George Bernard} Brady, Poet, Farmer,
Philosopher and Apostate !!

"That Night in Stradone"

If you heard each disaster of your poetaster
A foolish old chancer at a dance in Stradone
Through ticker tape dashing, his old ribs a smashing
My friends in compassion, your Brady bemoan

Oh! What a collection and such a selection
From old "Napper Tandy" to sweet Molly Malone
There were tinkers and tailors and men dressed like sailors
And quite a few flairers that night in Stradone

There were high brows and low brows and some had no brows
Not so with Brady they stood out on their own
But fate proved the master and so spelled disaster
"He got left on his arse in Stradone."

Though he cared not for Sambas or Ramlas or Bambas
Still, those graceful old timers at his heart strings they tore
He was just only Brady fast holding the baby,
He ne'r got his feet on the floor.

Then those ladies so fair, some with white arms bare
Not a few showed a good slice of shoulder
But when Brady made eyes they all flitted by
He was just an old thistle in clover.

That night it sped on, mid gay dancing and song
With Brady alone and deserted.
He was just an old relic of other days
And sorely and sadly he felt it.

But did not the harp tang on old Tara's Walls
Long after the days of its glory
He stroked his old jaws like a cat with her claws
As he watched the "Mau Maus" from Vairolic

Then the national anthem struck up like a phantom
It stirred his old heart to the core
With one wave of his hand he saluted the band
Then, wended his way to the door

Yet he caused not dissention or raised not contention
Just relaxed in his taxi going home
He sure got a squashing, darn near lost his washing
It was a lousy old night in Stradone.

Jim Brady (1955)

All for the Love of Theresa

By
James Brady

Why look askance at that wayward stranger
Scarred in the wars of an alien clime
If he led a fast life for the love of Theresa
T'was his craze for fair women and the red roaring wine.

He was just a young soldier, suntanned and brown
He first met Theresa in old Canton town
And her fair golden tresses and loving caresses
Were but links in the chain that fast pulled him down.

Teresa she wooed him and with passion imbued him.
While the wine it flowed freely like rain pouring down
There was pleasure unending and money for spending
Oh! Those were the days in old Canton town.

She led him to bowers bedecked with gay flowers
That cast their rich odors far out to the sea
And in that haven of glory…for so goes the story
Says she "Gallant soldier, now share life with me."

And he was a soldier of that once Noble Band,
That withstood charging troopers, with sword in right hand
But he fell for Theresa, he drank her cup deep
And entranced in her arms she lulled him to sleep.

She sapped his life's vigor in those moments accursed
As nudely prostrated, she reveled in lust.
Then followed the wine that drove him depraved
And night noon and morning for Theresa he craved.

Till one dismal day on the old barrack square
He fell into line and ne'er combed his hair
T'was the ceremonial parade and the major marched past
At the slovenly soldier he stared quite aghast.

To his words of command he failed to respond
When he called "The Salute" he raised his left hand.
At the order "Right Turn" he lurched to the left
His mind was a shipwreck and of reason bereft.

"Dismissed from the "Army" the words rang out clear
He summoned the guard "March him straight out of here."
For the love of Theresa he was drummed out the gate
And that once gallant soldier bowed obedience to fate.

Now why be unkind when he's wayward and old
In youth he was crazy and spent all his gold
In war he won glory, ne'er counting the cost
And for the love of Theresa …well he's just lost.